OPTING IN

Improving the
1992 Federal
Constitutional
Proposals

Bryan Schwartz

LL.B., LL.M., J.S.D.

82 Frontenac Street, Hull, Quebec J8X 1Z5

(819) 778-2946

First Published in 1992 by
Voyageur Publishing
Editor: Sean Fordyce
82 Frontenac Street, Hull, Quebec.
(819) 778-2946

Media and Publicity:
Elizabeth Jefferson
203-51 Grosvenor St.
Toronto, Ontario
(416) 515-1678

Production Coordination:
George McKenzie of GEMM Graphics
2022 Kingsgrove Crescent,
Gloucester, Ontario.
(613) 748-6613

Cover Design:
Kim Ford
Cover Photography courtesy of The National Capital Commission

First Edition May, 1992.

Second Printing August, 1992.

ISBN 0-921842-07-4

Printed in Canada on recycled paper.

For my tiny compatriots Mikie and Lainie, who made the writing of this book necessary and impossible; for Bevy, always.

Acknowledgements

This project was initiated and completed under severe time pressure and would not have been possible without the help of a number of people. Alvin Esau, Wes Pue and Butch Nepon all provided encouragement to do this project, but now that it is over, I forgive them. The Legal Research Institute of the University of Manitoba provided support on short notice. Leonard Schwartz devoted much effort to finding materials and reviewing the manuscript. Elliot Leven, Charles Schwartz and Stanley Poor also provided assistance for which I am very grateful.

Sean Fordyce has been an exceptionally co-operative editor and publisher, and has provided many useful insights into matters of substance as well as style.

Contents

Preface

This time, I hope the people of Canada have the last word on any proposals for constitutional reform. The intention of this study is to address a wide audience that includes the general public; my colleagues in the academic community, in the hope of contributing to the understanding of the current Constitutional crisis; and to officials and politicians who are actively involved in the hope of making a practical and positive contribution. I have tried to avoid technical jargon, case citations and footnotes.

The subject matter is the current round of constitutional reform, and in particular, the proposal released by the Federal Government in September, 1991 and its follow-up in March 1992. The aim is to look at the broad issues connected with Canada's constitutional destiny and focus on specific ways in which our system of government may be altered. In looking at the federal proposals, the goal has been to not only analyze and criticize, but provide specific suggestions for improvement.

The study was written in my role as a member of the academic community — a community whose role is to provide strictly independent analysis and judgment. Politicians, bureaucrats and advocates for special interest groups are all constrained by duties to others or self-interest. Members of the academic community have a special opportunity and duty to provide commentary reflecting the free movement of the individual intellect and conscience, rather than pleasing others.

The Federal Government seems to be proceeding with great haste to secure approval of a massive package of reforms that would irreversibly affect many important institutions and programs in Canada. I have tried to cover as many issues in as much depth as possible. There are many points on which I would have liked more time for research and reflection. With respect to several issues, it was not possible to provide even a preliminary discussion. Among these omissions are the proposed "double majority" rule for Senate voting and the proposed abolition of the existing federal power to assume regulatory control over certain enterprises by declaring them to be "for the general advantage of Canada." My inability to deal with such issues was the the product of time pressure, and does not reflect on their importance — which is potentially very great. I would not want the existence of this study, which is fairly extensive, to be taken as an indication that the pace being imposed by the federal government allows adequate time for study, reflection and public discussion. It most assuredly does not.

I do hope, however, that what follows will be of assistance to those who do care about or are involved in the process that is now unfolding.

Meech II: Mulroney tries again

In September, 1991, the Federal Government released a document called *Shaping Canada's Future Together* (referred to as the Federal Proposal). The document proposes sweeping reform of the Canadian Constitution.

The Canadian Obsession with the formal Constitution amendment.

The "constitution has two key purposes," says the Federal Proposal. One is functional: to set the ground rules for running the government. The other is symbolic: to describe the "defining qualities" of the country and its people. The Federal Proposal proceeds to tell us what amendments are required to the texts that compromise our formal Constitution.

Not so fast. It may be that we need new rules to operate our system of government but should they be set out in a formal Constitution? Should a constitution address "spiritual" needs, such as seeing oneself acknowledged in a sacred text? Should a constitution confine itself to the more modest task of establishing the most basic decision-making rules?

It is possible to think of our "constitution" as including the whole ensemble of rules, principles and practices that determine how government operates. Our system of government operates largely on the basis of political conventions — principles that are created and enforced primarily by political practice rather than by formal constitutional amendments or judicial decisions. Many of the most basic principles of our government have been established this way: e.g., the role of the Prime Minister in selecting the cabinet, the principle of cabinet solidarity, the ever-diminishing principle of Ministerial responsibility.

Our "constitution," broadly understood, extends not only to political conventions, but ordinary legislation on such matters as election financing, official language policy, and judicial and administrative appointments. It also encompasses judicial decisions such as the procedures that must be adopted by administrative agencies.

The informal aspects of our constitution are every bit as important to the practical functioning of our system as the formal Constitution. An overhaul of our system of government could very largely be accomplished through informal means. For example, by ordinary legislation, we could reform election financing to minimize the clout of those with money; we could outlaw party affiliation as a basis of appointment to government office (unless it is a bona fide occupational qualification for the job); we could provide for a rational, merit-based system of competing for government contracts. There is no need for a constitutional amendment to have referendums on the text of any constitutional proposal

— it would suffice for the federal government to hold a technically non-binding one but agree to abide by the result.

The Canadian constitution is, according to the *Constitution Act, 1867*, "similar in Principle" to that of the United Kingdom. However, the British constitutional tradition was to develop the constitution through ordinary political and judicial practice, rather than having a formal entrenched document. The British system is not really unwritten after all. It consists largely of legislation and judicial opinions amenable to fairly easy revision in light of experience and new ideas. It has no special obstacles to undoing mistakes. A law isn't working well? Repeal it, try something else.

Canada has become obsessed of late, with the formal Constitution which consists almost entirely of a set of texts that are supreme, entrenched and listed in the schedule to the *Constitution Act, 1982*. Supreme means that they have priority over any inconsistent laws. For example, the *Charter of Rights* is part of the Constitution, so any law that is inconsistent with it is, to that extent, invalid. The same goes with the federal-provincial division of powers contained (mostly) in the *Constitution Act, 1867*. Entrenched means that the text cannot be enacted or changed by ordinary legislative processes. It takes a higher level of consent. For example, some amendments must be approved or changed by the House of Commons and 7 provinces with 50% of the population (the "7/50" formula). Others require consent of the federal level of government and all ten provinces. "Included in the schedule" means that the 1982 amendments to the Constitution — the "Patriation" package — specifically provides a list of texts that are included in the formal Constitution. The list is actually longer than is usually realized. The popular conception of the Constitution may be that it consists of the federating Act of 1867 and the "Patriation" package of 1982. The Schedule actually lists thirty Acts or Orders, including measures dealing with the entry of new provinces.

The Less Said the Better?

"The less said in the formal constitution, the better" is a thought not without wisdom. There are disadvantages to entrenching new provisions in the formal Constitution: It is difficult to obtain the necessary level of consent; the numbers game is an obstacle in itself; it is hard to get the federal level and 7/50 worth of provinces to agree on anything. Nevertheless, it is the easiest of the two major amending formulas; often, you have to obtain unanimity among the provinces, either because the amending formula requires it, or because dissenting provinces can simply opt out of the amendment and scuttle its practical effect.

The pursuit of formal amendments raises the stakes higher than they need be. For many Canadians, the formal Constitution has sacred status. Amendments may be pursued, but also resisted, with a special vehemence when the proposition is raised from politics as usual to the loftier plane of Supreme Law.

The game is played more intensely because wins and losses tend to be seen as permanent. To score a "win," you may have to persuade the feds and ten provinces to your side. That is hard enough. To undo a loss is even harder; you have to persuade every one of those orders of government to reverse the position taken by their predecessors. That's almost impossible. How likely is it that a future federal government and ten provincial governments will all come to the opposite conclusions?

A disturbing feature of the Canadian Constitution is that the amending formula is rigged in favour of decentralization. The more amendments, the more likely federal powers are to disappear. Why? A centralizing amendment requires the consent of the federal level and all ten provinces; any dissenting province can either veto the change, or opt out — sometimes even with financial compensation. It is extremely difficult to persuade ten provinces, including Quebec, to yield any authority unless it is a part of a package of trade-offs which leaves Canada at least as decentralized as ever. It is not hard to persuade ten provincial Premiers to participate in a power grab; it only takes one federal government to agree, and the power is gone forever. The 1982 Constitution does not require the people to be directly consulted through a referendum.

The most powerful moral cause for restraint about constitutional amendment is respect for the democratic freedom of those in the future. Attitudes change, even about "sacred" principles. The Constitution should not unduly prevent new thoughts from becoming new deeds. The less-said-the-better principle can be overcome when it comes to certain basic rules of governmental functioning. Some may be of fundamental importance to a democracy. We can choose to entrench certain guarantees of individual or minority rights when there is reason to fear they may be trampled on by those in power.

The less-said-the-better principle may have extra force, however, with matters of symbolic self-portraiture. It may be necessary at times to spell out certain values and technical provisions. Sometimes, explaining the underlying purpose of an arrangement provides necessary guidance to those who must interpret and apply a constitutional provision. We should, however, avoid trying to entrench statements of fundamental political philosophy and ideals. Contrary to what is often claimed, the task of constitutional reform is not to get everyone to agree on the same moral vision but to provide a democratic, fair and peaceful process whereby people can live together and, when necessary, settle disagreements. If everyone agreed on all the fundamentals, we would not need a constitution — or indeed, much in the way of ordinary political and legal processes.

The reasons for the latest attempts at constitutional overhaul.

After the death of the Meech Lake Accord, the best thing this country could have done about the constitution would have been to spend a number of years doing nothing at all. We could have returned to the constitutional debate in a more relaxed, thoughtful and genuinely interested spirit having spent the interim trying to address social and economic issues through ordinary political processes.

Proceeding now means yielding a major role in reshaping the country to a government that most Canadians dislike in general, and distrust on constitutional issues in particular. Contrary to what the Spicer Report suggests, the Prime Minister is not merely a "lightning rod" for general discontent with the political system as a whole. Many Canadians believe that the Meech Package was one-sidedly favourable to Quebec nationalism at the expense of Canadian nationalism; towards Quebec's political interests and against those of western and northern Canada; towards provincialism at the expense of nation-building and individual rights; towards executive federalism at the expense of open and widespread public participation in government. The means used to sell the package were marked by a strong preference for back-room bullying and intrigue at the expense of honesty, openness and public participation.

Yet here we are again, reminded of the advertising slogan for the follow-up movie about demonic sharks. It went: "Jaws II: just when you thought it was safe to go back into the water." For Canadians, it is Meech II.

Constitutional reform can appeal to political egos as a rare opportunity to achieve something both transcendent and permanent; a chance to rise above the petty squabbles of the day, and make a lasting contribution to the "sacred text." There may still be some would-be Law-givers. Still, there must be some sensible people — even among senior political leaders — who are just as sick and tired as everyone else of the whole business. The federal government's record of shabby manipulation in the promotion of Meech — of turning constitutional reform into a matter of back-room wheeling, dealing, intimidation and brinkmanship — must have caused at least some participants to move constitutional reform from the "sacred" to the "profane" side of the spiritual ledger. So, ego may be part of the underlying causes, but only part.

If ego doesn't entirely explain the return to the fray, what about partisan politics? Couldn't a successful outcome on the constitutional front rescue the fortunes of the government? Isn't this another chance to embarrass and divide the Liberal Party, by making it choose between surrendering to provincialism on the one hand, or being wiped out in Quebec if the party actually asserts its traditional commitment to Canadian nationalism and individual rights? Constitutional reform does offer these prospects, but also creates the risk of antagonizing everyone, including Quebec nationalists. Political calculation is indeed part of what is going on; for example, some of the Federal Proposal (such as loosening party discipline) is borrowed from the Reform Party, in an apparent effort to reverse its capture of Tory support in western Canada.

Sincerity cannot be entirely discounted as a motivation — even in politics. Maybe politicians are returning to the constitutional agenda because they honestly believe the country needs it but what are the underlying conditions within Canada that cry out "once more into the Meech, dear friends?"

The Constitution is not the fundamental cause of separatism. Separatists are.

Obviously, a major concern of politicians is to counter the rise in support for Quebec independence. The actual workings of our constitution, however, are not the basic cause of separatism in Quebec. The desire to have a nation-state of one's own is felt as a primal and positive value by many people around the world. The specifics of the Canadian constitution cannot possibly explain the desire of many Quebecois for independence. Quebec has thrived, both economically and culturally under that constitution.

On the cultural front, the National Assembly of Quebec already has broad authority to entrench the position of the French language in Quebec. It is true that the Courts have poked some holes in Bill 101, but the basics of the program remain intact.

In the 1988 "sign law" case, for example, the Supreme Court spoke warmly of laws giving "marked predominance" to the French language on commercial signs and insisted only that "other languages" be permitted, at least in small letters. This ruling was entirely consistent with the position of Mr. Bourassa in the 1985 election. As a practical matter, the position of the French language in Quebec has never been stronger. The percentage of francophones is holding up and it is the anglophone population that is in demographic jeopardy. Federal agencies have not been hostile to the French language and culture of Quebec. On the contrary, the federal government has a policy of official bilingualism, and in his recent book *Quiet Resolution,* Georges Mathews, a Quebec nationalist, plainly acknowledges that "the federal government has done infinitely more for the cultural advancement of French Canada than has the provincial government."

On the economic side, association with Canada has brought many benefits to Quebec. One of them is direct subsidies from the rest of Canada. In *Deconfederation,* Professors Bercuson and Cooper observe that from 1961-88, the federal government spent about $136 billion more in Quebec than it removed, whereas it removed about $100 billion more from the western Canadian provinces than it spent. Union with the rest of Canada has provided Quebec with a "shock absorbing" effect. In hard times, Quebec, like other provinces, can turn to the rest of the country for help, through means such as increased equalization payments, unemployment insurance and job-creation funds. Union permits Quebec to benefit from the clout of Canada as a whole in negotiating trade deals and in establishing credibility for the currency it uses.

A major factor driving the return to the constitutional debate is a genuine anxiety among senior politicians about the break-up of Canada. It is not the operation of the constitution, however, that added new supporters to the independence movement in Quebec; it is the mythology of constitutional rejection fuelled by Prime Minister Mulroney and exploited by Quebec politicians.

The Prime Minister did not seriously attempt to engage in a genuine discussion with the Canadian people about the substance of the Meech Lake Accord. Rather, he attempted to justify the deal on the basis that Quebec was "left out" of the Constitution in 1982 and its people were "deprived...of a sense of fairness and tolerance and acceptance by the constitution." Refusal to ratify Meech, we were told, would amount to further rejection of Quebec. In order to sell the remedy, the Prime Minister helped create the disease. The 1982 package was not, in substance, unfair or disrespectful to Quebec. Indeed, the province gained enhanced authority and rights in some areas. The political drive behind the Patriation package came from a Prime Minister from Quebec, a ruling party whose parliamentary party was in large part from Quebec, and the support of almost every member of Parliament from Quebec. It produced no immediate popular discontent in Quebec and until the issue was revived by the current Prime Minister, indifference to constitutional matters was at a modern high, both in Quebec and the rest of the country.

There are, of course, reasonable concerns of the Quebec government that could be addressed through moderate changes to the constitution. It would have been one thing to consider Quebec's demands as part of a positive and forward-looking process of creating a better Canada; Prime Minister Mulroney chose instead to impugn the legitimacy of the existing constitution and join in presenting Quebec's demands as redress for past indignities.

After the death of Meech, the opinion polls showed a rise in support for independence among Quebec voters. In order to stave off demands for immediate separation, the Premier

Bryan Schwartz LL.B., LL.M., J.S.D.   11

of Quebec did the following. First, Mr. Bourassa set up the Belanger-Campeau Commission to study the appropriate course of action. That bought some time for public anger to cool off. He then assuaged nationalist demands within his own party by accepting the radically decentralist Allaire Report as the party's official position on the constitution. The Report says, in a nutshell, that the Quebec government should acquire jurisdiction over just about everything in the province while the federal government will retain the right to send it money. Mr. Bourassa appointed just enough federalists — or at least, enough people who did not want independence immediately — to the Belanger-Campeau Commission to prevent it from recommending immediate and outright sovereignty.

Allocation of Powers Under Allaire: excerpt from the Allaire Report (A Quebec Free to Choose).

4.   That the Quebec state move resolutely toward the political autonomy necessary for the full development of Quebec society, by implementing the following political orientations:

(a)   Quebec will henceforth exercise full sovereignty in its current areas of exclusive authority under the existing Constitution, in particular the following:

-Social affairs	-Family policy	-Municipal affairs
-Culture	-Natural resources	-Education
-Health	-Housing	-Tourism
-Recreation & sports	-Manpower & formation	

(b)   Quebec will also exercise full sovereignty in sectors not specifically enumerated in the Canadian Constitution, namely the residual powers, as well as in certain areas currently under shared jurisdiction or under exclusive federal authority, in particular:

-Unemployment insurance	-Environment	-Language
-Research & development	-Public security	-Agriculture
-Industry and commerce	-Income security	-Energy
-Regional development	-Communication	

(c)   the central government will exercise exclusive authority in certain areas, in particular:

-Defence & territorial security	-Customs & tariffs
-Currency & common debt	-Equalization

(d)   certain powers will be shared between Quebec and Canada according to the respective authorities of each level of government, in particular:

-Fisheries	-Native affairs	-Financial institutions
-Transport	-Foreign policy	-Taxation & revenue
-Justice	-Immigration	-Post office & telecommunications

As Professor Leon Dion put it, Canada would be given "one last chance" with a "knife at its throat." Belanger-Campeau proposed that a referendum on Quebec independence be held, either in June or October 1992. Belanger-Campeau also recommended that a special legislative commission be established. It would have a dual mandate: to analyze all matters relating to Quebec's accession to sovereignty and to study any "binding offer" from the federal government and the other provinces.

The National Assembly passed legislation based on "make us an offer or else" recommendations. It set up not one but two Committees: one to study sovereignty, the other to study "formally binding" offers from the federal government and the other provinces with respect to a new "constitutional partnership."

The option remains open for the provincial Liberals to use their legislative majority to repeal the referendum law for whatever reasons they choose. Premier Bourassa could, for example, announce that the latest federal proposal is not yet good enough, but shows some signs of promise. He could then use his majority in the National Assembly — assuming it stays loyal — to postpone the referendum and try to obtain yet more concessions from the rest of Canada. He might even call an election asking for a mandate to continue the negotiation process or hold a vote on the proposals rather than independence.

Some political analysts have suggested the following dance has already been choreographed by Prime Minister Mulroney and Premier Bourassa. The feds will propose something; Premier Bourassa will say "not good enough"; the feds will offer more; Premier Bourassa will say "see, I know how to negotiate with Ottawa," and call for a provincial election on the issue of who is best suited to extract even more. I cannot say whether such plotting has actually taken place, but the scenario is consistent with past attempts by federal strategists to carry out the real business in political back-rooms while presenting the public with well-scripted theatre.

Quebec's bargaining position is both powerful and perilous.

All this looks very threatening to the rest of Canada. In a way, however, the bargaining position of Quebec is also perilous. Quebec is threatening to bring down the roof on its housemate. If the vote is in favour of independence, Quebec is very likely going to separate. That would mean high transition costs for its people and a permanent loss of the benefits of confederation. Premier Bourassa may have only a lukewarm emotional attachment to Canada, but it is doubtful whether he is an ardent Quebec nationalist either. His main concern appears to be bringing lasting prosperity to the people of Quebec and he probably figures that staying in Canada is the best way to do that. If there is a referendum and the vote is against separation, then Quebec's power to threaten in the future will be minimized. So Premier Bourassa — whose highest aspiration appears to be lasting prosperity for his people rather than the trappings of independence — must be very eager to avoid a referendum. He is in a position, in other words, where he has every reason to find some merit in any federal proposal — at least enough to keep talking.

As I write several polls have found the pro-independence vote dropping below 50% for the first time since the death of Meech. Looking ahead, it is one thing to tell a pollster you are ready to separate; it is another thing to decide in favour of taking big chances with the economic stability of your society and your own family. In 1980, about 60% of the people of Quebec denied their provincial government even a "mandate to negotiate" something called "sovereignty-association." A decade later, will 50% vote for outright independence?

Perhaps they will. You can never tell for sure about politics. When Meech was signed, it had the support of the federal government, both opposition parties, and ten provincial premiers. Who thought it could be stopped? A little less than three years later, there was an all-party consensus in Manitoba insisting on change, and Premier Wells of Newfoundland was expressing strong opposition on the basis of deep personal conviction. Who at that time thought Meech could ever proceed without changes? Most thought the Accord was "so

Bryan Schwartz LL.B., LL.M., J.S.D.

much dead Meech." Yet in June 1990, Prime Minister Mulroney called together the First Ministers and held the Premiers of Manitoba and Newfoundland in a gruelling, week-long, closed meeting, hoping that the other Premiers would pound them into submission. The message was essentially this: do you want to be personally responsible for killing Canada? When an Accord finally emerged, calling for Meech to be passed in return for some vacuous promises about the future constitutional agenda, who thought Meech would not pass? Yet less than two weeks later, opposition by Elijah Harper, an aboriginal member of the Manitoba Legislature, ground the Manitoba process to a halt. Premier Wells was then able to rebound and successfully urge his Legislature to let Meech die without a vote.

It might be objected here that the example I just offered is largely a tale about First Ministers making decisions. What a small group of people will do may be highly unpredictable. What any one person will do is even more unpredictable, and changes in the conduct of one actor can drastically alter the overall chemistry.

Is the electoral behaviour of large groups of people more predictable? Look at the startling case of David Peterson, whose party had 50% in the public opinion polls when, understandably confident about the outcome, he called a provincial election well ahead of the normal cycle. A month or so later, his party was voted out of office and he resigned as its leader. Who would have thought that Ontario voters would have turned their backs on Peterson so suddenly? Many factors could affect an actual referendum campaign: among them are economic circumstances and the emergence of a charismatic leader.

It would be imprudent, therefore, to base any calculations on the confident prediction that the people of Quebec would not vote to separate in the near future. It is indeed possible, although from this distance I would consider it less probable than not, that the people of Quebec would vote to separate unless offered a highly decentralist package. At the same time, there is a possibility that the people of Quebec would actually accept a program of constitutional reform that built up the Canadian economic and social union rather than trying to buy off separation by further diluting the national community. My overall approach to the constitutional agenda is not based on discounting the possibility of Quebec's separating. It holds, instead, that the national unity problem cannot be solved by continuing to dilute the institutions, programs and symbols of national Canada. This would only accelerate the administrative and emotional detachment of the people of Quebec from the rest of Canada — and leave the rest of us without a nation of our own.

Should we feel threatened by the prospect of separation?

Suppose Quebec did separate. What would happen to the rest of us? We would have to absorb large transition costs ourselves. They would not be as severe in proportion to our wealth and population as Quebec's. Canada-without-Quebec would still be a very large and prosperous state and its economic credibility would exceed that of a new Quebec state with no track record of political or economic stability. These costs would be minimized if Canada-without-Quebec adopted an attitude of making the most of its new situation rather than seeking revenge in any way. No productive purpose would be served by trying to re-draw boundaries, for example. Native people in Northern Quebec might protest strongly but it might be possible to negotiate a Canada-Quebec-aboriginal treaty guaranteeing them fair treatment and self-government within an independent Quebec.

What about the longer run? The rest of Canada might actually derive new energy and self-confidence from separation. The national government of this country has been impaired by the constant need to assuage Quebec nationalism. The remaining provinces might be happy to have a strong central government under new circumstances. It would no longer be necessary that the Prime Minister be a bilingual person, and generally, from Quebec. There would no longer be massive transfers of wealth to Quebec for the illegitimate purpose of buying out separatism in addition to the laudable one of promoting the social welfare and economic development of fellow partners in confederation. The nation might find a new sense of national purpose, such as building its human capital — investing in the health, education and training of the people of Canada in the hopes of obtaining an exceptionally creative and productive society. Opinion polls suggest that the overwhelming majority of remaining Canadians would want to stick together even if Quebec left.

The fear of Ontario domination is not one that should be taken too seriously. The people of Ontario have a strong attachment to Canada as a whole, and could be relied upon to accept institutional arrangements (such as Senate reform) that would counterbalance its force within Confederation. Furthermore, it is not only Ontario that would increase its share of the population; so would all other parts of Canada. Currently, the population of central Canada (Ontario and Quebec) is over half of the total; if Quebec left, the people of the outer provinces would, for the first time, form a majority of Canadians.

Then again, there are risks. To many, Canada would seem like a smaller, less distinctive, or less interesting place. With Quebec having demonstrated that Confederation can be a way station, rather than a final destination, people in some other provinces might begin to ask whether their own destiny would be better served by independence or union with the United States. Once the sense of historic continuity and territorial contiguity has been disrupted, anything might seem possible.

A loss that is merely transitional in the great flow of history may be a grievous one in the short life of individual human beings. Maybe the two divorced polities — the rest of us and Quebec — would be better off a decade after the split but what about people who may lose their jobs because of economic uncertainties created by the split? As well, there is an appreciable risk of finding ourselves the citizens of tiny independent states or insignificant additions to the United States.

Despite the real risks, I think many ordinary Canadians would rather see Quebec separate than accept the prospect of their national community being steadily dismantled in order to accommodate Quebec nationalism. Whatever people want, the politicians are very likely to cut another denationalizing deal. Federal politicians have the usual electoral anxieties; if you take a stand against denationalist demands from Quebec, you chance writing off a quarter of the seats in the House of Commons. All of the politicians will be concerned about bearing moral responsibility for doing something that will break up the country.

Prime Minister Mulroney's tactic for securing the passage of Meech was not to attempt a reasonable accommodation with its critics; it was to isolate the Premiers of Manitoba and Newfoundland from their advisers and their constituents, and repeatedly have their colleagues pound into them the fact that they could be responsible for the destruction of the country. Constitutions are complex things and the future must be seen through a thick haze of uncertainty. It is almost easier, rightly or wrongly, to follow a course that leaves one with the majority of his or her political colleagues and avoids any immediate crisis. Agreeing to transfer more power to the provinces and allowing for plenty of opting-out of national programs and laws, can be seen not as denationalist but "bringing power closer to the people," or "valuing diversity." Who needs to bear personal responsibility for provoking an immediate rupture? Who does not want to demonstrate a spirit of good will and compromise to a national minority, the Quebecois? Is it not quintessentially Canadian to want to be praised for displaying a spirit of accommodation and compromise?

Many of the senior decision-makers are provincial premiers who tend to approach issues from the point of view of local leaders who have had frustrations in dealing with the national government. If the national parties are pushing power their way, it is difficult to expect them to assume a stance that is more oriented to promoting authority at the national level. The prospect of acquiring more authority personally must be a difficult one to discount.

It is certainly not impossible for a politician to support decentralist demands from Quebec believing that doing so is in the best interests of the country. The three national parties and almost all of the provincial premiers supported Meech Lake, despite strong opposition by most Canadians outside Quebec. It was almost impossible for the opposition to Meech to find a political exponent. This fact requires explanation.

It is logically possible that almost all the politicians were right about the merits of Meech and the people were wrong. My own assessment is otherwise; I do not think, as a general proposition, that the politicians involved were better informed or more insightful than the average Canadian and I do not believe that the politicians had a better case on the merits. Most of the factors that explain the near-passage of Meech still remain. The three national parties will still be eager to court electoral support in Quebec; all the senior politicians involved will find it difficult to resist the pressure to make a deal, any deal; the provincial premiers will still be attracted to acquiring more power for themselves and their provinces. The majority of Canadians, therefore, have every reason to be concerned that the current political system gives them no real voice in the outcome. A remedy must be found. I would suggest that it must include giving people the final say directly, through a referendum on any package that is negotiated by senior politicians.

Standards of Judgment

I would suggest that in making a final assessment on the constitutional front, it is important that all of us avoid locking ourselves into a mind-set that might be called "map syndrome." There is a tendency to think that Canada is being "saved" as long as Quebec does not formally separate but it avails a country little to maintain its monochrome colouring on a Rand-McNally Atlas if it loses its soul. The value of any political arrangement must be judged in terms of the material, emotional and spiritual returns it brings its people. An arrangement that technically holds the country together may leave Canadians poorer in all respects than would outright separation; it could leave us without the national institutions, symbols and programs necessary to produce a sense of community and the practical ability to promote prosperity, economic opportunity for all, and social justice. In the long run, an arrangement that denationalizes Canada may not be stable anyway.

As the institutional and programmatic bonds with the rest of Canada are weakened, it will become easier, both emotionally and administratively, for the Quebecois to take the final step out the door. Even the rest of Canada may become so unglued that it cannot resist the powerful natural forces of disintegration — which include immense geographic distance and the economic attractions of the United States.

We should also avoid the fallacy of decomposition. The mistake is to focus on diminutions of national community one piece at a time. It is hard to resist any single measure on the grounds that it is, in and of itself, lethal to the national community, even though the cumulative effect of the steady erosion of national programs, institutions and values will eventually destroy the viability of the country. At every stage, on every issue, doubters will be told something like "are you going to risk breaking up the country just because Quebec wants jurisdiction over labour market training?" To accept a break with Quebec is an onerous responsibility. It is tempting to constantly avoid a firm decision, and make just enough concessions to provincialism now to avoid it.

The situation reminds me often of the folk story about a matchmaker. He begins by telling a client about a prospective husband. The prospect is wonderful in every possible way. The woman is almost sold on the match. The matchmaker then says he has to admit "just one little problem." The man has a bad temper. The woman is concerned. The matchmaker points out that he is amiable enough most of the time, and "are you going to reject a perfect match just because he's a little chippy at times?" The woman says okay, why spoil a perfect match for just one little problem. The matchmaker then admits to another one. The man sometimes get drunk. Same reaction, same reassurance. And so it continues. One "little problem" after another. Finally, the matchmaker mentions that the man is bald. Finally, the woman says that's it, the match is off. The matchmaker concludes "I can't believe you're throwing away the perfect marriage for a few strands of hair."

One of the factors that may distort judgment among both politicians and the people is a weary longing for a "final settlement." A great many Canadians are utterly fed up with constitutional wheeling and dealing. They would love to have the matter settled, for better, or even for worse. In some ways, Prime Minister Mulroney is doing to the entire nation what he did to First Ministers during the Meech era: tell them that they can't leave the room until they sign something. There is a legal aphorism that "it may be more important for the law to be settled than for it to be settled correctly." There is something to be said for establishing a stable order, and getting on with things.

Depending on the settlement, the sense that it is final may be illusory. Many of the critics of the Meech Lake Accord believe that its passage would have settled nothing; Quebec's five conditions were the price it demanded for coming to the table. A further set of demands would have followed. The promise of an infinite series of annual First Ministers Conferences on the constitution would have provided a forum to press them.

Leading Quebec politicians, including Premier Bourassa, have certainly adopted this view in discussing this current round; they say that it should logically give Quebec more than it was offered in Meech, because the two phases (bringing Quebec to the table and satisfying its larger agenda) are now being combined.

A settlement is not final if the parties to it have a radically different understanding of what its terms mean. Nor is it final if it creates new avenues whereby one party can press for more and more concessions. The latest Federal Proposal creates mechanisms that would make it

Bryan Schwartz LL.B., LL.M., J.S.D.   17

much easier for the federal government to give away powers. Without a wall behind it — the necessity of obtaining the consent of other provinces — the federal government will be pushed backwards more easily. It is a safe bet that successive Quebec governments will be eager to exploit the opportunity.

In an eagerness to get on with other things we may also overlook the fact that a constitutional deal may make it impossible to get on with those other things. In his initial response to the Federal Proposals, Mr. Chrétien expressed his weariness with the whole constitutional reform business and his desire to move beyond it to other things — like jobs, competitiveness, the environment, health care. What if the constitutional deal has just impaired the ability of the federal government to act in these areas? As a matter of fact, the Federal Proposal actually does threaten to diminish federal authority over labour market training, the environment and health care.

Time pressure can also impair judgment. The Prime Minister tried to press First Ministers for important and difficult decisions at constitutional meetings without allowing them to go away, consult and reflect. In the current round, the federal government has tabled extremely complex and multifaceted proposals. Many aspects, such as reform of the Senate, could amount to a heavy round of constitutional reform in and of themselves. Substantial and practically irreversible changes to the structure of the country should be done with adequate deliberation not rushed through to accommodate arbitrary deadlines from a Prime Minister, one province or anyone else.

There are traps to avoid on the negative side as well as the positive one. The *ad hominem* fallacy is the discounting of a position by evaluating its proponent, rather than its intrinsic merit. The denationalist policies and manipulative tactics of the current government have earned it the distrust of many Canadians. It is disliked for many other reasons as well, including its overall handling of the economy and taxation. A successful constitutional deal may be both a political and morale booster for a government that, to a great many Canadians, deserves nothing but crushing defeat at an immediate election. The good of the country is more important than retribution on a few politicians, however misguided or devious they have been. A recent best-seller was called *When Bad Things Happen to Good People;* well, it is also possible that good ideas can happen to bad governments.

Mature political judgment does require a considerable willingness and ability to evaluate proposals independently of the motives of the proponent. We are not obliged, however, to read a proposal as though we knew nothing of the character and values of the current government. They tell us what to look out for. We should be open to the possibility that the proposals have surmounted or redefined the nature of the current government, but we do not have to be naive about the interest groups and ideologies that have consistently guided the government in the past. In looking at the package, it is legitimate to ask whether the government has attempted to entrench an outlook driven by the groups from which it derives its greatest intellectual and political support; these have included the big business lobby and Quebec nationalists.

Sometimes, it is not only legitimate but even necessary to reject a proposal on the basis of the process and methods used to create it. What a proposal means depends very largely on what people think it means. The most important effect of a constitution is the direction it gives to politicians and people, not the Courts. Sometimes a Court will have a chance to interpret a provision and occasionally, it may have the last word. Most of the action, though, is in the political arena. If a constitution is produced by inserting massive ambiguities and by offering different interpretations of them at different places, then nothing has been solved. What a constitution means in its largest emotional and political sense depends on whether people accept it as theirs, or as an imposition. Suppose that the Meech Lake Accord had been passed at the end of June, 1990. It would not have produced a lasting peace. It would have left most Canadians feeling that their opinions and interests had been treated with contempt; that the Constitution had been produced by the scheming and intimidation of a small political elite. There is no doubt that the government has learned a lesson from Meech, but is it that the judgment of the people should be respected, or merely that the government should go to greater efforts to create the appearance of public input?

Another factor that can distort judgment in the direction of a negative conclusion is perfectionism. Even if we all agreed on our constitutional vision, there are a variety of choices about drafting and mechanisms on which people would reasonably differ. Some of the aspects of actual amendments will be innovative and no one can predict with perfect accuracy how they will work. Of course there is a wide diversity of constitutional opinion that must be accommodated and all of us will have to accept some provisions which vary somewhat from our own notions of justice and pragmatics. A spirit of accommodation does not, however, excuse all. If we are truly shaping "Canada's future," there are some points on which people of integrity should not yield.

This evaluation of the Federal Proposal is the reflections of one whose occupation is teaching about the constitution at a law school. I believe that the standard of judgment one should expect from academics include: rationality in assessing facts and consequences, balance in the evaluation of the merits and demerits of a proposal, openness and independence in describing a vision of the nation There is, unfortunately, a serious problem in Canada with respect to the "independence" part of the equation, and therefore, with the rest of it. An "expert" who is prepared to sing the right song has excellent prospects to be paid for the tune. Even observing the "rest" marks for enough bars can earn its rewards. The patron may be a government or it may be a special interest group and the rewards may come in many forms: the financial reward of consulting contracts, the gratification of access to important political actors, the opportunity to spread the influence of your ideas. We already have enough politicians and lobbyists; the public can benefit from informed and nonpartisan judgment. There is cause for concern that even when holding forth in their academic capacity, academics may be tailoring their opinions to suit the needs of the marketplace. I can only assure you that I have always tried my best to be forthright.

It must be emphasized that independence does not mean scientific objectivity with respect to the overall evaluation of a proposal. On facts and predictions, we should try to be as reliable as possible. Some issues, though, are a matter of political philosophy which depend in part on values, not just facts. Do you believe in the supremacy of the rights of the individual or that group rights can sometimes outweigh them? Do you want a government that redistributes wealth or one that confines itself to maintaining efficient markets? Philosophies on these matters can and should be developed and revised in light of an examination of the facts, argument and reflection. At the end of the day, though, the political philosophy of every person depends on personal experience and commitments.

Bryan Schwartz LL.B., LL.M., J.S.D. 19

The perspective from which this book is written includes the following:

* a commitment to the supremacy of the individual, and the belief that groups and states must be judged solely on how they promote the liberty and welfare of individuals;

* individuals should be treated as political equals, rather than claiming special rights based on the history of the group to which they belong;

* political decision making should be open, honest and participatory;

* a major aim of political ordering is to facilitate co-operation among people who do not agree on abstract political philosophy. An aim of constitutional decision-making should be to devise practical arrangements that can be accepted by people with different "political theologies";

* the state is not merely a menace to be restrained. It has a legitimate role in protecting individuals from the oppression of others, in providing public services and in promoting social well-being;

* balanced federalism offers excellent prospects for promoting the protection of individuals, participatory democracy and providing for social welfare. Local government can sometimes provide more accessible and responsive decision-making; but it is also susceptible to be dominated by local factions and parochial outlooks.

* national government, properly utilized, can provide greater scope for individuals to achieve their personal, economic and political objectives, especially in a country as large and diverse as Canada; it can protect individual and minority rights from local oppression; it can maintain a framework of economic and social union that provides greater stability, security, and sharing.

I have attempted to find the positives as well as the negatives in the Federal Proposal, and where there are shortcomings, offer specific suggestions for improvement.

Shaping Canada's Future Together

The federal government released *Shaping Canada's Future Together* in September, 1991. Some of its proposals are set out in draft legal form. These allow for the most thorough analysis and specific suggestions for improvement. There are others on which the government takes a position, but in terms that are general and vague. In still other cases, the Federal Proposal indicates options, rather than stating a preference.

The Federal Proposal is the product of a series of closed meetings among federal cabinet Ministers. The government commissioned studies by various groups of deputy ministers, none of which have been released except in the form of controlled leaks. The government also commissioned an expensive series of public opinion polls at public expense, which it has chosen to keep secret as well. It appears that the process was an internal "mini-Meech" — a small group of individuals meeting in private, under great time pressure, crafting a "delicate compromise" which is presumably now untouchable in many respects.

A big difference, the government might tell us, is that it has consulted widely before formulating its proposals and is looking for further input now. The quality of post-Meech consultation, however, gives rise to concern about the future. The Spicer Commission and the Beaudoin-Edwards Committee have followed a familiar pattern: the government appoints a committee, dominated by those of its perspective; the committee travels the country asking people what they think; on many important issues, the majority on the Committee end up making recommendations that are congenial to the government's agenda, regardless of the fact that the people consulted had strong objections.

The Federal Proposal called for yet another Parliamentary Committee. It was supposed to "travel widely within Canada, to speak with Canadians and with their provincial and territorial representatives from coast to coast" and report in "early 1992." The Federal government is then supposed to "propose a plan" for Parliament's consideration. The time allotted in itself is inconsistent with a real concern for public input. How can members of the public reasonably be expected to study and respond to a proposal as complex and vague as the federal one in a matter of months? How can communities and organizations that take internal consultation seriously be expected to inform and canvass their members before the "deadline"? Yet the public hearings started almost immediately after the release of the Federal Proposal. Is this a selling job or a sincere invitaion to participate in the process?

As I write, there have been further causes for anxiety about the openness and responsiveness of the process. Political friends of the government have been hired to act as consultants. "Experts" and organizations who are known to be sympathetic to the government have been given invitations and plenty of "air time." Elected representatives of two parties representing a large segment of Canadian opinion — the Reform Party and the Bloc Quebecois — have been excluded, while unelected members of the Senate have been included. The government has declined to promise a referendum before pushing ahead. Indeed, it has not even promised an election before engaging in a major rewrite of the fundamental law of the nation. The "Special Joint Committee" has suffered from such poor organization that at least one of its stops, there was no one there to make submissions to it.

Even if nothing this study says makes any practical difference, I believe there is value in understanding for its own sake. If this study does nothing else but offer some information, insight or stimulation to others in their own attempts to appreciate the unfolding of important public events, it would accomplish one of its purposes.

Samual Johnson once defined an aquaintance's second marriage as the "triumph of hope over experience." There is certainly a strong case to be made for not getting involved at any political level; of "opting out" of any attempt to engage the merits of the Federal Proposal with a view to seeing it improved. Principled non-participation would be supported by the following specific considerations. The current federal government has no electoral mandate to rewrite the fundamental law of Canada; its past behaviour on constitutional reform do not justify confidence in either its constitutional vision or its respect for democratic process; the federal government has made no promise to even hold an election before proceeding with an overhaul of the constitution; it has not promised the people a referendum; it is proceeding with unreasonable haste to accommodate a deadline arbitrarily imposed by Quebec.

The "democratic deficit" in the process will indeed have to be addressed, and "public hearings" alone cannot do so. There is indeed a need to develop a process that permits adequate time for deliberation and advanced comprehension. In the meantime, though, proposals are being made that may reshape the fundamental law of Canada. This study proceeds in a spirit of trying to make a constructive contribution to that outcome. Whatever has happened in the past, or even the present, it may still be possible to hope that the future will be different. The Federal Proposals are entitled *Shaping Canada's Future Together*. Let us hope that we all will.

Bryan Schwartz LL.B., LL.M., J.S.D.   21

Putting Canada in the Canada Clause

The history of removing Canada from Canada Clauses

The "Canada clause" has an extensive history. It is a story of words that are missing because of a spirit that is dying. The "Canada clause" is supposed to be a statement recognizing the fundamental nature of Canada. What has historically met with the most resistance? Not the recognition of any of the parts; not the acknowledgment of aboriginal peoples, French-Canadians, women, multicultural communities. What has been most staunchly resisted is the recognition of a sense of shared national identity and community. The parts can speak for themselves. They do so loudly, well and effectively. Who speaks for a sense of national cohesion?

The 1867 Constitution: Structure without Decoration

As mentioned in the previous chapter, the *Constitution Act, 1867,* was functional and prosaic. It aimed to do no more than establish a spare legal framework for operating a federal union. It eschewed any attempts at prescribing high ideals or describing the national psyche. The preamble was laconic. It mentioned that provinces wanted to establish a union with a constitution "similar in Principle" to Great Britain's and that doing so would be good for both the locals and the Empire. The preamble adds that the Constitution should address matters of both legislative and executive authority and provide for the eventual admission of additional provinces. Only this, nothing more.

Trudeau's proposals during the Patriation era: From boldly affirming a transcendent national identity to silence.

In 1980, Prime Minister Trudeau proposed a First Ministers Conference on the constitution. He suggested an agenda that included a "Statement of Principles for a New Constitution." The statement began:

> We, the people of Canada, proudly proclaim that we are and shall always be, with the help of God, a free and self-governing people.

> Born of a meeting of the English and French presence on North American soil which had long been the home of our native peoples, and enriched by the contribution of millions of people from the four corners of the earth, we have chosen to create a life together which transcends the differences of blood relationships, language and religion, and willingly accepted the experience of sharing our wealth and cultures, while respecting our diversity.

No federal government would ever again formally propose as bold an affirmation of Canadian nationhood. The statement acknowledged aboriginal people, the two language communities, the multicultural heritage of Canada, the need for sharing and tolerance but it insisted that we were forging a distinctive national community "which transcends the differences."

As Trudeau recalled in his appearance before the Senate in 1988, in opposition to the Meech Lake Accord, the proposal created "one great scandal":

> The outrage of not only Premier Levesque but of the Quebec intelligentsia and the Quebec media was enormous. Somehow we could not even talk about "the people" of Canada. Of course, it was forbidden to talk about one Canadian "nation," but we found we could not even mention the people of Canada without offending the Premier of Quebec.

In October, 1980, apparently convinced that achieving unanimous agreement of the provinces was impossible, Trudeau announced his intention to unilaterally patriate the Constitution. While he claimed the legal right to proceed on his own, he obviously would have hoped to acquire a moral right as well by obtaining widespread support among the people of Canada and from a substantial majority of provincial governments. In this context, the resolution he proposed, for a *Constitution Act, 1980,* adopted a "less said the better" approach to the preamble; indeed, he settled on its logical conclusion, which was to say practically nothing at all.

The Constitution Act, 1982: Only God in the preamble.

While there was no symbolic preamble to Trudeau's initial Patriation package, its actual contents did reflect a variety of higher political ideals. Various constituencies within Canada responded in ways that forced Trudeau to incorporate their own visions. A review of how Trudeau responded will help to explain the dissatisfaction of the Quebec government, and its later demands for a "distinct society" clause; the response to Quebec's claims will in turn explain why the Federal Proposal has returned to where Trudeau started, with a proposal for a comprehensive preamble. Trudeau's initial Patriation proposal was not a something-for-everyone package; to a large extent, the package reflected Trudeau's philosophical preferences. He believed in a society of equal individuals, rather than assigning rights on the basis of group history. The *Charter of Rights* was forthrightly liberal and individualist and made few concessions to group rights.

Trudeau believed in the sovereignty of the people, rather than provincial governments; he proposed an amending formula that would allow legislatures to register consent, but also allowed the people to take matters into their own hands through a referendum.

> The idea of a shared Canadian identity was reflected in several ways: through a common standard of human rights, through a commitment to equalization payments for have-not provinces, through an amending formula that allowed a strong national majority to override the dissent of a few smaller provincial communities. Trudeau was concerned about Canada developing further into the "two solitudes": an English-speaking Canada, and a French-speaking Quebec. He urged the entrenchment of bilingualism at the federal level and the protection of linguistic minorities throughout Canada.

The original Trudeau package did offer some concessions to Quebec's concerns over its political autonomy. If an amendment was passing through the route of legislative ratification, the National Assembly could veto it; if an amendment was submitted to the people for ratification by a referendum, the people of Quebec could veto it. As a nod to the principle of the equality of the provinces, Quebec's veto was formulated as a veto for *any* province that had 25% of the population in 1981. The rights of aboriginal peoples were recognized, but only in the weakest possible form: a section of the *Charter* which declared that the affirmation of *Charter* rights did not detract from the existence of any other rights, including those of native people.

A Parliamentary committee held hearings on the Trudeau proposals. Eager to gain political support for the package, the federal government responded positively to a number of fragments of the mosaic who felt symbolically or substantially slighted. The changes it made were incorporated into the *Constitution Act, 1982*.

Let's look at the additions to the mosaic one tile at a time:

 * Multiculturalism: was not expressly affirmed in the initial draft; a s.27 was added to the *Charter,* encouraging that it be construed in a manner "consistent with the preservation and enhancement of the multicultural heritage of Canada";

 * Gender Equality: Trudeau's proposed *Charter* included a guarantee of individual equality in s.15, which specifically listed sex as a prohibited basis of discrimination but an energetic lobbying effort by women's rights organizations produced s.28 of the *Charter* as finally enacted, which re-emphasized the equality of men and women;

 * Mentally and physically handicapped: These categories were added to the list of prohibited grounds of discrimination in the final version of s.15;

 * Aboriginal rights: the initial Trudeau proposal contained only an acknowledgement that the *Charter* did not deny the existence of any other rights and freedoms, including those of "native peoples." The package was later changed in two ways. Section 25 was inserted in the *Charter;* it directs that the *Charter* should be construed in a manner that does not detract from any rights of the aboriginal peoples of Canada. Even more importantly, s.35 was added to the Patriation package. Section 35 positively acknowledges and protects "existing aboriginal and treaty rights." The Metis people eventually obtained an express *Charter* recognition that they, along with the Indian and Inuit peoples, were an aboriginal people;

 * Groups with denominational school rights: s.29 was added to the *Charter* in order to ensure that the *Charter's* guarantees of equality did not undermine the special educational rights and privileges accorded to some religious denominations by virtue of constitutional history;

 * Provincial rights: In order to attract greater support from provincial governments, Trudeau made some significant concessions to substantive demands for enhanced provincial jurisdiction. The authority of the provinces over the regulation and taxation of natural resources, including energy, was affirmed and expanded. At the insistence of the provinces, Trudeau eventually accepted, with minor modifications, the amending formula that had been pushed all along by most of them. It provided dissenting provinces with the ability to "opt out" of amendments which transferred power to the federal government and with respect to matters of education and culture, to obtain financial compensation for doing so. Quebec has sought a right to compensation in all cases. Trudeau agreed to the "notwithstanding clause" — a provision allowing a legislature to override many of the most important sections of the *Charter*, such as the guarantee of fair procedures in criminal cases and the right to freedom of expression.

 * Monotheists: One of the last political concessions Trudeau made was to the forces of monotheism. After the nine provinces and the federal government had worked out an apparently final deal, a vigorous lobbying effort induced the parties to introduce a short preamble to the *Charter* that recognized that "Canada is founded on principles that recognize the supremacy of God and the rule of law."

The mini-preamble in the *Charter* illustrates the perils of symbolism. It is not clear what the "God clause" is supposed to accomplish, or how it is to be reconciled with later sections that guarantee religious freedom and equality to every individual. Even as a factual claim about history, the theistic reference is dubious. The closest thing to a supreme being clearly recognized in the *Constitution Act, 1867* was the Parliament of Great Britain, which retained ultimate sovereignty over Canadian legal affairs. Whether an eternal moral consciousness exists is not an issue to be trivialized; nor is anyone's genuine faith. Glib avowals of theism that are motivated by politics and not conviction, are demeaning to all concerned.

Patriation and the theory of original sin: Was Quebec done a wrong that requires redress?

Both the provincial government and the legislature of Quebec rejected the Patriation package. It would have been surprising if a separatist government had not done so. One of Quebec's elected voices, the National Assembly, said no. The other, Quebec's representatives in Parliament, said yes. The federal government that brought about the Patriation package was led by a Prime Minister and Minister of Justice from Quebec. About half of Trudeau's caucus members were from Quebec and they represented almost every single riding in the province.

Even if the federal representatives of Quebec had a leading role in the Patriation initiative, what about the merits of the package? What about Quebec? Did it make any symbolic or substantial gains? Why did its government feel it necessary to pursue, among other things, a "distinct society" clause?

Quebec made as many gains as any other province and was subjected to one fewer restriction (it is not bound by guarantees of minority language rights with respect to immigrants from foreign countries). The Quebec economy is heavily dependent on hydro development; enhanced provincial jurisdiction over natural resources and energy development was hardly a minor gain. Quebec has been one of the biggest beneficiaries of equalization and other transfer payments; obtaining the entrenchment of the equalization principle was no small boon to Quebec. The "notwithstanding clause" has proved useful to Quebec in defending its laws against *Charter* challenges. The amending formula was very close to that sought by Premier Levesque himself as a member of the "gang of eight," a coalition of provinces opposed to Trudeau's initial package. It fell short of Quebec's aspirations as a member of the gang of eight in one limited respect: Quebec had wanted a general right to financial compensation in case it "opted-out" of constitutional amendments, whereas the package guaranteed compensation only in cases of language and culture.

As we have been reminded, the government of Quebec refused to endorse the final compromise package which later became the *Constitution Act, 1982*. Should we accept the theory of "original sin" — that Quebec was done an injustice in 1982, and that political justice now requires that Canada pay a certain "price" for Quebec's acceptance of the new Constitution?

While the oft-repeated claim by Quebec governments is that Quebec's powers were reduced by the Patriation package, it is impossible to demonstrate any substantial damage. On the amending formula front, Quebec obtained essentially what its own Premier had originally sought. Even if Levesque bungled the case by not insisting on wider veto powers, he was not giving up anything Quebec already had. In 1982, the Supreme Court of Canada re-affirmed that Quebec never had a veto power by law or by political convention.

As for the *Charter,* Quebec was subjected to it to almost the same extent as every other government; but even Gilles Rémillard, the Quebec Minister of Intergovernmental Relations, has characterized the *Charter* as a document of which the people of Quebec can, on the whole, be proud. Quebec was given special exemption from part of the minority language educational guarantees in the *Charter;* what did apply — only Canadians who themselves went to English schools in Canada can send their children to English schools in Quebec — went only minimally beyond what was allowed by Quebec's own language policies (which based rights on whether parents had gone to English schools in Quebec).

The guarantees of "fundamental freedoms" in the *Charter* could have had an impact on language policy. In the "sign law case" in 1988, however, the Supreme Court of Canada unanimously affirmed that Quebec's francization goals were legitimate objectives and could provide the basis for upholding restrictions on language freedom.

The overall conclusion must be that Quebec made significant gains in the Patriation package. The 1982 amendments did not present obstacles to Quebec's continuing protection of its linguistic and cultural heritage. Quebec's ability to protect its "distinct identity" already existed by virtue of being a predominantly French-speaking province.

To be fair, Quebec's desire for a "distinct society" clause of some kind was not unreasonable. The *Charter of Rights,* enacted in 1982, contained no explicit recognition that the promotion of the French language and culture was a legitimate basis for limiting the rights it protected. The Courts would not make it clear that the promotion of French language and culture was an acceptable basis for limiting *Charter* rights until the sign law case of 1988. Even now, a provincial government might want an entrenched safeguard, rather than allowing some future Court to move in the opposite direction. Furthermore, the *Charter* does expressly pay tribute to other cultural communities: specifically, aboriginal and multicultural ones.

While it was not unreasonable for Quebec to seek some recognition of its character, the most productive course might still have been to avoid insisting on the entrenchment of abstractions such as "distinct society." The greatest safeguard for the majority in Quebec was, and remains, that the provincial government is equipped with wide-ranging authority. The *Charter* already contains "reasonable limits" and "notwithstanding" clauses to help Quebec governments overcome claims that the rights of individuals and minorities take precedence over the safeguarding of the French language and culture. Quebec has more than its "rep-by-pop" share of Supreme Court of Canada positions (with only about a quarter of the population, it has a third of the judgeships). It could have contented itself with acquiring more of a role in the appointment of the judges who interpret the *Charter,* rather than trying to rewrite it in order to acquire yet another legal weapon to use against minorities and dissenting individuals. It might have been better for all concerned had Quebec advanced concrete proposals to enhance the powers of its legislature or government, rather than engaging Canada in a debate over a term as charged and abstract as "distinct society."

In any event, Quebec's demands, including "distinct society" recognition, should have been examined in the light of whether they amounted to improvements to a constitution that already treated the people of Quebec in a respectful and generous manner. Instead, Prime Minister Mulroney recklessly insisted that Quebec was owed something to compensate for its having been left feeling "rejected and isolated" in 1982. He was undeterred by the inconvenient fact that he had privately supported the Patriation package; that his own party voted for it; that Quebec was well-represented in the Trudeau government; that the package gave no new powers to Parliament, but enhanced fiscal rights and legislative authority of the provinces. In order to sell Meech as a "solution," Prime Minister Mulroney helped create the problem: a feeling among the ordinary people of Quebec that they had somehow been demeaned and rejected in 1982. Through his vigorous efforts, widespread indifference to constitutional affairs in Quebec turned into an unprecedented interest in independence.

"Distinct Society" in the Meech Lake Accord.

In February 1985, the Quebec Liberal Party's Policy Commission issued a paper entitled "Mastering our Future." It set out the five "conditions" for Quebec's acceptance of the political legitimacy of the *Constitution Act, 1982*. They were:

1. Express recognition that Quebec is a "distinct society";

2. A guarantee that Quebec would be consulted on Supreme Court of Canada appointments from that province;

3. A greater role for the province on immigration;

4. Limits on the federal spending power;

5. A veto for Quebec on Constitutional amendments.

The Meech Lake Accord

On April 30, 1987, after a one-day marathon session, the First Ministers surprised Canada (and many of themselves, who thought they were going for preliminary discussions only) by announcing they had reached agreement in principle on a constitutional accord. While a number of points were expressed in sketchy form, the "distinct society" clause was presented in full-blown legalese; the tortured drafting appears to be the result of secret Ottawa-Quebec dealings prior to the meeting. Further negotiations to draw up a formal legal text, culminating in the Langevin Block meeting of June 2-3, 1987, resulted in a series of qualifications to the original text. The final product read as follows:

2(1) The Constitution of Canada shall be interpreted in a manner consistent with

(a) the recognition that the existence of French-speaking Canadians, centred in Quebec, but also present elsewhere in Canada, and English-speaking Canadians, concentrated outside Quebec but also present in Quebec, constitutes a fundamental characteristic of Canada; and

(b) the recognition that Quebec constitutes within Canada a distinct society.

(2) the role of the Parliament of Canada and the provincial legislatures to preserve the fundamental characteristic of Canada referred to in paragraph (1)(a) is affirmed.

(3) the role of the legislature and Government of Quebec to preserve and promote the distinct identity of Quebec referred to in paragraph 1(b) is affirmed.

(4) Nothing in this section derogates from powers, rights or privileges of Parliament or the Government of Canada, or of the legislatures or governments of the provinces, including any powers, rights or privileges relating to language.

Among the other modifications to the Accord secured at the Langevin Block meeting was the addition of s.16. It provided that the "distinct society" clause did not "affect" the recognition of multiculturalism in s.27 of the *Charter*, or the rights of aboriginal peoples as recognized in section 25 of the *Charter* and other places in the Constitution.

The "distinct society clause" provoked more controversy than any other section of the Meech Lake Accord. My criticisms included the following:

* the clause could be read as giving an open-ended political mandate to Quebec to pursue its own separate development, rather than balancing its diversity with a commitment to the cohesion of Canada as a whole. There were no boundaries placed on what makes Quebec "distinct" and Quebec governments were free to interpret the mandate as justifying almost any departure from the national framework, whether it was opting out of national shared-cost programs or using the "notwithstanding clause" to override the language rights of minorities.

* the proposed clause did refer to Quebec's being "within Canada." Canada could be understood, however, as being merely a geographical or a legal framework incorporating quasi-independent states. There was no recognition of the necessity of building the country as a whole as well as building the province's own destiny. The word "distinct," in English, connotes "separate" as well as "distinctive"; the phrase "distinct identity" implies separate development much more strongly than a phrase such as "distinctive character." Should not the parts of Canada express some commitment to building the whole?

* the clause purported to "affirm" the role of Quebec, implying national approval of the approach Quebec was already taking to pursue its "distinct identity." Some of Quebec's policies, however, have been criticized for being parochial and oppressive. The use of the "notwithstanding clause" to ban English from signs was, to most Canadians, unacceptable. Some of Quebec's measures amounted to serious, and arguably unnecessary, restrictions on the freedom of members of the francophone majority as well as the anglophone minority. Provincial measures prevent francophone children from attending English-language public schools, and even limit the extent to which francophone children can obtain instruction about English;

* the clause was too heavily weighted in favour of the power of the francophone majority and against the rights of the anglophone minority. The only protection afforded to anglophones was to allow that they are "also present" in Quebec, and that the fact of their mere existence in Quebec should be preserved. There is no recognition that anglophones might be an integral and legitimate part of the Quebec society that is to be "preserved *and promoted*." The clause threatened to erode the legal and political position of anglophones beyond their already vulnerable position;

* the clause directed that the entire Constitution, including the federal-provincial division of powers, be construed in a manner consistent with Quebec's special role. The potential existed for Quebec to push, on both the legal and political fronts, a claim to special powers exercised by no other provinces; or at the very least, to push for legal or political recognition of greater powers for all provinces, in order to accommodate Quebec's special needs.

The beginning of the "Canada clause": early proposals to recognize other groups beside Quebec.

A series of spiralling events now led to a return to the concept of a comprehensive statement of Canadian values. The 1982 round had led to recognition of the claims of certain groups. Quebec responded by demanding recognition of its "distinct identity." The next upward twist came when some critics of Meech suggested that the recognition of Quebec's distinct identity should in turn be defined and moderated by putting it in the context of a larger portrait of the country.

A straightforward approach to Meech's perceived defects would be "cut-and-paste"; that is, delete certain phrases and try to replace them with better ones. A more subtle strategy was the "add-another-page" approach. Some reformers of Meech felt it was better to leave the existing language intact, but add some additional material to clarify the Accord and address the concerns of those who felt left out. The perceived advantage of "add-another-page" was that Quebec would be spared the indignity of having to surrender its preferred formulations. If a strict "add-another-page" approach were used, no legislature would have to withdraw its earlier approval of Meech. Instead, the remaining hold-outs — which by 1990, were Manitoba, Newfoundland and New Brunswick — would actually pass the Accord as is, and then everyone would pass the "additional page." Some called the latter a "parallel accord."

About half a year after Meech was proposed, the federal Liberal Party adopted a half-hearted combination of the two techniques. The House of Commons wing of the Party moved several amendments, but made it clear that it would vote for passage of the Accord anyway. With respect to the "distinct society" clause, the amendments mostly consisted of enlarging its scope. Amendments of this kind dealt with multiculturalism, aboriginal peoples, and the advantages of the "economic union." The Liberals also proposed language to directly moderate the impact of the "distinct society" clause, including an assurance that nothing in the Accord would derogate from any of the rights and freedoms guaranteed by the *Charter* or would affect Part II of the *Constitution Act, 1982* (i.e., aboriginal concerns).

On a few other issues, the Liberals proposed straight-out changes in wording. Among the notable revisions would have been the strengthening of the hand of the federal government with respect to national shared-cost programs. "Opting out" would only be permitted if provinces ran programs that met the "minimum national standards" of the federal government, rather than merely being "compatible with the national objectives," which was the requirement specified by the Accord.

In 1988, the Senate, then dominated by the Liberals, enacted a version of Meech that directly incorporated the proposals for amendments that the federal party had developed in 1987. The House of Commons responded by exercising its constitutional authority to override the Senate with respect to constitutional amendments.

Manitoba Task Force creates the Canada Clause: Other groups are recognized, but so is the Canadian community.

I had been an adviser to the Manitoba government during some stages of the negotiation of the original Meech Lake Accord, but for almost all of the 1987-90 period, my involvement in constitutional affairs was in the capacity of an independent academic. My suggestions for

Bryan Schwartz LL.B., LL.M., J.S.D.   29

improving and expanding the "distinct society" clause were advanced at various "public hearings" concerning Meech, including those before the Senate of Canada, the Legislature of New Brunswick, and the constitutional Task Force in Manitoba. The proposals were eventually published in 1989, in a Law Review article entitled "Refashioning Meech Lake."

The proposed redraft of Meech in "Refashioning Meech Lake" would have softened the quasi-separatist nuances of the "distinct society" clause. "Distinct society" and "distinct identity" would be replaced with "distinctive part of the Canadian nation." The nature of the "distinctiveness" of Quebec would be better defined by specifically identifying its salient components as its linguistic and cultural heritage. More recognition would have been given to the protection of the rights of individuals, and the role of various communities — including not only aboriginal peoples and our multicultural heritage, but linguistic minorities. The special features of Quebec's identity would be spelled out and defined, but it would be acknowledged that each of the provinces has a distinctive identity. The latter idea was eventually incorporated in proposals for reform advanced in January, 1990 by Premier Van der Zalm of British Columbia.

The proposed redraft sought to revive an idea that the Meech politicians utterly ignored. The idea was this: the Constitution should recognize the whole as well as the parts; that while we may have different aims in life as individuals, and affiliate with different communities, we all belong to a larger national community and we should be committed to building its distinctive character. Constitutional language committing all governments to "building the Canadian identity" would have provided a necessary legal and political counterbalance to the recognition of diversity in the Meech package.

Manitoba was one of the few provinces that held public hearings. It was the only one that fully acknowledged the widespread demands for changes in the Accord, accurately summarized the reasons for discontent and proposed substantial changes to the Accord before it was enacted. What it heard from many Manitobans was that their primary political identification was "Canadian"; not Manitoban, not English Canadian or French Canadian or Ethnic Canadian, but Canadian. In the fall of 1989, the Manitoba Task Force reported the following:

> The first step in transforming the [distinct society] clause into a Canada clause is to affirm the national identity and the character of Canada as a whole. The Task Force believes that the commitment of the provinces and the national government to uphold the national community and to foster a strong national identity must be first and foremost in a constitutional clause which celebrates Canada as a nation. Canada is comprised of many diverse parts but it is more than those parts. All governments should play a role in ensuring that the whole as well as the parts remain strong and united.

The Government of Newfoundland and Labrador adopted the Manitoba Task Force's "Canada clause" in its formal constitutional proposal of March 22, 1990. Premier Van der Zalm had adopted the Manitoba proposal to recognize a "distinct national identity" in his own initiative of January, 1990.

As the "deadline" for the passage of Meech approached, there were behind-the-scenes negotiations on a "Canada clause." The federal government encouraged Manitoba and Newfoundland to accept an ever more diluted version of it. While the federal government gave the impression that the Quebec government might actually accept a suitably diluted version, Quebec itself never directly offered the other provinces the slightest indication that it was even willing to discuss the matter.

In June, 1990, Prime Minister Mulroney invited the First Ministers to the infamous "roll of the dice meeting." The initial meeting was allegedly an informal dinner-time discussion, to see if there was sufficient agreement to proceed to formal negotiations. What actually happened is that First Ministers cloistered themselves in closed meetings, held every day almost all day, for a week, until the "hold out" Premiers could be pressured into submission. Mid-way through the sessions, drafts of "Canada clauses" were circulated by various delegations. By this point, the best that anyone was claiming for Canada was that its national identity was founded upon, and strengthened by, the diversity of the provinces. So much for bold affirmations that there is a national community that transcends regional differences.

The Prime Minister was not satisfied, however, with squeezing any meaning out of the Canada clause. History should not forget the political agreement that ended the June meeting — which ought to be remembered as the "Stockholm Syndrome" Accord. The "Stockholm Syndrome" refers to a phenomenon in which captives display a certain sympathy for their kidnappers. The "Stockholm Syndrome" Accord cannot bring itself to even speak of a "Canada clause." Instead, it refers to a "recognitions" clause, and snidely observes that no one has had much luck in developing a Canada clause in the past. The only "promise" that is made is an illusory one: a House of Commons committee would hold public hearings on a recognitions clause and report to a First Ministers conference the following year. Any recommendations would have to be "in a manner consistent with the Constitution of Canada" — which would include the Meech Lake Accord. In other words, no comprehensive "recognitions clause" could in any way moderate the impact of the "distinct society" clause.

In October, 1991, the Manitoba Task Force released its "post-Meech report." It re-affirms the commitment to making "Canada" foremost in the Canada clause:

> We recommend that the Canada clause begin with a clear statement expressing a commitment to a strong and united Canada. To advance this goal Canadians have chosen a federal governing structure which, while responsive to the provincial and community levels, remains committed to a strong sense of national identity.

Now, in 1991, the federal government is a convert to the "Canada clause." Or is it? Let us now take a closer look.

The Federal Proposal for a Canada clause — No Canada: The New National Anathema

Shaping Canada's Future Together, the Federal Proposal presented in September, 1991, does not present a draft legal text of the Canada clause. It does, however, prepare a "point form" list of values to be recognized. While allowing some room for adjustment, we may be sure that the formulations are considered ones and will be largely carried forward into the final federal proposal.

> While the discussion in the Federal Proposal says that:

> ...many who spoke to the Citizens' forum articulated a strong sense of a distinct Canadian identity

which sets us apart from any other country. They expressed a sense of deeply felt core values which they believe that *all* Canadians share...

What the Spicer Commission actually said, *inter alia,* was this:

> In fact, the desire of the majority of participants outside Quebec is for a strong central government which will act with resolution to remedy the country's economic ills, help to unify its citizens and reduce the level of division and discord among groups or regions.

The Spicer Commission, which consisted entirely of appointees by the Prime Minister, felt it necessary to go beyond reporting what the people said and provided its own comments. Not surprisingly, in view of how it was constituted, the conclusions are often more in line with the federal government's agenda, and even its catch-phrases, than with what the people of Canada said. The Report makes no recommendations in favour of strengthening or maintaining the authority of the national government. Instead, it calls for "responsible, honourable compromise," insists that the people of Canada are illogical and ill-informed when they stress the "equality of provinces" and recommends "special arrangements" to accommodate Quebec. The federal government had much earlier prepared a couple of "selling lines" for its decentralist agenda — "bringing government closer to the people" and "eliminating waste and duplication." The Spicer Report happily repeats these slogans, and they naturally show up in the Federal Proposal.

The Federal Proposal goes even further than Spicer in down-playing what the people had to say about the national identity and national government. Did the people tell Spicer anything about strong national government, institutions, programs? Apparently not; the "distinct Canadian identity" which "sets us apart from other nations" includes the following "core values":

> ...a belief in the need for equality and fairness as guiding principles for our society, a belief in consultation and peaceful dialogue, the importance of accommodation and tolerance, a respect for diversity, the need for compassion and generosity, the value of Canada's natural beauty, and the importance of a national conscience that spurs us to make our contribution to global peace and development.

Substitute "world" for "Canada," and you actually have a statement of the "core values" of the United Nations.

Let us now turn to the inspiring statement of shared national purpose that is the capstone of the Canada clause. The Federal Proposal would entrench a statement recognizing:

> ...a federation whose identity encompasses the characteristics of each province, territory and community.

Notice that there is no reference to a "distinct national identity." There is not even a "national identity." Come to think of it, there is not even a "Canadian identity." The word used is "federation" — a technical, unemotive term that refers to the partial union of component parts. Its "identity" is immediately said to "encompass" the characteristics of each and every subunit. Does the identity "encompass and transcend" the differences? We are not told.

So once again, we have no Canada in the Canada clause.

The failure is a symbolic and a spiritual one and will have a long-term impact on political rhetoric and psychology within Canada. It will also have a seriously adverse legal impact. A strong statement of shared national purpose and cohesion would help to moderate other parts of the Canada clause that grant special recognition to Quebec, aboriginal peoples and multiculturalism. The reference to "Quebec's distinct society," for example, will be invoked in court cases to argue that a matter should come under provincial, rather than federal jurisdiction; an affirmation that Canada is a national community would provide a counterbalance.

Aboriginal groups may define "self-government" in a manner that would (at least to some of us) be disruptive to notions of common citizenship and equality before the law. Does self-government mean, for example, that the *Criminal Code* does not apply within the territorial limits of an aboriginal government? Putting some "Canada" in the "Canada clause" would, again, help a Court to define a reasonable balance between accommodating diversity and maintaining unity.

To make what I have in mind a little clearer, let me make a specific suggestion. No doubt it could be improved, but here is a draft:

> Canada has a distinct national identity that embraces and transcends the diversity within it. All governments are committed to working together to ensure that the strength and coherence of the national community is maintained, and the federal government has a special responsibility to preserve and promote the symbols, institutions, programs and values that bring Canadians together as one people.

Yes, some of the provinces would resist something like this but the federal government should be putting forward the case for Canada, and fighting as hard as possible to ensure that the Canada clause does affirm the coherence of the national community. A federal government that believed in itself and in the future of Canada as one nation would challenge Quebec and the other provinces to explain and defend their objections, rather than starting with abject surrender to provincialism and division. Such a government would insist from the beginning and right through to the end that there will be no further recognition of diversity without a counterbalancing dedication to unity; that there can be no "Canada" clause unless it clearly and proudly proclaims that there is a strong and dynamic national community that includes us all.

Equality of the Provinces

Equality of the Provinces.

As we have seen, the Federal Proposal borrows the phrase "Canada Clause" but leaves out the "Canada." Another resounding omission in the Federal Proposal on the Canada clause is "the equality of all the provinces." Of course, an omission exists only in relation to an expectation. There is ample precedent, logic and public support for an "equality principle." Even the federal government has endorsed it on several occasions, both formally and informally.

We do not have to go far back for a formal recognition of the "equality of all the provinces" by the federal government and every single one of the provincial premiers. Here is the story. The Meech Lake meeting of April, 1987, produced only a "point form" agreement. Some points were addressed in a political accord that would accompany the draft amendments. After bureaucrats were unable to agree on several points, such as the exact wording of the spending power clause, a First Ministers meeting was convened at the Langevin Block in Ottawa to close the deal. Towards the end of the meeting, the Alberta delegation insisted that the political accord must recognize "the equality of all provinces." All the participants, including Prime Minister Mulroney and Premier Bourassa, agreed. The political part of the Meech Lake Accord stated that the Accord would "recognize the principle of the equality of all the provinces."

The "distinct society" clause of the Meech Lake Accord caused considerable concern among Canadians that Quebec was being given privileged status, both legally and symbolically. The remedy I proposed in "Refashioning Meech Lake" was this: recognize that each of the provinces is a distinctive part of the Canadian nation, and then spell out the specific features of Quebec (language, culture) that accounted for its distinctiveness. Premier Van der Zalm would later propose something along these lines.

The approach of the Meech-era Manitoba Task Force on the Constitution and of the Newfoundland government was to protect equality by altering and limiting the "distinct society clause." Around the time the "Stockholm Syndrome" Accord was being negotiated, there was some exploration of whether the same objectives could be accomplished by positively affirming the equality of provinces in the Canada clause, rather than putting constraints on the "distinct society." As we have seen, the federal government ultimately chose to try to pressure Manitoba and Newfoundland into ratifying the Accord without a comma being changed.

Two recent contributions to the "Canada round" have called for recognition of the equality of the provinces: On October 22, 1991, Premier Wells released a "Commentary on the Federal Proposals." It holds that:

> If there is to be a Canada clause identifying the essential values of the Canadian federation it would be unacceptable not to include recognition of the principle of the equality of the provinces.

Less than a week later, the Manitoba Task Force on the Constitution concurred; a Canada clause should include "a recognition of the fundamental equality of provinces." An "equality of the provinces" principle would not suggest that all provinces are the same. It could be reasonably understood in the following ways:

* provinces have the same powers to pass laws. They may use that authority to pass different laws, depending on local circumstances and values. Exceptions to the equality of constitutional authority have been few in number and limited in scope, and should remain so;

* the federal government cannot discriminate, economically or otherwise, against any the government or residents of any province. "Discrimination" means arbitrary favouritism or adverse treatment. Federal measures, such as equalization payments, that respond in a consistent and even-handed manner to special needs are acceptable.

The absence of equality in the Canada clause is matched by a commitment to inequality in the rest of the Proposal. Specifically:

* a major aim of the Senate reform movement has been more economic fairness for less populous provinces. The Federal Proposal would deny the Senate any power over money bills;

* the Federal Proposal calls for the entrenchment of an "economic union principle," but the principle is defined only in terms of the free movement of goods, services, capital and people. There is no explicit guarantee against discrimination in government procurement policies, or taxing and spending measures. On the contrary; the Federal Proposal entirely exempts equalization and regional economic development programs from the scope of the "economic union" principle;

* the only federal spending that would be rendered more difficult would be national shared-cost programs, which, along with equalization payments, tend to be among the most rational and even-handed forms of federal transfers;

* the Federal Proposal would allow Parliament to delegate any powers it wants. The federal government will be able to give away its powers to some provinces and offer them financial assistance in return for relieving the federal government of its responsibility. The door is wide open for "profitable separatism";

* the Federal Proposal would allow the federal government to enter into constitutionally binding agreements with provinces on immigration and culture. The federal government would reserve the right to make a deal that is "appropriate to the circumstances of each province." Again, the path is created for all sorts of inequality and for "profitable separatism";

* the Federal Proposal would allow up to three provinces to "opt-out," perhaps indefinitely, from laws that Parliament passes, and the proposed Council of the Federation approves, under the proposed new "economic union" power;

* the "Canada clause" singles out Quebec as a "distinct society," and describes its government and legislature as having a "special responsibility to preserve and promote" that society. In the absence of an "equality of the provinces" principle, there is a limited risk that the Courts will interpret the general provisions of the Constitution in a way that gives Quebec, but not other provinces, authority over certain subject matters. The far greater risk lies in how the clause will be

read at the political level. The federal government may cite it as a justification for handing over money and power to Quebec on terms that are not available to any other province and which amount to "profitable separatism."

* The distinct society clause" of the *Charter* will provide that Quebec has special authority to limit *Charter* rights in order to promote its "distinct society." The Courts have already decided that the preservation and advancement of French in Quebec may justify limiting some *Charter* rights to a limited extent; for example, the National Assembly may require that commercial signs contain French, although other languages cannot be banned outright. It is possible, though not certain, that the formulation of the "distinct society" clause in the latest Federal Proposal will tip the balance even further against the anglophone minority. The issue will be discussed further in the next chapter.

While the Federal government has at times paid at least lip service to the principle of the "equality of provinces" (for example, in the Meech Lake Accord) it has manipulated events in this round to discourage recognition of the principle. Look at what happened with the Spicer Commission.

Purportedly formed to solicit the opinions of the people, the Spicer Commission was appointed entirely by the Prime Minister, without consulting with the other federal parties. Among the appointees were people such as a senior constitutional adviser to the Prime Minister during the Meech Process. From the beginning to the end, the Commission went out of its way to discourage and dismiss public opinion on one key point: the equality of the provinces.

The interim Report of the Spicer Commission, dated March 20, 1991, found that Canadians were insisting on the equality of provinces, but were apparently unaware of the extent to which the existing Constitution makes special arrangements. The same "finding" is repeated in the final Report of the Spicer Commission.

It is the people who have it right, not the Spicer Commission. The general principle of the Canadian constitution is that provinces have the same legal powers. The 1982 amending formula was established in strict adherence to the principle that no province is intrinsically entitled to a greater vote than any other. True, there are exceptional provisions for certain provinces; the fact that the federal government habitually cites such examples as a promise of railway service in the *British Columbia Terms of Union, 1871,* shows just how limited the exceptions are. There are no significant exceptions with respect to the Constitutional definition of the areas in which provinces can legislate; they are the same for all provinces. The exceptions under the existing Constitution relate to matters such as minority language rights (Manitoba, Quebec and New Brunswick have varying degrees of official bilingualism) and denominational school rights. Entrenching the principle of the equality of the provinces would not rule out recognizing some special linguistic or cultural arrangements for Quebec. The exceptions, however, should remain rare and limited. They should be structured so that any economic or political inequality that follows is minimized.

The existence of the "equality of provinces" principle is hardly disproved by showing it is not absolute. It is not inconsistent with the nature of a principle that it admits of exceptions. We have not refrained from proclaiming religious liberty and individual equality in the *Charter of Rights and Freedoms* even though some denominations retain special constitutional privileges under earlier arrangements.

Perhaps the drafters of the Federal Proposal were concerned that if they recognized the "equality of the provinces," it would be impossible to resist strict equality in the Senate. Not so. The principle of the "equality of provinces" does not necessarily dictate strictly equal Senate representation, in addition to equal legal authority for provinces and non-discriminatory treatment by the federal government. The principle of the equality of the provinces should be understood in light of its underlying justifications.

There are strong foundations in principle for saying that all provinces have jurisdiction over the same matters. Canadians should have an equal measure of local self-government. Lack of equality would also undermine the democratic legitimacy of Parliament. If Quebec had, say, jurisdiction over labour market training, but no other province, how could it be proper for Quebec members of Parliament to have an equal say in national policy? Determining policy for others, when it does not apply to yourself, amounts to colonialism. All provincial governments and their residents should be treated in an even-handed manner by the federal government.

On the other hand, it is not obvious that all the units of a federation must have equal representation in an upper Chamber. The American system works this way, but it is not the only way. It is impossible to find any democratic first principle that explains why Prince Edward Island should have as many Senate Seats as Ontario, which has eighty times the population. Strict equality of provincial representation arguably departs excessively from the principle of "one person, one vote." I understand Senate reform as a way of ensuring that all provincial governments and their residents are treated fairly by the national government. Giving all the power to a rep-by-pop House of Commons seems to result in political impotence, and adverse economic treatment, for less populous parts of the country.

The European Community observes the principle of legal equality of its members. It also observes a non-discrimination principle. Political decision-making is not always done on the basis of strict equality of states. The European Council often uses a weighted voting system; smaller states have more clout than they would under "rep-by-pop," but less than they would under strict equality of states.

If agreement can be reached on an equitable Senate, rather than a strictly equal one, it is possible that the federal government will be less negative about recognizing the "principle of the equality of all the provinces."

The entrenchment of the principle of "equality of provinces" would have several salutary effects. It would help to ensure that the Constitution is not interpreted or applied in a way that leads to more and more inequality in the powers of different provinces. It would discourage judicial and political action that would arbitrarily discriminate in favour of one province over another.

The Federal Proposal's disregard for equality in its specific suggestions for new governmental arrangements should be remedied by:

* eliminating the massive loopholes in the economic union package, and positively affirming that non-discrimination with respect to every province and its residents is a fundamental principle of the economic union;

* giving the reformed Senate real power over economic issues, including oversight of whether federal taxing and spending is consistent with the non-discrimination principle;

* affirming that Canada is a social union, and requiring provinces to at least observe minimum national standards in the shared-cost area, rather than being able to "opt-out" and still claim federal money;

* eliminating provisions of the Federal Proposal that would allow Parliament to freely delegate its legislative authority — that is, to hand over whatever powers to whatever province on whatever terms it wishes.

Chapter

4

The Distinct Society Clauses

Distinct Society Clause

The Federal Proposal would respond to Quebec's demands for recognition of its "distinct society." There would have been great advantages in avoiding the phrase altogether, and trying a different formula. The 1991 Progressive Conservative policy convention referred to Quebec as "unique." It was a promising idea and would have given constitutional drafters a fresh opportunity to avoid the obscure, unbalanced or provocative aspects of the Meech Lake draft. By hauling out the "distinct society" phrase again, the federal government has invited minute comparisons with Meech Lake and at least some parties are going to think they have lost something in the transition. It would appear that the federal government eventually figured that the phrase has too much emotional significance in Quebec to be replaced and senior federal cabinet Ministers have suggested that the phrase is now sacrosanct.

The Federal Proposal would recognize the "distinct society" in two places. It would be part of the "Canada clause" and would be embedded in the *Canadian Charter of Rights and Freedoms*, with other interpretive sections.

Actual text of the Federal Proposal

The "Canada clause" would recognize:

the special responsibility borne by Quebec to preserve and promote its distinct society.

The *Charter* would be amended to include the following new section:

25.1 This Charter shall be interpreted in a manner consistent with:

(a) the preservation and promotion of Quebec as a distinct society within Canada; and

(b) the preservation of the existence of French-speaking Canadians, primarily located in Quebec but also present throughout Canada, and English-Speaking Canadians, primarily located outside Quebec but also present in Quebec.

(2) For the purposes of subsection (1), "distinct society," in relation to Quebec, includes:

(a) a French-speaking majority;

(b) a unique culture; and

(c) a civil law tradition.

In an earlier book, *Fathoming Meech Lake*, I devoted sixty-nine pages of close analysis to how courts and politicians might interpret the Meech version of the "distinct society" clause. No doubt the latest version would sustain an effort of similar breadth and intricacy. I think, however, that I am protected by some sort of intellectual double jeopardy principle, the same one that says you only have to figure out a Rubik's cube once. They can't just give it a couple of twists and make you do it again, can they? Anyway, here's some brief observations:

* this time, there are two "distinct society" clauses, one in the "Canada clause" and one to be inserted in the *Charter*. The "Canada clause" could be worded so that it does not affect the interpretation of the Constitution, but generally speaking, anything in a Constitution — even a preamble — has some interpretive weight. The "Charter d.s.c." (distinct society clause) is expressly stated to be interpretive, and therefore will carry extra weight. The fact that there is no d.s.c. expressly attached to parts of the Constitution dealing with the division of powers, as opposed to the *Charter*, may encourage courts to conclude that Quebec receives no more areas of jurisdiction than any other province;

* There is some risk, however, that the "Canada clause" d.s.c. will lead the courts to interpret the Constitution so as to allow some special legislative powers for Quebec. There is no "non-derogation" clause to protect the powers of Parliament (as there was with Meech) and no reference to the "equality of provinces";

* The disruption to the federal system from the "Canada clause" d.s.c. is more likely to come from politicians than from the courts. It is easy to imagine the federal government using the "Canada clause" d.s.c. to justify making special deals with Quebec to transfer legislative and administrative powers and generous funding to handle the new responsibilities;

* Notice that the "Charter d.s.c." gives a definition of the "distinct society," but the "Canada clause" d.s.c. does not. It cannot be assumed that the "Charter" definition carries over into the "Canada clause." The language of the Federal Proposal may even suggest otherwise. The "Charter d.s.c." expressly says that the definition offered is "for the purposes" of *Charter* interpretation. A possible inference is that "distinct society" has a wider meaning in the Canada clause and that this more expansive meaning affects such matters as the division of powers;

* The "Charter d.s.c." says that Quebec has a "French-speaking majority." My suggested redraft of the "distinct society" clause in "Refashioning Meech Lake" would have said that Quebec has a "French speaking majority and an English speaking minority." My version would have made it clear that the anglophone minority is an integral part of Quebec's evolving society. The latest Federal Proposal will be read by Quebec politicians, and probably the courts as making it clear that anglophones are merely a "presence" whose existence is to be "preserved," in contrast with the francophone majority, which is to be "preserved and promoted";

* Anglophones may draw some consolation from the fact that the Federal draft refers to a "French-speaking" majority, rather than Quebec's being a "French-speaking society." The reference to "majority" immediately reminds us that there are minorities as well. A Court looking at the proposed s.25.1, the "Charter d.s.c.", would readily notice that it is placed in proximity with sections acknowledging a series of minorities: aboriginal peoples (s.25), anglophones (s.25.1.(1)(b)), multicultural communities (s.27);

* Anglophones may draw some consolation... but not that much. The "Charter d.s.c." is going to say that Quebec's "distinct society" will be "preserved and promoted"; that multiculturalism will be "preserved and enhanced"; but the anglophone presence is merely to be "preserved." The politicians and the courts will use the contrast to the detriment of anglophones;

* The second-class constitutional status that is assigned to language minorities (anglophones in Quebec and francophones outside of Quebec) cannot be justified on the basis that Quebec's majority is itself a threatened minority in the context of North America. The fact of the matter is that the proportion of the Quebec population that is francophone is holding up very well. The

anglophone minority does not have a high birth rate and is threatened by continuing out-migration, partly due to uncongenial social and political circumstances;

* The "reasonable limits" clause of the *Charter* already provides Quebec's majority with ample opportunity to promote the French language. The "Charter d.s.c." threatens to tip the balance even further in favour of the majority and against individuals and minorities. Currently, the Supreme Court decisions on whether Quebec language laws are justified limitations of *Charter* rights are based on the "reasonable limits" clause alone. The same general test of justification thus applies equally to all provinces; what varies is how the Court will apply the test to the particular social circumstances in a province at a given time. In the "sign law" case, the Supreme Court of Canada agreed that the Quebec legislature could limit *Charter* rights to serve the objective of enhancing the position of the French language in Quebec. At the same time, it found that a total ban on languages other than French exceed the bounds of "reasonable limits" of *Charter* rights in pursuit of that objective. In the "sign law" case, the Court accepted that the French language in Quebec was in a vulnerable position. If the Courts continue to rely on the "reasonable limits" analysis alone, they might someday find that the position of the French language has become more secure and assess restrictions on the use of other languages accordingly. By contrast, the "Charter d.s.c.", with its fixed and sharply contrasting value system — French language majority first, anglophones second — may tend to push the Courts to provide even less protection for Quebec language minorities than they currently do;

* The Meech Lake d.s.c. would have "affirmed" the role of the Quebec government and legislature in "preserving and promoting" the "distinct identity of Quebec." The latest Federal Proposal does not use "affirmed." The deletion of "affirmed" amounts to progress — at least for those of us who are concerned about maintaining national cohesion and the protection of individual rights.

The use of "affirm" in Meech might have sent several messages that most Canadians would never wish to endorse. As a general matter, the word "affirm" implies an endorsement of something that already exists. (Section 35 of the *Constitution Act, 1982,* uses "affirm" to extend constitutional protection to the rights aboriginal peoples had acquired by historical usage or treaty).In the Meech Lake d.s.c., the word "affirmed" could have been read as endorsing the way Quebec's National Assembly had been defining and implementing its "distinct society" role.

Bill 101, the *Charter of the French Language,* refers to French as the "distinct language" of Quebec. Ratification of the Meech Lake Accord could have been interpreted as a recognition that Bill 101 was entirely appropriate, even though some of its provisions may amount to undue restrictions on individual freedom.

In 1988, the National Assembly overwhelmingly voted in favour of Bill 178, which used the "notwithstanding clause" to overturn rights the Supreme Court recognized in the "sign law" case. Had Meech been passed in 1990, it would have wrongly implied that Canadians generally accept the more separatist and exclusionist connotations of "distinct society."

The latest Federal Proposal does more than simply drop the word "affirm." It also recommends making the "notwithstanding clause" more difficult to use. A simple majority vote in a legislature would no longer be sufficient to invoke it. A sixty per cent vote by all members of the legislature (and not only those voting) would be required. The reform of the "notwithstanding clause" goes nowhere near far enough but at least it sends the message that the rest of Canada is uncomfortable with Quebec's use of the "notwithstanding clause" in the Bill 178 episode;

* The Meech Lake d.s.c. contained no explicit definition of "distinct society." In the Federal Proposal, the "Charter d.s.c." (but not the "Canada clause" d.s.c.) gives some indication of the key elements. The distinct society is said to "include" (or in the French version, "*comprend*

notamment") these three elements: a French speaking majority; a unique culture; and a civil law tradition.

The use of "includes" allows that there may be elements to Quebec's "distinctness" apart from language, culture and civil law. On the other hand, by singling out three elements for special mention, the Federal Proposal would make it more difficult for Quebec to argue that its "distinctness" includes, for constitutional purposes, other major elements, such as economic, financial and social arrangements. The limitation of the scope of "distinct society" does not, of course, imply that Quebec has no authority in these areas. The significance is that the "distinct society" concept will be less available to justify attempts by Quebec to extend its existing powers in these areas.

It must be emphasized again that the Federal Proposal includes a definition of the d.s.c. only for the purposes of *Charter* interpretation. Unless the definition is extended to the Canada clause, it offers very little comfort to anyone worried about how constitutional recognition of a "distinct society" is going to be exploited in the future to promote decentralization in general and special arrangements for Quebec in particular.

Suggested Improvements

If the federal government is determined to push ahead with its attempts to constitutionally entrench the term "distinct society," it should at least:

* make sure the definition of "distinct society" applies for all constitutional purposes, and not only the interpretation of the *Charter*;

* put the recognition in proper context, by balancing it with express recognition of Canada's nationhood, the equality of the provinces, and respect for individual rights;

* eliminate the stark contrast between "preserving" linguistic minorities, as opposed to "preserving and promoting" multiculturalism and "preserving and promoting" the distinct society. The Constitution should affirm that the "existence" of language minorities should also be "preserved and *promoted*" throughout Canada. The anglophone minority in Quebec should be recognized as part of its "distinct society";

* remove the aspects of the package which allow special status for Quebec to be established by the back-door. These include proposals such as: allowing constitutionalized agreements on immigration and culture, without any guarantee that other provinces will be offered equally favourable terms and conditions; allowing Parliament to delegate its powers to any province it chooses, on any terms and conditions it chooses; allowing any province (which in reality is especially likely to be Quebec) to opt-out of national shared-cost programs and out of the "economic union"; giving the Quebec government far more influence than the federal government over Supreme Court appointments from Quebec.

Individual and collective rights

The Federal Proposal makes a definite commitment to enhancing the "collective rights" of the francophone majority in Quebec. The proposed "distinct society" clause in the *Charter* would entrench a two-tier value system in which "preserving and promoting" the French language majority in Quebec is priorized over "preserving" the anglophone minority. The clause could be used to tip the balance in favour of laws that favour the French language and culture at the expense of individual rights and freedoms.

The Meech Lake "distinct society" clause was similarly groupist in nature. The perceived threat to individual rights under the *Charter* was a focal point for much of the opposition to the Accord. The federal Liberal Party and the Manitoba Task Force on Meech, among others, recommended amending Meech by inserting a clause that would expressly protect the *Charter* from the "distinct society" clause. A compromise approach that emerged from other quarters would have tried to moderate the impact of the "distinct society" clause by placing it in a larger context. The Ontario Committee on the Constitution, for example, recommended that Meech be passed but that the Constitution should eventually be amended to recognize that the "fundamental characteristics of Canada" include:

> a recognition that the commitment to the protection and guarantee of the rights and freedoms of all Canadians constitutes a fundamental characteristic of Canada.

The Ontario proposal could certainly be dismissed as vacuous in one sense. It proposed a fairy-tale process whereby Quebec would acquire a "distinct society" clause under Meech, and then, in return for nothing, risk weakening the clause by re-affirming the *Charter*. If it actually had been passed at the same time as Meech, the Ontario amendment would have had a positive effect. It would have encouraged judges and politicians to read the "distinct society" clause in a way that was respectful of individual and minority rights. It would not be easy to read the "rights and freedoms of all Canadians" as including the "collective right" of the Quebec majority to limit the rights of its minorities. The "rights and freedoms of *all Canadians*" would most likely be construed as encompassing the universal human rights guaranteed in the *Canadian Charter of Rights and Freedoms,* but not the collective rights of one language group in one part of the country.

The Federal Proposal contains two "distinct society" clauses, one in the "Canada clause," the other in the *Charter*. The rest of the Canada clause is drafted with scrupulous care to make sure that it cannot in any way act as a counterbalance to the rights-limiting effect of the "distinct society" clause.

Notice the following features of the proposed "Canada clause":

* "Canada" is defined as a "federation" whose "identity encompasses the characteristics of each province, territory and community." The special character of Quebec is implicitly affirmed as being part of the Canadian identity. By contrast, a commitment to rights and freedoms, or the dignity of the individual, is not;

* the phrase "fairness, openness and full participation in Canada's citizenship by all people, without regard to race, colour, creed, physical or mental disability or cultural background" contains no reference to language. The only explicit reference to minority language communities relegates them to the status of a second-class constitutional concern; they are to be "preserved," whereas the "distinct society" is to be "preserved and promoted";

* the phrase "the importance of tolerance for individuals, groups and communities" makes no concessions to the supremacy of the individual over the group and the community. If the phrase were invoked in Court by an individual seeking protection against "distinct society" legislation, Quebec would respond that "tolerance" for the Quebec "community" is no less important than "tolerance" for its minority;

* the phrase "respect for the rights of its citizens and constituent communities as set forth in the *Canadian Charter of Rights and Freedoms*" is again drafted with a view to ensuring that no recognition of individual rights can be cited as a counterbalance to the recognition of Quebec's "distinct society." Anyone saying "respect my rights as set forth in the Charter" will meet this response from Quebec: "your rights as set forth in the Charter have to be interpreted in light of the 'distinct society' clause. Indeed, the 'distinct society' is not only a limitation on your rights; it amounts to an implicit affirmation that the Quebec majority has 'collective rights'".

* the phrase "the balance that is especially Canadian between personal and collective freedom on the one hand, and on the other hand, the personal and collective responsibility that we all share with each other" is again drafted to put individual and "collective rights" on the same plane. The phrase "responsibility we all share with each other" would appear to invoke the earlier reference to "the special responsibility borne by Quebec to preserve and promote its distinct society."

The Federal Proposal for a "Canada clause" marks a major step forward for the "collective rights" ideology. The English version refers variously to rights of "constituent communities" and to "collective freedoms" and "collective responsibilities." The French version explicitly uses the phrase "collective rights." Those who believe in the supreme importance of the individual have reason to be concerned.

There can be no denying that the Constitution already recognizes certain rights that are enjoyed only by members of particular groups. The primary examples include: denominational school rights, minority language educational rights and aboriginal and treaty rights. Each of these rights has its own peculiar features. The Constitution has never before recognized the general category of "collective rights."

"Collective rights" may be invoked against non-members of the group; for example, the "collective rights" of the French-speaking majority of Quebec have been cited as a justification for restrictions on the rights of the anglophone minority. "Collective rights" may also be invoked to justify restrictions on members of the group themselves; the same "collective rights" thus may be used to justify limitations on the freedom of Quebec francophones to obtain English-language instruction for their children.

Constitutional recognition of the general concept may give renewed impetus to the promotion of "groupism" at the expense of political equality for all Canadians, and the freedom of individuals.

Individualism versus Groupism in a Historical Context.

Canada has always experienced a tension between two political visions. One is the liberal individual vision; that Canada is a society of free and equal individuals. The other may be called "groupist." It holds that certain groups have rights that are equal or superior to those of individuals.

The groupist perspective in Canada has tended to include a large element of historical reasoning. Adherents of the "history-based groupist" vision may believe that aboriginal peoples have special rights to self-government by virtue of a history of self-government pre-dating European contact. Similarly, the French-Canadians of Quebec have a special right to retain their language and culture by virtue of being a founding people. Some advocates of preferential treatment for members of "minorities" argue in historical terms: that past injustices against the group should be redressed by special measures to help its current members, regardless of whether they have personally experienced discrimination.

Today, groupist thinking seems to hold that groups are the fundamental unit of moral account, regardless of any historical claims. The "representational" theory of social justice is common now; it is often asserted that the demography of various occupations or political institutions should roughly match the demography of society as a whole. The Federal Proposal on the Constitution urges that the method of electing people to the reformed Senate should "give expression to the social diversity of the Canadian population, keeping in mind the history of the inadequate political representation of women, aboriginal peoples and ethnic groups." No doubt the response of various advocacy groups will be to demand that a fixed quota of seats be set aside for women, aboriginal people and other "minorities."

The tension between individualism and groupism is reflected in our founding texts. In several crucial respects, the *Constitution Act, 1867,* reflected liberal individualist thinking. The *Act* created a federal order of government based on representation-by-population in the House of Commons; almost no special guarantees of representation were extended on the basis of ethnic or linguistic background. The Senate, by contrast, guaranteed extra representation for the wealthy and for those in less populous parts of Canada. The fact that the Senate was a chamber for the privileged, and that its members were not elected, meant that it never acquired the political legitimacy to be really effective.

The 1867 Constitution dealt with the political aspirations of the French-Canadian people in a subtle way. The constitution eschewed symbolic characterizations of Quebec; it refrained from taking sides on issues such as whether Quebec is the homeland of the French-Canadian nation or a province like the others. Instead, a practical arrangement was created that could satisfy people with a variety of different political visions. Quebec would be a province with powers equal to the others. The Constitution did not establish special privileges for the French-Canadians of Quebec; but by recognizing a political unit in which French-Canadians were numerically predominant, it ensured that there would be a government that would be responsive to their political aspirations.

The 1867 Constitution stopped well short of amounting to a triumph of the liberal individualist perspective. A major departure was the absence of any guarantees of universal human rights, such as freedom of expression or religion. Furthermore, the 1867 Constitution did make some explicit concessions to "history-based" groupism. It guaranteed

Bryan Schwartz LL.B., LL.M., J.S.D.   4 5

that whatever rights a religious denomination happened to enjoy at the time of Confederation would continue. Parliament was given exclusive legislative authority over "Indians and the Lands reserved for Indians." Individuals were guaranteed the choice of which language, French or English, they wished to use in Parliament and federal courts, or in the Quebec legislature and its provincial courts.

The unilateral Patriation package of Prime Minister Trudeau, presented in 1980, exhibited the liberal individualist perspective of Trudeau himself. The proposed *Charter of Rights* incorporated the ideas, and often the language, of the outstanding legal proclamations of that perspective: the American *Bill of Rights*, the *Universal Declaration of Human Rights*, the *European Convention on Human Rights*. Under the *Charter* proposed by Trudeau, and eventually adopted, "everyone" is guaranteed freedom of thought and expression (s.2); "everyone" has the right to "life, liberty and security of the person and the right not to be deprived thereof except in accordance with the principles of fundamental justice" (s.7); "every individual" is "equal before and under the law and has the right to the equal protection and equal benefit of the law without discrimination..." (s.15).

The initial Trudeau package did contain some "made-in-Canada" language provisions. Only two languages, French and English, were recognized as official languages, and only official language minorities were guaranteed the right to public funding for their schools. It can be argued, however, that the recognition of two official languages does not have to depend on the "two founding peoples" ideology. It might proceed from the recognition that a functioning democracy needs some shared channels of communication; that the number of official languages also has to be limited for reasons of efficiency and economy; and that the obvious choice for official status would be the two languages which overwhelm any others in terms of the numbers of native speakers.

Trudeau's package offered a possible concession to "groupism" in s.15(2). It stated that the guarantee of individual equality in s.15(1) does not preclude programs that aim to "ameliorate the conditions of disadvantaged individuals or groups." It is not clear whether s.15(2) of the *Charter*, as it was eventually enacted, gives *carte blanche* for any or all "affirmative action" programs. In my view. section 15(2) should be read together with the guarantee of individual equality.

The Trudeau proposal for the *Charter* was modified in response to the advocates for various groups and communities. Among the alterations:

* s.23 (minority language rights) was altered so that it is of limited application in Quebec;

* s.25 calls for the *Charter* to be interpreted in a manner consistent with the rights of aboriginal peoples;

* s.27 requires the *Charter* to be construed in a manner that is "consistent with the preservation and enhancement of the multicultural heritage of Canadians";

* s.29 provides re-assurance that existing denominational school rights are not diminished by the *Charter*;

* s.33, the "notwithstanding clause," allows legislatures to shield their laws from the application of many of the most important sections of the *Charter*. All a legislature has to do is enact that a particular law operates "notwithstanding the Charter," and the law is immune from challenge for five years. The immunization can be renewed indefinitely. The "notwithstanding clause" allows legislatures to act in favour of politically powerful groups at the expense of unpopular individuals.

Since the *Charter* was patriated, the cause of individual freedom has scored some triumphs in the Supreme Court of Canada. The Court has, however, too often tilted in the groupist direction. Its decision in *Andrews* may have turned a guarantee of equality for "every individual" into a guarantee of "non-discrimination" for members of certain groups only. In the *Mahe* case, the Court held that s.23 of the *Charter* guarantees separate school boards for minority language groups. In the *Ontario Denominational Schools* case, the Court found that the *Charter* in no way inhibited Ontario from extending special school rights for Roman Catholics. On the contrary, the Court found that Ontario was obliged to under the Constitution. In the "sign law" case the Supreme Court of Canada firmly endorsed the right of Quebec to force all commercial signs to be predominantly in French. The Court accepted uncritically the contention that the French language continues to be in a vulnerable position in Quebec. It flatly endorsed the notion that the language on all commercial signs should "reflect the demographic reality" that French is the "predominant language," and it would be proper to require that French be exhibited with "marked predominance" over any other language.

The theory that every sign must reflect overall demographic reality is remarkable. Would anyone suggest that the majority must reflect the demographic reality of the minority? In a liberal state, every individual would express his or herself freely and the overall picture would correspond to that demographic reality. In any event, it is not clear that any state intervention is still required to ensure that the overwhelming majority of signs in Quebec include French. The francophone majority would freely choose to use their own language. Most minorities would use French out of respect for the majority and in the interests of attracting their business. A fraction of the people would continue to use minority languages only but what harm would that cause beside offending political orthodoxy?

The Supreme Court was not necessarily wrong to find that the National Assembly has the authority to require French on signs. The issue involves many difficult judgment calls on matters of principle and fact; it is sometimes justifiable for a Court to say "this is the sort of judgment call that is better left to the elected representatives of the people." My more modest point is that the Court should not have taken sides with the collectivist position.

In any event, the Court did not go far enough in the collectivist direction, however, to satisfy the political needs of Mr. Bourassa. Although the Supreme Court had endorsed the language policy on which Mr. Bourassa successfully campaigned in 1985, Mr. Bourassa was anxious to avoid an issue with which the hard-line nationalists could bludgeon him. Accordingly, he used the "notwithstanding" clause to reinstate the ban on outdoor bilingual signs. In doing so, Mr. Bourassa told the National Assembly that there was a contest between "individual rights" and "collective rights," and he had no hesitation in arbitrating in favour of the latter.

In Defence of the Supremacy of the Individual

In other books and articles, I have explained why I remain committed to the view that the individual is the ultimate unit of moral account. For present purposes, I will make a few observations and refer interested readers to the elaborations I have provided elsewhere.

As I see it, each of us moves in time through a succession of thoughts, experiences and sensations that are profoundly our own. Around that core, each of us tries to develop and

Bryan Schwartz LL.B., LL.M., J.S.D.

express ourselves in our own unique way. We should each be free to do so without any group or state imposing an orthodoxy about what individuals must make of themselves. No "groupist theory" can do justice to the underlying diversity of individual human beings and the fact that each of us is a world of experience and beliefs that is worthy of respect in and of itself, rather than being incidental to a larger community. Each of us should not only be free, but equal; no one should have special advantages by virtue of being affiliated with one group or another.

Believing in the supreme importance of the individual is not inconsistent with recognizing a value in groups but that value is not intrinsic; groups, communities, states, must be judged in terms of their impact on the freedom and welfare of the individuals who comprise them. It can readily be acknowledged that most people want and need the co-operation, friendship, love or partnership of others. Individualists can support many community-building projects, precisely because of the benefits that redound to individuals. The "social welfare" state should not be concerned only with the material well-being of individuals but with the needs individuals have for the support, affection and co-operation of others. It is wrong for a child to live in material poverty. It is just as wrong for a child to lack dependable and loving parents. We should be helping the aged avoid suffering economic deprivation but we should also be trying to find ways to rescue them from loneliness and neglect.

A great deal of common ground can be found between individualists and "groupists." One of the tasks of Canadian statecraft is to find practical arrangements that are satisfactory to people with differing views, rather than trying to force everyone to share the same political ideals. Sometimes, however, hard choices have to be made; they should be in defence of the freedom and equality of individuals.

You do not have to be a "groupist" to believe that aboriginal people should have substantially enhanced self-government. All Canadians should have local governments that respond to their needs and counterbalance the authority of the national government. Fiscal support for aboriginal governments need not be based on some historical claim to special privileges; it may be sufficient to place aboriginal governments in the context of the equalization and transfer payment system that is available to provincial governments generally. The political equality of Canadians should be a constraining principle on the way aboriginal governments are established and operated. People within the jurisdiction of aboriginal governments should continue to enjoy many of the rights, and share many of the responsibilities, of other Canadians. The *Charter of Rights* should apply to aboriginal governments; many federal laws of general application, including criminal law should continue to apply; aboriginal governments should be expected to raise their own taxes, rather than accepting fiscal transfers only, and the extent to which aboriginal lands are "havens" from general tax laws should be limited.

You do not have to believe in the "representational theory" of society to support many measures that will better ensure opportunity for women and "minorities." Individualists can readily support rigorous enforcement of anti-discrimination laws, more flexible working schedules and career paths to accommodate the needs of those with family responsibilities. They could agree with facilitating opportunities for newcomers by improving the pension and early retirement benefits of those who feel they have made their contribution and would like to try something else. But as a general matter, giving hiring preferences on the basis of group affiliation should be opposed.

Just about everyone understands that most francophones in Quebec wish to learn, live and work in their own language. Those who believe in individual rights can accept many measures by the provincial government to ensure that francophones have reasonable opportunities to learn, work, receive public services and govern in French. Many Canadians, however, would reject any theory of "collective rights" which suggests that the majority have a moral right to demand linguistic conformity from the minority; or that a bilingual elite is justified in fighting "assimilation" by restricting the opportunities of francophone public school children to acquire a knowledge of the other official language.

"Collective rights" may sound good. The phrase has the superficial attraction of appearing to be something new and progressive. It is in fact an old idea in Canadian constitutionalism, and has often fostered privileges for established and powerful communities at the expense of newer and more vulnerable ones. "Collective rights" may sound even better when combined with a claim of historic victimization. The validity of the historic claim may range in various cases from exaggerated to unclear to true; but we should be concentrating on where we are going, not where we have been. The redress of past grievances does not justify doing wrong to individuals now, or entrenching political inequality in the future.

Some people seem to think that "minority groups" must necessarily be the victims of majoritarian political processes. Not necessarily. It depends on the group. Some of them have significant political advantages over other groups or unorganized individuals. They may have established institutions that make it easy and economic to canvass their own members and lobby politicians and they may have force of numbers in some political districts, if not on a province-wide or national basis. Members of groups with a strong sense of identity may be "single-issue" voters; a politician who resists the group related concern may be at great risk of political retribution.

The Court system should be a place which is exquisitely sensitive to the need to do justice to individuals. Litigation can offer the opportunity to fully and dispassionately examine the facts and pressures on the Courts to view things in more groupist terms. Litigation is expensive, and the most active and effective advocates may be those for special interest groups. Judges are not always immune either from the desire to be popular with political vocal groups, or at least to avoid criticism from them. Still, the *Charter* stands as a powerful symbol of our concern for the individual, and sometimes it even produces justice for the single, even unpopular individual. It would be unfortunate if the "Canada Round" erodes that role for the *Charter*, and leaves even less protection than ever for the "minority of one."

The Canada clause should be revised to:

* include one statement which clearly affirms a commitment to respecting the fundamental rights and freedoms of each and every Canadian. It should not be diluted with references to "collective rights";

* whatever is said about the specific situation of Quebec and aboriginal peoples, the general concept of "collective rights" should not be given constitutional recognition, and put on the same plane as individual rights.

Bryan Schwartz LL.B., LL.M., J.S.D.   49

Chapter

6

Specific changes to the Charter

The Charter of Rights and Freedoms: The Notwithstanding Clause

When Quebec enacted Bill 178, Prime Minister Mulroney was challenged to criticize it by the opposition Liberals. The response of the Prime Minister consisted partly of trying to blame the episode on former Prime Minister Trudeau. By agreeing to the "notwithstanding clause," Trudeau had made the Constitution "not worth the paper it is written on."

Mulroney's attack came up short on an internal consistency count. He was in the midst of trying to force through the Meech Lake Accord, which did nothing whatsoever to limit the use of the notwithstanding clause. On the contrary, the "distinct society" clause contained a subsection 2(4) which made it absolutely clear that it did nothing to limit the power of legislatures; there was no such assurance for the rights of individuals and minorities, and Meech Lake might have pushed the Courts in the direction of interpreting those rights more narrowly. All the while, Prime Minister Mulroney was insisting that it was of the utmost national importance to pass the Accord.

The Federal Proposal briefly identifies the arguments for and against the existence of the "notwithstanding clause." On the one hand, it dilutes the guarantees in the *Charter*; on the other, the final say on public policy and social needs should rest with elected members of the legislature. The Federal Proposal does not take sides. Whatever happened to "not worth the paper it's written on?" The Proposal concludes that as a "practical matter," the "notwithstanding" clause will remain in the Constitution but it should be put under tighter control. The Federal Proposal suggests changing the rules for invoking it requiring 60% of the "members of Parliament or the legislature" rather than the current 50% of those voting.

The change could make a difference when a government is in a minority situation or that of a narrow majority, which happens at times in Canada. In such situations, however, there is at least some chance of having the decision reversed at the next election. The 60% rule is not going to be of much comfort to a minority that can expect little sympathy from either of the two biggest parties. When the National Assembly used the "notwithstanding clause" an overwhelming majority of the members of the Assembly supported doing so.

Whether the notwithstanding clause should be abolished is a very difficult question. My view is that there should be some "safety valve" in case of Supreme Court decisions that are wholly unreasonable. The issue is not as simple as saying that politicians should be able to override rights. The politicians may believe that the Courts have adopted a wrong-headed approach to interpreting rights under the *Charter,* and that they are, in good faith, insisting on a better one. The "safety valve" should be used only in the rarest of cases, and the procedures connected with the "notwithstanding clause" should ensure that legislatures are fully aware of the seriousness of what they are doing and that they openly and explicitly acknowledge it. It would therefore be appropriate to amend the "notwithstanding clause" in the following ways:

* the legislature invoking it must include a "notwithstanding" declaration on each and every piece of legislation to which it applies. (In the "sign law" case, the Supreme Court of Canada ruled that under the existing "notwithstanding clause," a legislature can pass a single law that applies the "notwithstanding clause" to every single piece of legislation in force at the time);

* the legislature invoking the notwithstanding clause must include in its legislation the text of the constitutional safeguard it is overriding. It should not be good enough to simply refer to section numbers. (In the "sign law" case, the Quebec Court of Appeal took this approach to the existing "notwithstanding clause." Unfortunately, it was overruled by the Supreme Court of Canada).

Another change is warranted as well. Under the current system, a "notwithstanding" declaration operates for up to five years, and then automatically expires. A legislature can renew it indefinitely, but at least it is obliged to actively pass legislation in order to do so. Five years is too long for an override to last without further consideration. The normal life of a government is about four years, and is often less. It will sometimes be possible for a government to rely on a previously-passed "notwithstanding" declaration, and never have to take responsibility for renewing it. A three year renewal period would make it more likely that a government relying on a notwithstanding clause will have to renew it at least once, and perhaps twice, during its mandate. The more often a "notwithstanding clause" has to be renewed, the more likely it is that the renewal issue will occur close to an election, and the people will hold the government accountable for its decision.

Property Rights

The Federal Proposal states that property rights are not currently guaranteed under the *Charter*, and they should be. No specific draft is suggested, no further elaboration provided.

We should not rule out protecting property rights because of a theoretical notion that property is inherently unworthy of protection. As Justice Stewart of the Supreme Court of the United States once said: "The dichotomy between personal liberties and property rights is a false one. Property does not have rights. People have rights..."

Controlling and enjoying part of the material world is necessary to all sorts of human aspirations including emotional, artistic and spiritual goals, not only narrow materialistic ones. The abstract word "property" may sound soulless compared to "freedom" or "liberty" or even "security"; but the moral imagination should extend to concerns about whether individuals are able to enjoy a home they have worked half a lifetime to own.

Protection from arbitrary state interference with property is a legitimate human rights concern, and not necessarily confined to a "right wing" agenda. Canada voted for the *Universal Declaration of Human Rights,* adopted by the General Assembly of the United Nations in 1948, which includes:

art. 17. 1. Everyone has the right to own property alone as well as in association with others.

art. 17. 2. No one shall be arbitrarily deprived of his property.

The Canadian *Bill of Rights* guarantees the right to the enjoyment of property, and the right not to be deprived thereof without due process of law. The *Bill*, which was enacted three decades ago, applies to the federal level of government and is still in force; it has so far not caused any disruption to federal regulatory schemes.

Although he did not pursue the initiative in the Patriation package, Trudeau's 1978 constitutional proposals would have included:

the right of the individual to the use and enjoyment of property, and the right not to be deprived thereof except in accordance with law.

It is true that the "property clause" idea is being revived by a right-of-centre government that is strongly influenced by the big-business lobby. There is a real risk that if the general idea of a "property clause" is accepted, the government may present a draft that unduly favours private wealth and power. Moreover, even assuming the best of intentions, there are no absolute guarantees about what the Courts will make of a new plaything. There are weighty considerations, therefore, in favour of just saying "no."

At this stage, however, my view is that it is at least worth thinking about what a satisfactory property clause might look like. It is first necessary to identify more specifically what kind of government abuses we wish to discourage; they might include:

* the taking of property without procedural fairness; for example, making a tax ruling against someone without providing for fair avenues of appeal to an impartial body;

* expropriation without just compensation;

* use-of-property regulation that is arbitrary; e.g., a law that impairs the owner's enjoyment of the property to a great extent while doing practically nothing to advance the public interest.

Legal language should then be chosen with a view to preventing the abuses we have targeted. The clause could specifically refer to the enjoyment of property by individuals, thereby discouraging claims by corporations. It might be a good idea to expressly pre-empt certain misinterpretations of the clause; for example, to provide in plain terms that the clause does not impair the right of a government to enact stringent laws on the use of property, even outright bans, as long as the government has a reasonable basis for believing that the measure is in the public interest. This would help to counteract arguments that property rights might lead to, for example, a general right to own and possess firearms free of governmental regulation.

Chapter

7

Bilingualism and multiculturalism

Bilingualism

The proposed "Canada clause" is strangely silent about bilingualism. There is no mention of official bilingualism, even though the Constitution already recognizes that French and English are equally the official languages of Canada. It may be that the drafters of the Federal Proposal thought it politically safer to avoid mentioning bilingualism in any form. The Spicer Commission stated that "Canada's use of two official languages is widely seen as a fundamental and distinctive Canadian characteristic." It also found, however, that "the application of the official languages policy is a major irritant outside Quebec, and not much appreciated inside Quebec." It proposed an "independent review" of the application of the official language principle (not the principle itself) to ensure that there is "fairness and sensitivity."

The "duality clause" speaks of preserving the existence of "French-speaking ... and English Speaking Canadians." There is no mention of bilingual Canadians, or the desirability of offering children the opportunity to acquire a knowledge of both official languages. The Spicer Commission states that:

> We believe that all children should have the opportunity to learn both official languages in school.

In 1987, in *Refashioning Meech Lake,* I had suggested that the "duality clause" be amended by mentioning the role of federal and provincial governments in:

> providing Canadians with opportunities to acquire a knowledge of the other official language.

The proposal would encourage efforts such as publicly-funded but voluntary French immersion programs for anglophones and help to encourage a positive attitude towards providing solid instruction in English for Quebec francophones.

It is well possible that a review of official language policy would reveal some excesses and injustices. The policy should be administered in a way that requires no more bilingual jobs than are necessary to serve the public and make the environment welcoming for people from both language groups. Reasonable efforts should be made to provide opportunities for unilingual people to compete for positions and promotions on an equal basis with the federal government providing whatever language training is necessary to equip people to fill those positions. In re-affirming official bilingualism, it should be possible to insert some words of re-assurance, such as the following:

> The official languages of Canada are English and French, and Canadians from both language groups should have fair and equal opportunities to participate in the public service.

Bryan Schwartz LL.B., LL.M., J.S.D.   5 3

The proposed "Canada clause" would promise "full participation in Canada's citizenship" by all people "without regard to race, colour, creed, physical or mental disability or cultural background." It is not clear whether the last-mentioned phrase refers to linguistic background which should be specifically enumerated in the list as a characteristic that does not impair a person's ability to fully participate in public life.

To sum up, the long-term cohesion of Canada is not going to be served by its reverting to two unilingual linguistic blocs. There should be some mention in the Canada clause of the existence of official bilingualism at the federal level of government, and of the desirability of giving those who so wish an opportunity to acquire a knowledge of the other official language.

Multiculturalism

The "Canada Clause" in the Federal Proposal would recognize:

...the contribution to the building of a strong Canada of peoples from many cultures and lands.

The *Charter of Rights* already recognizes "multiculturalism," in s.27.:

This Charter shall be interpreted in a manner consistent with the preservation and enhancement of the multicultural heritage of Canadians.

The Spicer Commission reports that:

While Canadians accept and value Canada's cultural diversity, they do not value many of the activities of the multicultural program of the federal government. These are seen as expensive and divisive in that they remind Canadians of their different origins rather than their shared symbols, society and future.

The Spicer Commission recommends that federal multicultural funding be confined to "immigration orientation, reduction of racial discrimination and promotion of equality." Provincial education departments should:

...maintain some heritage courses, but only for young elementary-school immigrant children. Such courses should be concise and be given for no more than a year or so for each immigrant child, to assist young newcomers' transition to their new land's culture and society.

Multicultural policy can be a cynical exercise in government pork-barrelling. It can amount to financial hand-outs in the hope of gratitude at the next election. A multicultural policy that respects the equality of Canadians can build a sense of identification with the larger Canadian community.

If parents wish to expose their children to another language and culture, so much the better. Another cultural perspective is intrinsically enriching and offers the possibility of acquiring a critical perspective on the mainstream. Canada as a whole would benefit from drawing on its multicultural resources, rather than trying to stifle them. If the child of an immigrant from Hong Kong receives extensive education in Chinese, along with the usual Canadian curriculum, we will have an adult who may not only be more cultured, but able to take advantage of educational or business opportunities that will end up benefiting the Canadian community as a whole.

A model of how individual equality, shared Canadian values, and multicultural diversity can be combined is the "Heritage Language" program in Manitoba schools. Under this program, any group with sufficient numbers and interest can work with the public schools and establish a program whereby their students can learn a "heritage" language — be it Ukrainian, Hebrew, Cree or German — as well as English or French. The program takes place in public schools, so students can mix with children from other heritages. The program is strictly voluntary; it enhances the options of students and parents, rather than restricting them. The school system is not fragmented into different boards, with the extra costs and inefficiencies that would result.

The Federal Proposal avoids using the word "multiculturalism," perhaps because of the current controversy over it. The formulation stresses that people of diverse origins contribute to a "strong Canada"; the emphasis seems to be on building the whole, rather than enhancing the parts. It is not entirely clear whether the "contribution" mentioned is historic only, or an on-going one. Those who favour multiculturalism need not worry too much about the latter ambiguity, because s.27 of the *Charter* makes it clear that multiculturalism has on-going vitality. The "people of many lands" clause does make it clear that the Constitution has not entirely endorsed the "two founding peoples" ideology.

As noted, Section 27, the "multicultural heritage" clause, will remain in the *Charter*. It will be juxtaposed with the proposed s.25.1., which recognizes Quebec's "distinct society." Both will have the status of interpretive rules under the *Charter*. One refers to "preservation and enhancement" of the multicultural heritage of Canada, the other to the "preservation and promotion" of the distinct society.

There are several reasons, however, to be concerned about how the "distinct society" clause will be interpreted by the Quebec cultural majority:

* Quebec's government and legislature are said to be have a "special responsibility" for the "unique culture" of Quebec; no such role is attributed to the federal government with respect to multiculturalism;

* it is not certain that the "distinct society" clause recognizes minorities as part of Quebec's "unique culture." It can be argued that the clause could be interpreted this way. The "distinct society" is "within Canada," and we are told by s.27 that Canada has a multicultural heritage. The "distinct society" clause refers to a "French-speaking majority," but that implicitly recognizes that there are minorities. There is a risk, however, that some people will interpret "unique culture" as referring exclusively to the one developed by the historically-established French speaking community (rather than including the contribution of French-speaking immigrants, anglophones and others.)

Some members of the cultural majority in Quebec may argue that their contribution to Canada-wide multiculturalism consists of promoting their own culture, rather than nurturing the diversity within their society.

The rather fuzzy treatment of multiculturalism in the "Canada clause" may be tolerable in light of the clear affirmation of multiculturalism in the *Charter*. The threat that the Federal Proposal presents to multiculturalism lies in its formulation of what makes Quebec a "distinct society."

Chapter 8

Gender equality

This Chapter addresses several points concerning gender equality:

* why did sexual equality become an issue in the context of the Meech Lake Accord?

* does the latest Federal Proposal avoid any threats to existing constitutional guarantees of sexual non-discrimination?

* why does "gender equality" receive separate and special billing in the Canada clause, compared to other types of equality — such as racial and religious?

The Meech Debate

Among the most effective campaigners for reform of the Meech Lake Accord were women's rights organizations. Many of these groups expressed concern about Section 16 of the Accord. It stated that the "distinct society clause" did not affect certain provisions of the Constitution that protect aboriginal peoples and multiculturalism but by contrast *did not mention "sexual equality"* as being among the values protected.

Some argued that s.16 might weaken the protection of women's rights in Quebec, or send a more general message that "sexual equality" is a second-tier constitutional value. As a remedy, they suggested the following: add sexual equality to the list of values protected by s.16 as well as a specific mention that s.28 of the *Charter* — which affirms sexual equality — is not adversely affected by the "distinct society" clause.

Some of the women's equality groups in Quebec did not agree, however, that the "distinct society" clause was a threat to women's rights. The *Federation de Femmes de Quebec* took the position that the "distinct society" concept was neutral with respect to sexual equality but while it perceived no threat to sexual equality, it would not object to the measure proposed by other women's rights organizations: adding s.28 of the *Charter* — which affirms sexual equality — to the list of provisions shielded from the effect of the proposed "distinct society" clause.

When the First Ministers met at the "roll of the dice" meeting in June, 1990, sexual equality was one of the very few areas in which they promised to enact actual amendments to the Meech Lake Accord. The "Stockholm Syndrome" Accord (as I have named it) indeed included a commitment to the amendment of s.16.

Does the latest Federal Proposal avoid any problems?

The existing Constitution makes special reference to gender equality. The general "equality" norm is s.15 of the *Charter*. It includes a reference to non-discrimination on the basis of sex but there is a second "sexual equality" guarantee in the *Charter*, section 28:

> Notwithstanding anything in this Charter, the rights and freedoms referred to in it are guaranteed equally to male and female persons.

This follows two other "interpretive clauses." Section 25 directs that the *Charter* should be construed in a way that does not derogate from the rights of aboriginal peoples; section 27 directs that interpretation of the *Charter* be consistent with multiculturalism. One of the original functions of s.28 may be to ensure that the accommodation of these other values is not accomplished at the expense of women. It will almost certainly have the same effect if a "distinct society" clause is placed in the *Charter*.

Special Mention of Gender Equality in the Canada clause

After the "Canada Clause" (which omits any reference to Canada as a whole), the Federal Proposal recognizes two kinds of equality norms:

* the equality of women and men;

* a commitment to fairness, openness and full participation in Canada's citizenship by all people without regard to race, colour, creed, physical or mental disability, or cultural background.

Why would the proposal single out gender equality for special mention? Part of the answer may be political. Women represent over half the electorate, and many men are sensitive to equality concerns as well. In addition to the power of the ballot, women's rights organizations have a demonstrated history of success in mobilizing during constitutional rounds. During the Patriation round, advocacy organizations secured the insertion of s.28 (re-affirmation of sexual equality) in the *Charter*. During the Aboriginal Rights round, one of the few amendments that emerged was s.35(3), which guarantees sexual equality in the enjoyment of aboriginal and treaty rights. During the Meech Round, one of the very few issues on which any improvements were promised was sexual equality. The federal government is clearly anxious to avoid any confrontations this time. By mentioning gender equality separately in the proposed Canada clause, the intention of the federal drafters may have been to re-affirm whatever priority sexual equality already has under the Constitution.

The existing priority of "sexual equality" is based primarily on s.28 of the *Charter*. Does this singling out of sexual equality imply that other forms of discrimination, such as racial and religious, are less invidious? Not necessarily. Rather than placing sexual equality above all other values in the *Charter*, section 28 can be read as ensuring that sexual equality is itself not downgraded by other provisions. Specifically, section 28 ensures that interpretive provisions favouring "multiculturalism" (s.27) and rights of aboriginal peoples (s.25) do not result in adverse treatment for women.

Reading section 28 in light of its political history, rather than dwelling exclusively on its legal language, suggests another effect the section might have: to make it difficult for Courts to uphold sexual discrimination as a "reasonable limit" on *Charter* rights. Section 28 could be understood as a directive to put sexual discrimination alongside race in the category of "extremely hard to justify," rather than in the same category of age discrimination, which (according to a recent Supreme Court of Canada decision on mandatory retirement) can be somewhat easier to defend.

Yet another potential consequence of Section 28 could be to make sexual equality immune from the "notwithstanding clause." That is, Courts might decide that the "notwithstanding clause" can not be utilized by governments to override the sexual equality rights in the *Charter*. Arguments can be made on both sides here. A decisive objection to the "immune-from-override" interpretation of s.28 might be this: it would make no sense for the Constitution to put sexual equality on a higher plane than racial equality, and racial equality is nowhere protected from the override clause.

What section 28 certainly does not do is guarantee that men and women can *never* be treated differently by the state. Some forms of "positive discrimination" are permitted. Section 15(2) of the *Charter* allows for affirmative action programs, including those to remedy sexual inequality; surely the women's groups that lobbied for s.28 did not seek to prevent special consideration from being given to women in certain circumstances.

Will the distinction between "gender equality" and "other kinds of equality" disadvantage women in any way? What about the fact that sex is not mentioned in the next part of the Canada clause? Is there a concern that the omission of any reference to sex will be understood as implying that women do not have the right to expect "fairness, openness and full participation in Canada's citizenship?" Again, the risk appears to be nil. The "equality of women and men" is the very first value listed in the Canada clause, right after the recognition of the federation itself. The omission could hardly have been intended to implicitly demean the concept in the phrase which is second only to the recognition of the federation itself. Finally, the "Canada clause" must be read in conjunction with the rest of the Constitution, which gives extra attention to sexual equality, rather than in any way relegating it to a second-class constitutional concern.

One might ask why the federal drafters did not list "sexual equality" in the "commitment to fairness" clause. Why not be on the safe side? Perhaps the drafters were afraid of giving the impression that equality for others counted less than sexual equality. The question that would then be asked is this: what higher level of protection is gender being given that is denied to other forms of equality? By putting the "equality of women and men" in one place and "equality for everyone else" in another the federal drafters have tried to give gender equality special recognition without giving offence to other forms of equality.

So far, the discussion has taken a look at the special references to sexual equality in both the existing Constitution and in the proposed new "Canada clause" and what the implications are of singling out sexual equality from other types of equality. The next question to consider is whether the Federal Proposal would in any way undermine the extent of the protection offered to sexual equality by the existing Constitution.

Section 28 would have the effect of shielding sexual equality from the "distinct society" clause in the *Charter*; and would ensure that any interpretive weight given to promoting Quebec's "distinct society" is not at the expense of sexual equality.

The current draft of the "distinct society" clause does not appear to pose any threat to guarantees against sexual discrimination. The proposed "Canada clause" would strongly affirm it.

While the latest Federal Proposal does not appear to diminish any constitutional guarantees against sexual discrimination, there may be other issues of concern to women's rights organizations:

* Some groups may be concerned about the impact of the proposal on the federal presence in the social welfare area. This study concludes that there is very serious cause for concern on this count;

* Some may take issue with the proposal to entrench property rights, and the effect it might have on state attempts to regulate and redistribute in the interest of the less powerful.

* Some organizations may cite the commitment to gender equality in the Canada clause as support for a 50% quota for women in the reformed Senate. This study argues for reforms to ensure real equality of political opportunity but opposes the implementation of quotas based on ethnicity, gender or other personal characteristics.

Chapter

9

Aboriginal issues

The Federal Proposal for a "Canada clause" would include:

> ...recognition that the aboriginal peoples were historically self-governing, and recognition of their rights within Canada.

Aboriginal peoples are unlikely to be satisfied with this statement. It says that they "were" (not are) "historically" self-governing. It stops far short of proclaiming that the right to self-government is on-going and unbroken.

The political history of every aboriginal group varies. As a matter of historical fact, it appears that some Indian groups had sophisticated structures of self-government; other peoples were free and independent, but may not have had group-wide systems for making decisions and enforcing them.

The Metis people who developed around the Red River settlement area were the descendants of both aboriginal people and Europeans. Prior to 1870, when Manitoba became a province, the Hudson's Bay Company was the owner and effective governing body of a vast territory that included the Red River Settlement. In 1845, its Governor stated officially that, unlike Indians, Metis people were subject to the same laws as those born in the British Isles. A number of Metis actively participated in the government of the territory, as magistrates or as members of the Council of Assiniboia. It does appear that at times, groups of Metis did establish political structures to carry out collective activities such as the Buffalo hunt or military excursions. Early in Confederation, the Metis aspiration for self-government, however, was channelled into the creation of provincial status for Manitoba, rather than creating any sort of "reserves" with ethnically-based governments.

The sort of "self government" that the federal government is now considering amounts to limited political autonomy within the Canadian state. That falls far short of the political independence enjoyed by many aboriginal groups prior to European contact. There is a potential for confusion to arise from the use of the same term, "self government," to describe both the arrangements of the distant past and of the near future.

In any event, the Federal Proposal includes a plan for advancing the cause of aboriginal self-government. The right of aboriginal peoples to self-government would be entrenched in the Constitution and enforceable in the Courts. The right would not be completely undefined:

> ...it will be important to express the nature of the right in terms that guide the courts toward an interpretation of self-government that is consistent with the understanding of both aboriginal and

non-aboriginal peoples. For example, such a right would provide for recognition of the differing circumstances and needs of the different aboriginal peoples in Canada and would be exercised within the Canadian constitutional framework, subject to the *Canadian Charter of Rights and Freedoms*. Many federal and provincial laws of general application would also continue to apply.

There would be a ten-year delay on the Court enforceability of the right. The Constitution would:

* entrench a commitment by government to negotiate agreements with particular communities;
* provide for regular First Ministers' Conferences to discuss aboriginal self-government;
* provide for constitutional protection for whatever agreements are reached.

The Federal Proposal has already been condemned by aboriginal leaders who contend that aboriginal peoples have the inherent right to self-government, rather than it being something granted to them. They argue that a ten-year delay in the Court-enforceability of the right implies that they do not already have such a legally enforceable right.

A series of constitutional conferences on aboriginal issues were held from 1983 to 1987 and many of the ideas in the latest Federal Proposal are based on ideas circulated at that time. My own account of the process is contained in the book *First Principles, Second Thoughts*. By the end of 1987, the federal government was making proposals that recognized a right to aboriginal self-government but fudged the issue of whether it could be enforced in the absence of an agreement. The federal proposals would have entrenched a commitment by governments to community-level negotiations and constitutional protection for any agreements.

I believe that the most productive approach for both sides to take would be focusing on practical measures aimed at securing a better future for aboriginal peoples. Both sides should make an effort to find common ground without forcing the other to agree to any particular "political theology." Self-government agreements are a useful mechanism for this purpose. Aboriginal peoples can, if they wish, maintain the position that they have an inherent right to self-determination but would be prepared to enter into negotiations on power-sharing. Some federal or provincial governments might have a different theory of why power-sharing negotiations are necessary. The essential requirement is to achieve common, satisfactory and practical arrangements.

Neither side has to agree with the other's abstract theories. They have to agree on the jurisdiction of aboriginal governments, checks and balances that will be put in place to safeguard individuals and minorities within aboriginal communities and the fiscal arrangements that will exist with federal and provincial governments. It should not be necessary for either side to insist on its version of history being accepted by the other.

The First Nations people on reserves should have greater self-government, regardless of what version of history you subscribe to. Canadians generally have the benefits of local self-government in the form of municipal and provincial government. The restrictions and paternalism of the *Indian Act* are not consistent with a respect for the democratic rights and political equality of all Canadians. The assumption of enhanced responsibility by aboriginal peoples for their own affairs should produce better government because it would be more responsive to local needs and opinion. Self-government should enable aboriginal peoples to move on from past injustices and current strictures and devote their energies even more to specific measures to improve human welfare within aboriginal communities.

In my view, however, aboriginal governments should amount to federal units within a large political community, not quasi-independent states. Canadians are sometimes inconsistent in their approach to self-government for aboriginal peoples on the one hand and the Quebecois on the other. Many people think (and I agree) that the "distinct society" should be defined before it is entrenched; that the Quebecois cannot consistently claim to be immune from federal jurisdiction while claiming to fully participate in national government; that the Quebecois cannot expect to practically eliminate the economic and political bonds of nationhood with the rest of Canada while continuing to receive transfer payments from other Canadians. Yet some of these same people seem relatively unconcerned about entrenching an undefined right to aboriginal self-government or political arrangements that offer aboriginal peoples full autonomy while retaining all the political rights and fiscal benefits of being Canadians.

Conversely, some Quebec nationalists seem to think that their claims to self-determination are incontestable while those of the aboriginal peoples within their midst are unthinkable.

It is understandable that the emotional appeal of the aboriginal cause may be more compelling to many people. The people of Quebec already have constitutionally entrenched self-government, a relatively prosperous economy and powerful influence over national affairs. Many aboriginal communities are still suffering the effects of misguided, even repressive, policies of the federal and provincial governments, and are still restricted in their ability to govern their own affairs. Apart from any emotional considerations, there are legal and practical differences between the aboriginal and Quebec situations that would justify some differences in the arrangements we devise. Some broad principles should apply to both cases.

One principle of general application is that individuals enjoy certain safeguards against the abuse of local authorities. No government is immune from the temptations of power, including favouring one's friends, discriminating against one's opponents and stifling political dissent. Small communities of any sort, including towns and cities, are prone to having their politics dominated by one faction. Our existing system protects local individuals and minorities in two ways. First, there are safeguards of specific rights. The *Canadian Charter of Rights and Freedoms* should apply to aboriginal governments. The issue of whether aboriginal governments would have access to the override is a difficult one, both theoretically and practically. Aboriginal leaders may protest loudly if their governments are denied this tool that has been made available to the provinces and deployed by Quebec to protect its "distinct society."

The second safeguard that should apply to aboriginal governments and to Quebec is the checking and balancing effect of having different orders of government involved in its affairs. Different orders of government, be they provincial and federal, or aboriginal and federal, help to keep each other "honest." Local governments can correct insensitivity to local conditions on the part of central governments. Central governments can counteract political abuses occurring at the local level and provide support for those who are on the "outs" with the local powers-that-be.

In addition, the federal government will provide fiscal assistance for "have-not" governments but the principle stated in s.36 of the *Constitution Act, 1982,* is that the federal government will try to "ensure that provincial governments have sufficient revenues to provide reasonably comparable public services at reasonably comparable levels of taxation." Aboriginal communities should be expected to raise some of their own revenues, and make a fair fiscal contribution to the federal and provincial governments in which they participate as equals.

Aboriginal people and the Quebecois should have the right to participate in the life of the national community but it would be unjust to allow anyone the right to be politically active — to vote or hold office — in federal and provincial institutions without accepting the authority of those institutions.

Every resident of an aboriginal community has a right to take up residence elsewhere in Canada; the rest of the Canadian community has a very significant and practical stake in the health, education and welfare of that person. Matters may also arise in which the interests of aboriginal communities directly compete with those of other communities; it will often be appropriate for provincial or federal governments to arbitrate these disputes. For the reasons just outlined, I believe that aboriginal communities should, as the Federal Proposal outlines, continue to be subject to many federal and provincial laws of general application. These could include the *Criminal Code,* laws for environmental protection, and taxation laws.

It is doubtful whether the Constitution should explicitly or implicitly promise self-government for aboriginal peoples living within urban centres, rather than their own land bases. The objection is not merely practical. It would indeed be difficult to organize a separate, general-purpose, government for aboriginal people living in the cities. Too many transactions cut across ethnic lines. It would be possible, however, for aboriginal peoples to operate their own schools or social welfare agencies. The issues that must be addressed include not only "what is practically possible?" but "is it a good idea?" In my view, the fragmentation of some of our public institutions has already gone too far. How many separate school systems and boards do we want? In some places, schools and boards are already divided along both linguistic and denominational lines. The fragmentation of systems can be costly and inefficient. It also can prevent the development of mutual understanding that occurs when families from different backgrounds participate in the same structures. I would support adaptations within the school system to meet the needs of aboriginal peoples. The development of Cree-English bilingual programs in the public school system is to be welcomed but the extent to which separate structures are necessary or appropriate should be left to ordinary processes; we should not entrench a "right" to urban aboriginal self-government that could lead Courts to order separate structures in all sorts of contexts.

It would be irresponsible and undemocratic for governments to recognize a general right to "self-government" and leave it to the Courts to have the final say on what that means. Politicians may be tempted to "look good" now, and leave it for future Courts to make the real choices and future politicians to deal with the fall-out from them. The people of Canada generally should have the opportunity to make an informed choice about how they wish their governments to respond to aboriginal claims for enhanced self-government.

Bryan Schwartz LL.B., LL.M., J.S.D.

Aboriginal peoples should not be given false expectations; the parties entering the community negotiations should have some idea of what the other side is seeking. It will not be an atmosphere of trust and respect if aboriginal peoples are led by unqualified affirmations to expect quasi-independence and then discover that federal and provincial governments have a more modest notion of self-government in mind.

The Federal Proposal calls for "terms that [would] guide the courts towards an interpretation of self-government that is consistent with the understanding of both aboriginal and non-aboriginal peoples." The idea is an attractive one, but it may not be easy for both sides to reach agreement on a formulation that actually means anything. The conundrum is the same one that is presented by Quebec's demand for recognition as a "distinct society." The rest of Canada can only properly respond to the demand by putting some limits on the concept; these limits, in turn, may be unacceptable to the government of Quebec. Similarly, the demand of aboriginal peoples for recognition of their "inherent rights" can only be accommodated by putting some constraints on the scope of those rights; and aboriginal peoples may find these constraints to be insulting.

In 1987, the Inuit Committee on National Issues at one point made an intrepid suggestion for finessing the problem. It was called the "silent option." The proposal was as follows. A constitutional deal would make no mention of a general right to self-government. Aboriginal peoples could continue to assert that the right is already implicit in s.35(1) of the *Constitution Act, 1982,* which recognizes the "existing aboriginal and treaty rights" of the aboriginal peoples of Canada. As the proposed deal would not expressly mention the right to aboriginal self-government, federal and provincial governments would not feel obliged to try to limit it. The "silent option" proposal would have skipped over the whole "political theology" debate, and moved instead to the nitty-gritty. It would have called for federal and provincial governments to enter into negotiations with aboriginal communities on self-government and provided constitutional protection for any agreements that resulted.

The "silent option" did not gain sufficient support in 1987, and it probably will not do so now. It will be difficult, perhaps impossible, to find "diplomatic language" that can somehow re-assure the general Canadian public about the meaning of self-government while at the same time boldly affirming a general, existing and enforceable right of aboriginal peoples to self-government.

To sum up, the further development of aboriginal self-government will not solve all of the social and economic problems of aboriginal communities, but it is a necessary step forward, and long overdue. It would best be facilitated by an honest and open dialogue. There does not have to be agreement on symbols and theories, but there should be a shared understanding of the general form that practical arrangements for self-government will take.

Chapter 10

Economic and social union

General Reflections

The Federal Proposal talks about the "economic union." There is no explicit reference to the "social union" but many Canadians regard our programs and attitudes towards social justice as important bonds of shared nationhood. An "economic union" is not a nation. A sense of belonging and sharing cannot be based primarily on the fact that people share a central bank and a free market. Canada should try to maintain and build its sense of identity as a social union.

The term just introduced here, "social union," does not appear anywhere in the Federal Proposal. The concept has several implications. One is that Canada should have national institutions and programs that can share prosperity among Canadians; that the sense of community and caring among Canadians should be concretely expressed in programs like nation-wide Medicare or equalization payments. Another is that a defining characteristic of Canada should be that it invests in "human capital"; that we realize that Canada's economic future will depend critically on whether it has a healthy, ambitious and educated workforce. Some people might consider "investing in people" as part of the economic union. All the better. My view is that the economic and social union have to be seen as complementary.

An efficient and productive economy is necessary to create the wealth to support a social union. Conversely, attention to human welfare helps to create the "human capital" that supports a productive economy. It is unfortunate that the economic value of investing in people is so often overlooked in practical politics. Investing in the health and education of children can produce productive adults; failing to do so can create huge costs in the form of welfare payments, strains on the medical system and costs of policing and imprisonment. Nation-wide standards with respect to matters such as pensions and unemployment insurance can enhance the mobility of capital and labour. People can feel freer to exploit opportunities in an economic union if moving does not jeopardize income support and benefit plans.

The economic and social union should support each other. The disproportionate emphasis on one can undermine the other. Eliminating all barriers to trade within Canada can undermine social welfare in Canada unless minimum national standards of employment and welfare are established. In a free market environment, there is a risk that provinces will be pressured to constantly bring the level of regulation and social welfare down to the lowest

Bryan Schwartz LL.B., LL.M., J.S.D.   6 5

common denominator. Provincial governments may be afraid that the taxes needed to maintain programs, and the restrictions needed to protect such values as worker safety and the environment, may encourage industries to locate elsewhere.

This study has tried to maintain a due regard for the merits of maintaining flexibility, rather than trying to entrench everything in the Constitution. We should generally avoid entrenching any particular program in the Constitution. The current system of Medicare may be a good idea now, but need adaptations later on. Canadians of the future should have considerable choice about how much of a "social welfare" state they want. There are always difficult trade-offs; governments can be wasteful, arbitrary, even oppressive and intervention can stifle individual effort and creativity. It should be possible to constitutionally affirm some general principles about our commitment to sharing and to investing in people.

Premier Rae of Ontario has proposed that the Constitution include a "Social Charter." His government's discussion paper, "A Canadian Social Charter," calls for constitutional recognition of "broad objectives of national policy" — such as providing adequate housing — that would be generally interpreted and applied by political bodies, rather than Courts. The paper discussion accepts that the many taxing and policy choices involved in realizing "broad objectives" should generally be left to democratically accountable bodies. The discussion paper does allow that some very specific "negative rights" — simply-stated things that governments cannot do or allow — might be suitable for court enforcement. An example of a "negative right" would be that no one should be subjected to extra-billing by doctors who participate in Medicare. The Ontario discussion paper is open-minded about the method of political oversight that would be involved in implementing the Social Charter; the process might involve "intergovernmental co-operation," the Senate or mechanisms that governments would devise after the Social Charter is enacted.

There is merit in Premier's Rae's ideas that the principles of the social union should be recognized in the Constitution but in my view, the proposal has to be developed in a way that recognizes two points:

* the social union cannot be maintained unless the federal government has a leading role in shaping and funding some actual programs;

* providing for more joint federal-provincial decision-making in some areas may be desirable, but the joint process should, produce results that are binding across the country. A real social union does not permit provinces to freely "opt-out."

There is no point in calling for a social union if some provinces do not have the resources to participate. The federal government has a necessary role in making equitable redistributive decisions. Furthermore, aspects of the social union will have to be spelled out; having eleven jurisdictions committed to shared platitudes may not result in any real accomplishment, such as ensuring that there is adequate vocational training across the country or universal access to health care. The federal government will be needed to help define and enforce minimum national standards.

There may indeed be areas in which more joint federal-provincial decision-making is desirable but the social union is going to be largely meaningless if any one province can veto decision-making, or opt-out if it doesn't like the results. Medicare was created without the agreement of all provinces; the *Canada Health Act* of 1984 helped maintain the system by pressuring some dissenting provinces into banning extra-billing.

If the definition and financing of the social union were left to a consensus among the provinces, it would quickly be reduced to the lowest common denominator — which is almost nothing at all. It may be suggested that the federal government should confine itself to making bloc grants to have-not provinces, and letting each individual province make its own social policy choices but it is unrealistic to suppose that the federal government is going to effectively participate in a system whereby it absorbs the political flak for raising taxes, while the provinces spend the money as they choose.

It is legitimate for a national government to want to devote its thinking and political energies to arenas in which it can influence policy. Furthermore, the social union is going to be financed by the residents of the more prosperous provinces. How long would they tolerate being told, in effect: "you should send money to people in distant provinces because they are your fellow Canadians. Your fellow Canadians, however, do not feel enough community with you to share in a national political process that influences how the money is spent."

The Ontario discussion paper is sound in emphasizing the importance of not leaving the leading role in the enforcement of the Social Charter to the courts. Choices about taxing and spending, about who-gets-what, is the main business of government. Turning such decisions over to judges would excessively undermine democratic control over social decisions. Ideally, everyone would have the opportunity to achieve an excellent post-secondary education, and everyone would have access to the best possible medical care; but what if there is not enough money to fully support both? What if there is not even enough money to ensure adequacy in both areas? Would investing in post-secondary education help to produce more productive citizens who could generate wealth to pay for things like Medicare?

Hard value choices have to made; so do complex calculations about how society really works, and how well-intentioned policies may actually operate. The decisions involved should generally be left to politicians, not non-elected judges. Politicians are electorally accountable to the people, and obliged out of self-interest, if nothing else, to try to find out how people are really living and what they are thinking. While courts see one isolated "slice of life" at a time, governments can try to see social problems in the context of a whole system and try to fashion remedies accordingly. Politicians can obtain information from direct contact with real people and the bureaucrats who actually deal with them. Judges are generally confined to considering the material that is put before them by contesting parties to suit their own purposes and then screened through legal rules of admissibility.

The economic-and-social union and the devolution of power.

The Business Council on National Issues may be the most influential lobby group in Canada. It is composed of big businesses, including Canadian subsidiaries of powerful multinationals. It has backed, and perhaps to some extent inspired, many of the current federal government's economic and constitutional initiatives, including Canada-US Free Trade and the Meech Lake Accord. Contributions from its members helped fuel the massive advertising campaign in the 1988 election to "sell" the Free Trade deal.

In April, 1991, the BCNI released its official position on constitutional reform. It is remarkably similar to the Federal Proposal released half a year later. Among the proposals anticipated by the BCNI are the strengthening of the economic union, the use of various techniques ("opting-out," delegation, bilateral deals) to enable provinces to "cut their own deals," more provincial input in federal bodies, a reformed Senate, some concessions to aboriginal peoples. Like the Federal Proposal, the BCNI position is almost entirely indifferent to the Canadian social union. About the only "people" issue in which the BCNI position displays much interest appears to be better systems for education and training. The federal government itself was making noises about assuming more leadership in education and training, until pressure from Quebec resulted in its promise to recognize provincial authority over labour market training.

The BCNI position paper is not overtly decentralist but clearly endorses the creation and deployment of various mechanisms (e.g.delegation, "opting-out") whereby massive decentralization could be achieved.

Whatever the actual motivations are behind the Federal Proposal (and those of its big business allies), Canadians should be aware that decentralization is consistent with an overall right-wing agenda. Decentralization reduces the net ability of Canadians to regulate business in order to protect the general welfare. Governmental power taken from the federal level dissipates when transferred to the provinces.

The laws of physics include the "conservation of matter and energy"; There is no principle of the "conservation of governmental power"; often the operative principle is "divide and conquer." It is easier for business to "manage" provincial governments than the federal one. Provinces can be played off against each other; they can be encouraged to offer subsidies, or relent on regulations, in the interests of preventing business from going elsewhere. Provinces may have fewer financial and technical resources to monitor the behaviour of business, and enforce laws to ensure fair competition or equitable treatment of employees and consumers. A big business in a small "provincial pond" may be in a position to make a very big splash if it is dissatisfied; it can conduct a province-wide advertising campaign attacking the government (which is far cheaper than doing so on a national basis); it can relocate; it can withdraw its financial support for the campaign activities of the government. Federal governments are often in a better position to regulate in the interests of the people. An interest group that is very powerful locally may be far less so nationally.

Many of the same principles apply with respect to provincial versus municipal regulation. It is relatively easy for local special interests, such as property developers, to acquire excessive power in local government. The right to appeal to a provincial body is sometimes the only chance for many local residents to obtain a fair hearing for their views.

It has been about a year since the federal government trotted out the slogan "bringing power closer to the people" to justify its decentralist agenda. It was floated through friendly journalists, repeated in the Spicer Report and makes an encore appearance in the Federal Proposal. The slogan is a gross oversimplification. The federal government is sometimes in a position to protect the people against powerful local interests. Terminating federal authority can amount to taking power away from the people. Agencies of the federal government can indeed be "out of touch" with local conditions, but maintaining local offices and staffing them with local people can help.

So can reforming the structure of the policy-making branches of the federal government, to better ensure that programs are designed with more sensitivity to local conditions. Among the institutional reforms that would help in this regard is the creation of a triple-E-ish Senate.

There is a special irony in the way the Federal Proposal states the "closer to the people" slogan. It is presented as a way of promoting "simplicity." Simplicity? Having ten different provincial regimes in Canada, plus federal rules, does not make life "simpler" for anyone, including business people. On the contrary, the existence of different and unharmonized regulatory regimes is regarded as a barrier to trade by a number of important agreements, including the U.S.-Canada Free Trade Agreement and the treaty establishing the European Economic Community. One of the best ways to promote an economic union is to authorize the central authority to legislate common rules. The *Constitution Act, 1867,* was originally intended to authorize Parliament to enact one nation-wide regulatory regime with respect to a vast range of business issues.

The Federal Proposal contains many proposals for bolstering the powers of the provinces at the expense of the authority of the national government. Among other things, the Federal Proposal would:

* recognize exclusive provincial authority over labour-market training;

* authorize the federal government to enter into binding agreements with provinces on matters of language and culture. If the latest immigration deal with Quebec is any example, the agreements will shift the balance of responsibilities to the provinces;

* enhance the role of provinces with respect to broadcast regulation;

* authorize Parliament to delegate any of its powers to any province;

* identify ten specific areas for immediate "streamlining," which will often mean delegating authority to the provinces;

* identify six areas of existing provincial jurisdiction from which the federal government is prepared to withdraw;

* require Parliament to obtain the consent of 7/50 provinces before enacting any new national shared-cost programs and allow provinces to "opt-out" of them, with compensation, provided they meet the "national objectives" of the program;

* abolish the existing power of Parliament to establish its regulatory authority over "works and undertakings" (that is, transportation and communication systems) by declaring them to be for "the general advantage of Canada."

There is only one "nationalizing" thrust to the package. A strong statement that Canada is an economic union and that the federal and provincial governments cannot pass laws that restrict the free movement of goods, services, capital and labour. Parliament would have the authority, with the consent of 7/50 provincial governments, to pass laws for the "efficient functioning of the economic union." The "economic union package," however, is shot through with loopholes and opportunities to "opt-out."

Bryan Schwartz LL.B., LL.M., J.S.D. 69

How the specifics of the Federal Proposal will affect the Economic and Social Union

To conclude this chapter, here is a review of how the Federal Proposal would deal with three elements of building the economic-and-social union in Canada: internal free trade, social programs and the division of powers.

The general idea behind the federal "economic union" proposal is admirable, even necessary. Prosperity and national unity will be served by trade liberalization. In all respects our internal freedom of trade should keep pace with, or exceed, our freedom to trade internationally. Unfortunately, the details of the Federal Proposal do not translate an excellent idea into reality. There are too many loopholes, too many opportunities to "opt-out." It is very much to be hoped that the federal government will strengthen and elaborate its proposal. Sadly, the most likely scenario is that the federal government will further dilute its proposal to soften criticism from provincial quarters, especially Quebec. The next chapter will explore the specifics of the "economic union."

The "social union" is little discussed in the Federal Proposal. The proposed "Canada clause" contains one vague mention of a "commitment to the well-being of all Canadians." There is no mention in the Canada clause of the social union, any of its specific elements, or even a restatement of the equalization principle already contained in the *Constitution Act, 1982*, s.36.

The only major substantive change to the "social union" may be seriously for the worse. The Federal Proposal presents a new obstacle to the creation of national shared-cost programs in areas of provincial jurisdiction: the consent of the "Council of Federation," which means 7/50 provincial governments. That constraint was not even proposed by the Meech Lake Accord. The idea is not necessarily a bad one. The requirement of provincial involvement would ensure that programs are preceded by adequate consultation with the provinces who must, to a very large extent, fund the programs out of their own treasuries and put them into practical effect. The support of 7/50 provinces would guarantee that a program has widespread political support and legitimacy, even though it intrudes on provincial jurisdiction. The potential "killer" is that the Federal Proposal offers the prospect for a province to "opt-out" of the program, even after it has been enacted by Parliament and supported by 7/50 provinces. The practical effect of "opting out" would put an end to national shared-cost programs as an effective instrument of nation-building.

A great deal depends on how the legal provision for "opting-out" is drafted. The Federal Proposal says that opting-out provinces would be able to receive financial compensation only if they run programs that "meet the objectives" of the national program. A requirement of "meeting the objectives" of the program would be reasonably demanding. The federal government would be able to insist that its policy directions had some real "bite." By contrast, the Meech Lake Accord allowed opting-out for running programs that were merely "compatible." At least one commentator has been very much encouraged by the movement to "meet." I regret to report that federal officials tell me that the wording change is not necessarily going to be reflected in the final draft. The word "compatible" may re-appear. If it does, the latest Federal Proposal will be even more hostile to new national shared-cost programs than Meech.

With respect to the division of powers, we have seen that the package is decentralist. The federal government makes some immediate "give-aways," and asks for the legislative authority to delegate even more power. The long-term prospects for Canada are not heartening. The Federal Proposal is liable to produce a Canada that is more and more decentralized; in which various delegations and bilateral deals (and various opt-outs under the "economic" union and "shared-cost" provisions) would produce a crazy-quilt Canada. All of the provinces would have different rights and operate different programs. Depending on how the final package is drafted, the federal level of government could wind up unable to establish nation-wide programs and regulations to promote either the economic or the social union.

The building of the social union is an essential part of maintaining a balanced federation. A process of constitutional "reform" which consists of constantly splitting the difference between the status quo and sovereignty-association is futile. There will always be hard-line Quebec nationalists, and the provincial government of Quebec will always be asking for more. The steady "ratcheting down" of the national community will not "solve" the national unity problem; it will leave the people of Quebec ever more detached, emotionally and politically, from the rest of Canada. It will leave other Canadians with the sense that their nation has been diluted into incoherence. Those who are interested in maintaining Canada must present a positive agenda that can appeal to a very broad range of Canadians, including many Quebecois. It must be a "people's agenda." An "economic union" is necessary, but not sufficient to build a community that can attract the profound and lasting loyalty of its people. There is no future in a "social union" that consists entirely of taxing residents of some provinces in order to underwrite the provincial governments of others. The federal government must have the legal authority and the political will to be a leading and visible partner in the creation and financing of programs that improve the day-to-day life of Canadians. Constitutional reform must build the national community as well as recognize diversity.

The federal package should be revised and clarified in the following directions:

* the "economic union principle" should be defined to include such matters as discrimination by governments in their taxing and spending measures. The Senate must be given real authority in money matters, including the right to monitor federal spending to ensure it is even-handed. The "loopholes" in the economic union principle should be eliminated and the new federal authority to pass laws "for the efficient management of the economic union" should not be subject to "opting-out";

* a revised federal authority to establish shared-cost programs in areas of exclusive provincial jurisdiction, subject to approval by 7/50 provinces, should include the right to insist that all provinces conform to minimum national standards;

* the "division of powers" package should not include the surrender of authority over labour market training. Federal authority over the environment should be enhanced, or at least, not undermined by other features of the package;

* the offer by the federal government to "clarify" existing provincial jurisdiction in a variety of areas should remain a statement of intent, to be dealt with later. The package is too big and complicated already, and important matters should not be dealt with as hastily-assembled "add-ons" to an already oversized package;

* the provision allowing the federal government to delegate any of its legislative authority to any province it chooses is intolerable. It opens the way to more and more decentralization, special status, and inequality. It would enable the federal government and provincial governments, including Quebec, to dismantle Canada one step at a time, through low-profile and discriminatory side-deals.

The economic union

The decline of federal authority over the economy

The *Constitution Act, 1867,* s.121, states that after Confederation, goods originating in any one province should be "admitted free" into each of the other ones. The statement can be understood as a modest guarantee that there will be no tariffs and other customs barriers between provinces. So far, whether through lack of opportunity or inclination, the Courts have not done much in the way of using s.121 to strike down federal or provincial laws that interfere with internal free trade in other ways. What about Parliament, though? Could it not use its existing powers over the economy to promote internal free trade?

The wording of the *Constitution Act, 1867* is very clear in granting the federal government the primary role over economic matters. Section 91 establishes the overall scope of federal authority. It begins by saying that Parliament has the general authority to pass laws for the "Peace, Order and good Government of Canada" — that is, to run the country. The only limitation is this: Parliament cannot intrude on a short list of provincial powers, contained in sections 92 and 93 of the 1867 Act. The nature of the provincial items is indicated by section 92(16): "Generally all matters of a merely local or private nature in the Province."

The framers of the original Constitution wanted to make extra sure that Parliament's general authority was not narrowed by an overly generous interpretation of provincial rights. So they added to s.91 a list of things that are deemed to come under Parliament's general authority, no matter what the provincial lists appear to say. The items on the federal list include many broad-ranging economic powers, including taxation, the regulation of trade and commerce, banking, money and interest, agriculture, inter-provincial and international transportation and communications.

The 1867 Constitution gave the federal government extraordinary authority to intervene in provincial matters to protect the national interest. Parliament can unilaterally assume regulatory authority over any local "work or undertaking" by declaring it to be "for the general Advantage of Canada." The federal government has the authority to disallow any provincial legislation of any nature.

What actually happened is much different. From early in Confederation, the provinces asserted their authority politically. The Trade and Commerce power, for example, was steadily chopped down by Court decisions until it was rendered almost meaningless. It was only in the 1980s that Supreme Court decisions began to breathe new life into it.

Federal authority over the economy has been impaired in other ways. The price that Trudeau paid for the Patriation package included the recognition of enhanced provincial authority over the management and taxation of natural resources. The 1988 Canada-United States Free Trade deal had the practical effect of sharply limiting federal authority over many areas, including energy export policy, government procurement and control of foreign investment.

What could the federal government do to promote the economic union with its existing powers?

Still, a determined national government would have a chance to succeed if it attempted unilaterally to cut back on barriers to trade within Canada.

The Supreme Court of Canada has held that Parliament's "Trade and Commerce" power does include the authority to regulate trade that might ordinarily be within provincial jurisdiction. Five factors have to be examined. No single factor is decisive, but a "good overall score" will help to persuade the Courts that a federal law is within federal jurisdiction. The factors are:

* public scheme: the law establishes a public scheme to regulate economic activity;

* oversight agency: the scheme is overseen by a federal regulatory agency;

* across-the-board application: the law is aimed at regulating trade and commerce in general, rather than a particular business;

* provincial inability: the provinces do not have the constitutional authority to put the scheme in place on their own;

* need for scheme to apply to all provinces: the efforts of provinces who wanted to establish the scheme among themselves could be undermined by the non-co-operation of one or more of the other provinces.

Suppose the federal government attempted to set up a scheme along the following lines. It would establish some general principles of the economic union, such as guarantees of free movement of goods, services, people and capital, and a guarantee of economic non-discrimination against any Canadian on the basis of provincial residence. An administrative board would be established to investigate departures from the norm, and order corrective measures.

There would be political protests from some of the provinces, but a federal government with a sense of national mission might be able to sell the idea to the people. Almost all of the provincial governments supported the U.S.-Canada Free Trade Agreement; would they not agree that national unity requires that trade within Canada should be at least as free as North-South trade? Should not Canadians enjoy at least as much economic freedom within their own state as Europeans do within a Community market that is many times larger?

The hypothetical federal scheme would appear to meet the above tests of public scheme, administrative oversight and across-the-board application. The "provincial inability" test would weigh in favour of the hypothetical scheme. There would be gaping holes in an economic union established by mutual agreement of the provinces. The provinces have limited or no authority over matters such as inter-provincial and international trade, industries under federal regulatory jurisdiction (such as banking, broadcasting and telecommunications) and the economic activities of the federal government itself. It is questionable whether a body established by the provinces jointly could be empowered to make decisions that are legally binding on private enterprises and individuals. Finally, the non-cooperation of one province could frustrate the "nation-building" aim of establishing a Canada-wide free market.

The legal case for the federal scheme would be assisted by other considerations. Parliament has, under its foreign affairs and trade and commerce powers, exclusive authority to enter into international trade agreements. It probably has substantial authority to implement these agreements in areas of provincial jurisdiction. The Courts might find some merit in the proposition that Parliament should at least be in a position to keep free trade within Canada on a par with evolving international standards. The case for the constitutionality of the federal scheme would also be assisted by Parliament's recognized authority over "inter-provincial trade and commerce."

The legal case for Parliament would still be far from "open-and-shut." The Courts might still find that federal "economic union" initiatives do intrude excessively on provincial jurisdiction. The possible "bite" of existing federal powers is a factor that should not be overlooked. Provincial resistance to the Federal Proposal might be softened by pointing out that the federal government may already have substantial authority to act on its own.

The Federal Proposal would make available to Parliament a new mechanism for promoting the economic union. To operate this mechanism, it would not be enough for Parliament to pass an ordinary law. There would be two other conditions. First, Parliament must declare the law to be "for the efficient functioning of the economic union." Second, the law must be approved by the "Council of the Federation." The Council of the Federation would be a body composed of ministerial representatives from the federal, provincial and territorial governments. All decisions of the Council would require the approval of at least seven provinces with half the population of Canada. The second condition would not always be easy to meet.

Currently, Parliament can exercise practically all of its legislative powers without provincial consent. Once the Senate is reformed to provide more input for smaller provinces, the moral authority of Parliament to act should be greater than it is at present. A more legitimate Parliament should not lose any of the powers it already possesses with respect to the economy. In preparing any legal text for the proposed "economic union" power, the federal government should make it clear that it is an additional power that does not detract from any existing ones. In particular, the requirement of approval by the Council of Federation should not apply to any of Parliament's existing powers over the economy.

Proposals in the Modern Era to Build the Canadian Economic Union: the Trudeau proposals of 1980.

The building of the economic union was part of Prime Minister Trudeau's constitutional agenda. In 1980, before he gave up on trying to achieve a consensus with the provinces (and announced his unilateral Patriation plans), Trudeau proposed a plan that provided as follows:

* individual economic rights would be protected, including "mobility rights";

* s.121, the existing "free movement of goods clause," would be expanded. Its protection would extend to persons, services and capital, and to both "direct and indirect" barriers to movement;

* there would be some exceptions to s.121. The "breathing room" for Parliament would be broad; it could continue to enact restrictive legislation if justified by a variety of considerations, including international obligations, equalization, regional development or "overriding national interest." Provinces would not be offered the same flexibility.

The provinces rejected the federal approach for a variety of reasons. It was contended that the expansion of s.121 left too much decision-making to the Courts; they, not politicians, would have the final say on what the "free movement" norm meant and whether an exception applied. Some provinces were critical of the relatively more expansive "escape hatches" allowed the federal government.

Trudeau did not pursue the larger "economic union" agenda when he announced his unilateral Patriation plans. He confined his efforts to having personal "mobility rights" entrenched in the Constitution. His proposal included the right to move to other provinces and to pursue the gaining of a livelihood in any province. Although eventually diluted somewhat (provinces with higher-than average unemployment are allowed to maintain hiring preferences for their residents) the proposal survived subsequent federal-provincial negotiations and became s.6 of the *Charter*.

The "MacDonald" Royal Commission of the Economy, which reported in 1985, found that the Canadian internal market operated reasonably well, but could and should be improved. The Report thought it premature to entrench an "economic union" principle in the Constitution. The Commissioners proposed that instead the federal government and the provinces should negotiate a "Code of Economic Conduct." At first, it would be enforced by political pressure. After some experience was gained, the scheme would be given more teeth by creating a commission of experts with enforcement powers. Finally, with enough experience gained and confidence built, the Code could be entrenched in the Constitution. According to the Royal Commission:

A constitutionalized code formulated today would probably include so many opting-out, *non obstante* and exemption clauses that it would perhaps only legitimize what it was designed to prevent.

The MacDonald Commission also recommended that Canada enter into a Free Trade Agreement with the United States. We have seen that the Commission recommended caution and incrementalism in building up free trade within Canada; but on the Canada-U.S. front, they recommended the immediate negotiation of a comprehensive and legally binding code. If disputes arose over the interpretation of the Canada-United States code, senior officials from both governments would try to reach agreement; but either side would, at the end of the day, be able to submit the matter to the binding arbitration of an impartial tribunal.

The MacDonald Commission's proposal on Free Trade was a major stimulus for Canada's entering into negotiations with the United States, and ratifying a deal in 1988. In the meantime, there have been some limited attempts to bolster internal economic union. The Western Premiers signed a political agreement in 1989 that promised to eliminate many forms of discrimination in government procurement. In 1990, a Premiers' Conference produced a similar agreement with nation-wide scope. Quebec did not attend the latter conference, nor did the federal government, and the implementation of the agreement seems to be somewhat stalled while the nine provincial (and two territorial) signatories wait for the federal government and Quebec to "get on board."

Perhaps the Commission was dishearteningly perceptive; it has indeed proved easier for Canada to make a comprehensive and legally binding free trade deal with a foreign power, the United States, than to take similar steps internally. The paradox cannot be dispelled by saying that the US-Canada Free Trade Agreement can be cancelled by either side on six months notice, whereas constitutional amendments are almost impossible to change. In reality, there can be no going back on a comprehensive trade agreement with the United States. Once put into force, the heightened flow of trade makes Canada more dependent than ever on the U.S.-Canada relationship; unilaterally terminating the treaty would cause disruptions, up to and including American economic retaliation, that no future Canadian government is likely to risk.

The Federal Proposals on the Economic Union

The Principle of the Economic union.

The Federal Proposal would strengthen s.121, the "common market clause." The proposed new s.121 would begin with a declaration of the "principle of the economic union." The definition provided is a welcome expansion on the current scope of s.121, but is still too restrictive.

Compared to the existing s.121, the Federal Proposal adds the following features:

* it states a general principle: that Canada is an economic union;

* the principle is expressly defined as applying to not only goods, as *per* the current s.121, but to people, services and capital;

* it prohibits generally "barriers or restrictions" based on provincial boundaries; the current s.121 might be read as being essentially confined to banning tariffs.

These are steps in the right direction but s.121 should be drafted in a more encompassing way. The current draft is ambiguous about whether the "economic union" is a larger principle that *includes* "free movement" or whether it is confined to the principle of "free movement." The accompanying text of the Federal Proposal seems to contemplate a larger meaning than merely "free movement." It suggests that establishing nation-wide standards for "labour market training" would be one aspect of "efficient functioning of the economic union." So would "fiscal harmonization." The legal draft should be revised to make it clear that the "economic union" extends well beyond "free movement."

One approach to better defining the economic union principle would be to provide a general definition and then say "here are some, but not all, of the specific things it includes." The list of specific items would guide the interpretation of the general definition. This approach may offer the best combination of retaining flexibility while ensuring that a broad range of specifics are covered.

There should be a guarantee that the federal government not discriminate against any province, or any part of a province, in its taxing, spending and procurement policies.

Bryan Schwartz LL.B., LL.M., J.S.D.   77

One of the biggest distortions of the Canadian economic union comes from governmental procurement, taxing and grant subsidy policies that arbitrarily favour some provinces or parts of provinces. A proper role of federal government is to extend special assistance to a part of the country on the basis of genuine needs. Favouritism based on partisan politics, however, has no legitimate place in Canada's future. It wastes scarce resources, and provokes bitter and lasting resentment. Albertans have not forgotten the National Energy Program of the 1970s. Manitobans will not soon forget the CF-18 scandal. (A multimillion dollar contract for servicing Canadian fighter aircraft was given to a Montreal facility, despite the fact that a Winnipeg operation submitted a superior bid. While the federal opposition parties criticized the tender procedures used by the federal government, they did not challenge the actual result. There was, after all, one calculation that the Winnipeg engineers could not overcome: the Montreal area has far more seats in the House of Commons than the entire province of Manitoba.)

The issue here is not only economic distortion and inter-regional resentment. Cynicism and contempt for the Canadian system of government is exacerbated every time a government deposits extra loot on the constituencies of government members.

The draft Federal Proposal offers excellent prospects for federal governments to continue regional favouritism and constituency pork-barrelling. The principle of the "equality of provinces" has been left out of the Canada clause. There is no explicit guarantee of non-discrimination in the "economic union clause." Perhaps some hope is offered in that the proposed Canada clause does refer to:

...the free flow of people, goods, services and capital throughout the Canadian economic union and the principle of equality of opportunity throughout Canada.

It is not clear from this statement whether the "principle of equality of opportunity" is an aspect of the economic union. In any event, statements in the "Canada clause" have no direct legal effect; what they do is influence how other parts of the Constitution are read. The vague reference in the "Canada clause" to "equality of opportunity" is hardly a guarantee that s.121 will be interpreted as prohibiting a broad range of discriminatory laws and practices, including discrimination and favouritism for provinces or constituencies based on partisan political considerations.

Among the programs that are most exploited for displaying political favouritism are regional economic development programs. Yet the Federal Proposal provides that the "economic union principle" does *not* render invalid a federal law "enacted to further the principles of equalization or regional development." That is a loophole that could be almost as wide as Canada. Most of the provinces are "have-nots" and are entitled to equalization payments under federal legislation. Even "have" provinces may have less prosperous regions. So the federal government can throw money at virtually anyone it wants, and call that an attempt to "further the principles of equalization or regional development."

The Federal Proposal in its current form offers almost no legal, court-enforceable limitations on the federal government's ability to distribute largesse where it pleases. It also avoids establishing any new political safeguards. The major purpose of the Senate reform movement has been to ensure the fair distribution of Canada's wealth among all parts of the country; but the Federal Proposal denies the Senate "any legislative role" over taxing and spending measures. The Federal Proposal suggests a new Council of the Federation as a check on federal authority. It would consist of representatives of the federal, provincial and territorial governments, and its decision-making rule would require the approval of not only the federal level, but of seven provinces with at least half of the population of Canada. The mandate of the Council is confined to three areas, none of which seem to include equalization payments or regional development programs:

* the Council can screen federal decisions under s.121(4), a new authority to pass laws declared to be "for the efficient management of the economic union" but the federal government does not need to resort to this route in order to continue making equalization payments and regional development grants;

* the Council can pass "guidelines" on "fiscal harmonization." The Federal Proposal is not clear about what the term means, but the examples provided include: maintaining a fixed schedule for the release of budgets, regular annual meetings of finance ministers, the publication of pre-budget fiscal outlooks by the federal government and its provincial counterparts and common accounting conventions. It does not appear that "fiscal harmonization" in any way involves deciding the size and distribution of equalization payments or regional economic development payments;

* the Council can screen new Canada-wide shared-cost programs and regional transfers. This category would not apply to either equalization payments (which are outright grants, not shared-cost or conditional transfers) nor to regional economic development programs (which are not "Canada wide"). In actual operation, the national shared-cost programs tend to be among the least suspect forms of federal spending. They are generally based on formulas that are fixed for a considerable period of time, and less liable to be manipulated by the political preferences of the federal government.

A broad anti-discrimination principle should be expressly included in the definition of the economic union.

A ban on discriminatory economic behaviour is a bedrock principle that is suitable for constitutional entrenchment. The aim is not to dictate the future direction of government policy but simply ensure that whatever policies are chosen conform to a standard of political fairness and honest government. The U.S.-Canada Free Trade agreement contains a number of guarantees of fair treatment with respect to government procurement and non-discrimination. The Treaty of Rome, which established the European Economic Community, is explicit:

Article 7. Within the scope of application of this Treaty, and without prejudice to any special provisions contained therein, any discrimination on grounds of nationality shall be prohibited...

This provision is directly enforceable by individuals and enterprises in national courts and before the European Court of Justice. In addition, the political organs of the European Community are authorized to establish binding rules to prohibit discrimination. As mentioned earlier, the "free movement" language chosen by the federal government in its current draft of s.121 does not go anywhere near far enough in striking at economic discrimination.

The Federal Proposal's draft section 121 might be interpreted by the Courts as applying to such matters as provincial government procurement policies that openly and expressly adopt a "buy local" policy but even that is not entirely clear. Non-discrimination should be expressly written into the definition of the economic union. It should be made clear that "discrimination" encompasses favouritism for provinces or parts of provinces based on partisan political considerations. In other words, the Constitution would make it clear that we are no longer prepared to accept the enormous economic and political distortions caused by "pork-barrelling."

A major role in the interpretation and enforcement of the anti-discrimination principle should be assigned to the reformed Senate. It will sometimes be very difficult to prove to the satisfaction of a Court that a particular spending amounts to favouritism rather than a reasonable response to differing needs. The Courts would no doubt accept that politicians have considerable discretion in deciding how to shape economic policy. A particular measure would have to be examined in the broad context of government programs. A political body such as the Senate would have some advantages over Courts in making wide-ranging assessments of political fact and value. The Senate could be assigned the role of reviewing government taxing and spending every year to ensure that all parts of Canada are treated fairly. The Senate would be charged with identifying and condemning programs that exhibit favouritism based on the boundaries of provinces or political constituencies. As a participant in the enactment of new legislation, it would be well-placed to ensure that there are no recurrences. The Constitution should also provide that individual enterprises who have been injured by economic discrimination may obtain remedies in the Courts. I would expect that judges would allow governments considerable leeway in the design and delivery of programs but would be prepared to intervene in cases of flagrant unfairness. Reports by the Senate would be helpful in proving these cases.

Suggested Improvements in the Definition of the Economic Union

* the "economic union" should be defined in a way that specifically includes guarantees of economic non-discrimination.

* it should be made clear that the "economic union" principle applies to government procurement and to taxing and spending measures;

* it should be made very clear that pork-barrelling is a form of economic discrimination. No area or enterprise should be economically favoured or disfavoured to reward it for supporting the government, or to coerce it to do so in the future;

* the principle should expressly state that every jurisdiction in Canada must extend to other jurisdictions all due recognition of their official acts on matters such as professional and educational credentials, legal judgments and products testing;

* the "loophole" for equalization payments and regional economic development programs should be severely limited. Only programs that respond to genuine needs, and exhibit even-handedness in doing so, would be permitted;

* the Senate of Canada should be given a specific role in reviewing government spending to ensure its conformity with the "economic union principle." It would have, at the very least, a suspensive veto over taxing and spending programs. If the House of Commons overrode the Senate, it would remain possible to bring the matter before the Courts, who would be able to take into account the Senate's decision in arriving at a final decision on whether discrimination has occurred.

Exceptions to the Economic Union Principle

Free Trade Agreements often provide for exceptions to various norms. The Trudeau proposal on the economic union ran into difficulty in 1980 with respect to the issue of exceptions. The provinces objected that much wider latitude would be given to the federal government. It is difficult to anticipate and formulate all of the possible reasons that might justify departing from the norm; the Federal Proposal avoids trying to exhaustively list all of them. Instead, it creates two "escape routes":

* loopholes: some laws are, by the their nature, expressly exempted from the application of the principle. Parliament would be free to enact laws "to further the principles of equalization or regional development." Provinces could enact laws to reduce disparities within the province, as long as they treat the interests of non-residents no worse than they treat less-favoured regions within the province;

* waivers: exemption for other laws could be obtained through a political process. A federal or provincial law can validly deviate from the "economic union principle" if Parliament declares the law to be in the "national interest" and the Council of the Federation agrees.

On the first count, the Federal Proposal allows far too much room for evasion. It has just been argued that the "equalization payments" and "regional economic development" exceptions could allow the federal government to dispense money in just about any arbitrary manner it chooses. The loophole for provincial "disparity" reduction within a province is also too broad. Such programs may have adverse impacts on out-of-province residents which outweigh any social benefit within the province. Furthermore, the economic union principle should apply within provinces, and not merely between them; for example, pork-barrelling within a province is just as corrupt and wasteful as pork-barrelling by the federal government.

Indeed, there are good arguments for establishing legal safeguards against provincial discrimination which are even tougher than those to be applied to federal misconduct. With a reformed Senate in place, the federal government would be under direct electoral pressure from all parts of the country; a federal government that discriminated against any particular part of the country could be chastened by the political response at the next election. On the other hand, provincial governments do not enjoy an electoral relationship with anyone but their own residents and are more likely to discriminate against people from other provinces. I would suggest, therefore, that either:

(a) the specific exception for intra-provincial "reduction of economic disparity" should be eliminated. Any province needing an exemption for its program would have to follow the general procedure for obtaining a waiver. Under the Federal Proposal, that would be an application to Parliament for a declaration that the program is "in the national interest," to be followed by the requirement of approval of the Council of the Federation;

or (as a much less preferable alternative):

(b) the exception should be severely narrowed. Provincial governments would be allowed to pass a law that discriminated within a province only if a series of conditions were met. The law would have to be a genuine attempt to address disparities within the province. It could not be part of an overall government program that exhibited favouritism for the special needs of one part of the province over another. It would have to be designed in a way that posed the least possible disruption to the economic opportunities of residents of other provinces.

Bryan Schwartz LL.B., LL.M., J.S.D. 81

As mentioned earlier, the Federal Proposal offers another "escape route" from the "economic union principle." A province or the federal government can win a waiver for any law if a special procedure is followed. Parliament must first declare the law to be in the "national interest" and the Council of the Federation must agree.

Is there a need for a waiver procedure? Probably. It is difficult to anticipate all of the circumstances that might justify an exception to the economic union principle. Before agreeing to entrenching a stronger "economic union" principle in the constitution, federal and provincial governments will want some re-assurances that the new principle will not be interpreted and applied in a way that is too rigid or harsh. It may be better to allow for the occasional waiver than to build in a raft of specific exceptions.

Should the "waiver" be granted by political bodies, or by impartial judges? Courts could be given a mandate to determine whether an exception to the economic union is warranted by "compelling economic or social circumstances." The germane analogy is the "reasonable limits" clause of the *Charter*. It is worth noting that the only survivor of Trudeau's economic union initiative of 1980, the "mobility rights clause" (which is in Section 6 of our *Charter*) is not subject to the "notwithstanding" clause. Parliament and provincial legislatures cannot grant themselves "waivers" from mobility rights. The only possible escape is the "reasonable limits" clause of the *Charter*. The Courts, not political bodies, have the final say on whether that clause can validate any particular law.

There is some merit to the view, however, that the social and economic value judgments involved in assessing a waiver application should be left to political bodies. The latter have certain advantages over the Courts, including accountability to the electorate and officials who may be in closer touch with social realities.

The Senate, as part of Parliament, might have a crucial role to play in the waiver process. The provinces may be too eager to grant each other exemptions. Premiers will tend to share the view that provinces should have some "breathing room" from national strictures and that doing a colleague a favour never hurts if you need one yourself. The federal government is too likely to yield to pressures for exemptions from the most populous parts of the country. Members of a reformed Senate may be inspired by their membership in a national institution to adopt a more Canada-wide perspective than Premiers. At the same time, the Senate may be more resistant than the House of Commons to pressure from the larger provinces. If an exemption-seeker has to win the support of the House of Commons, the reformed Senate and seven provinces, there may be enough resistance to prevent the economic union from being smashed into fragments.

It is understandable that national bodies should be involved in screening provincial attempts to deviate from the economic union principle; provincial legislatures are only accountable to their own residents and so cannot be counted upon to put the national interest ahead of the local one. So why is it necessary to involve other provinces, rather than leaving the scrutiny strictly to Parliament?

Similarly, why does the Federal Proposal grant provinces must have a role in reviewing waivers that Parliament proposes to allow itself? The Federal government will be answerable to all Canadians, through a "one person, one vote" House of Commons and a Senate that provides extra representation for less populous provinces. The law for which a waiver is sought may be in an area that is exclusively within federal jurisdiction. Why is it always necessary to have provincial governments passing judgment on a waiver sought by Parliament?

A good case could be made for letting Parliament act as the sole judge of whether a waiver is appropriate, whether sought by the provinces or by the federal government itself. We should not assume that the will of the nation can only be expressed by a supermajoritarian process that resembles the amending formula. Specifically, Parliament should not generally be required to obtain the approval of the Council of the Federation before it can act.

Analogies with other systems should not be applied uncritically. For example, it is true that European Community laws must often be approved by a Council which is composed of representatives of national governments but European laws are not generated by a democratically elected parliament. They are proposed by the European Commission, which is composed of unelected bureaucrats. The European Parliament remains a junior partner in the law-making process and involving the Council is necessary to ensure adequate political accountability. In Canada, we are aiming at establishing a Parliament whose two chambers are both directly accountable to Canadians.

There is a good case for the consistent involvement of the Council of the Federation in granting waivers. The fact that Parliament must abide by the same waiver system imposed on provinces should make it easier to entrench the economic union principle and should help to avoid suspicion and resentment later on. It will be easier for provincial governments to accept a "no" from Parliament if they can sometimes say "no" to Parliament. It will also be easier to accept a "no" if it is backed up by other provinces, who cannot be accused of being insensitive to the provincial point of view. When a province is seeking a waiver, the involvement of other provincial governments will ensure that their views and experience are thoroughly canvassed. Giving a party a role in the decision making process may not be the only way to ensure that the party is consulted, but it is the surest way.

Another way to improve the "economic union" proposal: provide that individuals and business enterprises may seek its enforcement in the Courts.

As presented in the Federal Proposal, it would appear that any "law or practice" that violates the "economic union" principle would be unconstitutional. How would an individual or a business enterprise go about gaining redress for violations of the "economic union" principle?

The Federal Proposal does not set out specific means of enforcement or remedies. By contrast, the *Charter of Rights and Freedoms* contains a section 24, which clearly establishes that:

> Anyone whose rights or freedoms ... have been infringed or denied may apply to a court of competent jurisdiction to obtain such remedy as the court considers appropriate and just in the circumstances.

The Federal Proposal should be revised by providing a similar "enforcement section" under the economic union principle. Doing so would send a clear signal to the Courts that they have a full and legitimate role to play in enforcing the economic union principle. If there is no "remedies clause," the Courts may be tempted to adopt an excessively "hands-off" approach. A Court might reason that it should intervene only in the most flagrant of violations of the economic union principle.

Another advantage to a "remedies clause" is that it will establish that Courts can grant damages, or other compensatory measures, to those who have been injured by violations of the "economic union" principle. Otherwise, Courts might think that their only recourse is to declare a law or government decision invalid. Such a result may be small comfort to an individual or business that has already been economically devastated.

Should Enforcement Lie With a Specialized Trade Tribunal, Rather than the Ordinary Courts?

There are a variety of advantages to leaving the interpretation and enforcement to the ordinary Courts system, which puts the final say in the hands of the Supreme Court of Canada. The existing institution is experienced in constitutional matters and has a broad base of credibility among governments and ordinary people. The immediate advantage of leaving things to the existing Courts system during this round is that it obviates the need to design and "sell" yet another new institution.

Later on, it may prove desirable to set up some specialized Courts to hear and decide disputes about the economic union. It would be possible to staff the Court with individuals who are knowledgeable in both constitutional and economic affairs. The Economic Union Court should not be given the final judicial say. It should be possible to seek reconsideration of its decision in the Supreme Court of Canada. The fracturing of ultimate authority over constitutional issues would create messy procedural complications; for example, what if a particular lawsuit raises some "economic issues" and some other issues?

If a special Court is to be established later on, who would create it? Parliament has authority under s.101 of the *Constitution Act, 1867,* to establish "additional Courts for the better Administration of the Laws of Canada." That authority might permit Parliament to establish a specialized Court to interpret and enforce the "economic union" principle. The most consistent course of action, however, might be to provide in the Constitution that any specialized "economic union" Court must be established by Parliament under its new power to make laws for the efficient functioning of the economic union. As with other laws enacted under the proposed new "economic union" power, it would not be valid unless approved by the Council of the Federation.

The Economic Union Power

The Federal Proposal calls for a new s.91A to be inserted in the *Constitution Act, 1867.* It contains the following elements:

* exclusive authority for Parliament to pass laws in relation to any matter that it declares to be "for the efficient functioning of the economic union";

* a requirement that the law be approved by the Council of the Federation;

* a province can "opt-out" of the law by a resolution supported by 60% of the members of its legislature;

* an opt-out can only last for a maximum of three years.

The explanatory material in the Federal Proposal calls upon the Parliamentary Committee studying the proposal to determine whether the "opt-out" should be renewable.

Neither the draft legal text nor the Federal Proposal explain very well what the scope of "efficient functioning of the economic union" is. One example that is offered is a measure to establish consistency in how federal and provincial governments release their budgets. The other is establishing national standards for "labour market training."

Let's look at the first example, "budgetary harmonization."

The Federal Proposal calls for the increased "coordination ...and harmonization of fiscal policies." When discussing the general objectives, the Federal Proposal expresses concern about establishing a common direction to policy, and not merely procedures. The Federal Proposal speaks of "the tax and spending policies of the provinces and those of the federal government," which may be at "cross purposes" and that this "conflict can reduce the growth of the economy and affect an individual's standard of living."

Perhaps the drafters of the Federal Proposal had in mind the heated controversy which arose over the 1990 budget of Premier Rae's government in Ontario. The policy of the federal government and a number of the provinces has been to slow down government spending in order to reduce deficits. The Ontario government, by contrast, chose to accept a ten billion dollar deficit in the hopes that foregoing spending cuts would prevent a bad recession from getting even worse. The Ontario government also argued that cutbacks at the provincial level would not necessarily improve the state of overall public finances; it might simply mean "off-loading" the problems on municipalities, just as federal "restraint" may amount to transferring burdens to the provinces. Prime Minister Mulroney and Premier Rae were sharply critical of each other over the issue, until a truce was declared to work on a constitutional settlement.

When making specific suggestions, however, the Federal Proposal shies away from matters such as common policies on deficits. It retreats into calling for more consultation among governments, more sharing of information, and the adoption of standard budgetary processes. The Federal Proposal speaks of using its "economic union" power to establish "guidelines" for the scheduling of budgets, the accounting conventions employed, and a fixed schedule of meetings among finance ministers.

Would the economic union power, as presented in the Federal Proposal, actually authorize laws that controlled the size of provincial deficits? The answer is not clear. There should be more direction for Parliament and the Council of the Federation, and perhaps the Courts. It may be that the Courts would uncritically accept that any law declared to be "for the efficient functioning of the economic union" is valid, regardless of its subject matter. It is also possible that the Courts would "look behind" a declaration, and ask whether a law has strayed beyond what was intended when the declaration provision was drafted. Whether the Federal Proposal, taken at face value, encompasses harmonization of policies such as deficits is not worth exploring in great depth.

First of all, a number of provinces are going to make very sure that the "economic union" power does not go so far. Their objections will be justified. Allowing the federal government and 7/50 provinces to dictate fiscal policy to an unwilling province would amount to a profound impairment of provincial autonomy. The amount of money a government can spend in a year influences almost every decision it makes. There is no comparison at all with the constraint on sovereignty imposed by an economic union principle. An analogy: to tell a private business it can not discriminate on the basis of age, race or sex is a very limited constraint on its economic freedom, whereas to tell a business how much of a debt or surplus it can accumulate in a year would be drastically more intrusive.

Second, the mechanics of the Federal Proposal would make it impossible to impose a common policy on deficits anyway. Any province that is unhappy could opt-out for three years. After three years, economic conditions will likely have changed the fiscal policies of every government in Canada.

Third, this particular Proposal is impossible to take at face value, no matter how willing one is to suspend disbelief about the current government's commitment to nation-building. The Federal Proposal asks the Joint Parliamentary Committee to consider whether the "opt-out" should be "renewable." How's that for leading with your chin? Once Quebec tells the federal government that the provision must be renewable — at least if it involves matters as profound as the size of budget deficits — the federal government will agree, and the "bottom line" will be this: the "fiscal harmonization" rules will apply to whichever province accepts them. The process will not have advanced in any serious way beyond what could be accomplished through voluntary co-operation and co-ordination.

The Federal Proposal should be improved along the following lines:

* there is a legitimate role for a federal power to pass laws for the "efficient functioning of the economic union." Recall the way that Article 7 of the Treaty of Rome works. It states the general norm of "non-discrimination," but provides two means of enforcement: judicial intervention for violation of the general norm, and a mandate for political bodies to pass more specific rules. There should be a mechanism for Parliament to establish guidelines to promote the economic union in areas that partly involve provincial jurisdiction. Parliament, in conjunction with the Council of the Federation, should be able to establish laws providing for the recognition of professional credentials, common requirements of product labelling and testing etc;

* the economic union power should be defined by examples of what it includes;

* budget harmonization is a matter that can be left to voluntary co-operation. It does not require constitutional amendments. The economic union power of Parliament should be defined in a way that makes it clear that the provinces retain their ultimate authority to decide on budgetary balances;

* the provision for any "opting-out" should be eliminated. Any "adjustment time" that is needed can be provided in the laws enacted under the "economic union" power.

The Monetary Union

There were complaints prior to the release of the Federal Proposal that the high interest rate policy of the Bank of Canada had been geared to meet the problems of an overheated Ontario economy, rather than responding to the needs of other regions, most of which were in various forms of economic distress. The Federal Proposal offers more opportunity for "regional input" into the operation of the Bank.

The Federal Proposal prefaces everything by promising to amend the *Bank of Canada Act,* to make it clear that the "mandate of the Bank is to achieve and preserve price stability." The current mandate of the Bank is less restrictive. The Bank can pursue various policy objectives, such as lowering the price of the Canadian dollar in order to promote exports and employment, or increasing money supply to stimulate a stagnant economy. Economists have differing views on whether monetary policy can be effectively used in this way. It is questionable whether the Act should preclude the Directors from considering other economic factors. It is unacceptable to constitutionally entrench a particular economic theory about the proper role of central banks. We do not know that much about how existing economies actually work and even less about how they will operate in the future. The Constitution should not prohibit future governments or central banks from trying new approaches to monetary policy. It may be that the Federal Proposal has constricted the role of the Bank precisely because it is afraid of the consequences of its other reforms. Perhaps the federal approach is that there can be lots of regional input as long as there is not too much that the Bank can do about it.

The Proposal offers to "solicit the views of provincial and territorial governments and consult with them before making appointments to the Board." It sounds reasonable, unless you remember the Meech experience with Supreme Court appointments. Quebec's initial "five demands" included "consultation" on judicial appointments. In the Meech Lake Accord, the federal government offered Quebec far more than it asked for: primary control over the appointments. The federal government would have reduced its own participation to that of choosing from lists of nominees provided by Quebec. There is far more clout in choosing the short list than in making the final selection. If you are presented with a list of five judges of the same philosophical stripe, it may not matter much which one you choose.

The Federal Proposal calls for "regional panels" to advise the Directors on regional economic conditions. The Federal Proposal would give the reformed Senate the power to ratify or reject the appointment of new Governors of the Bank. There is merit in requiring prospective Governors to demonstrate their qualifications and explain their economic philosophy but the banking policy is an area where a coherent policy should be worked out at the national level. Instead of relying so much on provinces and territories to provide that input, why not give Senators the role of ensuring that regional perspectives are being blended to produce a national policy? For example, the constitution could provide that one of the responsibilities of Senators is to keep the Bank of Canada informed of local conditions. Giving elected people something to do would be better than setting up additional institutions, which may be expensive, unnecessary and end up being filled with patronage appointees.

The Federal Proposal is not clear on whether it is proposing to actually amend the Constitution to carry out its central banking reform, as opposed to merely amending the *Bank of Canada Act*. It may be appropriate to constitutionally specify a role for the reformed Senate, but beyond that, the federal government should confine its experiments in banking reform to ordinary legislation. It should leave future federal governments free to examine how new policies and systems have worked out and make appropriate adjustments in light of experience and new ideas.

Chapter

12

Federal spending power

The Spending Power and the Social Union

Over the years, the federal government has been able to use its "spending" power to help build the Canadian social union. Even in areas where the federal government's constitutional authority to directly regulate is limited, it is often able to influence policy by setting the terms and conditions under which it will spend money. Over the years, there have been relatively few court tests of the right of the federal government to spend money in areas where legislative authority has been assigned to the provinces but several decisions in recent years have, in a variety of contexts, upheld the exercise of the federal spending authority. There is a long history of federal spending in provincial areas and of provincial governments actively agreeing to it or at least acquiescing; the Courts will likely consider the precedents established by other branches of government as a weighty factor on the side of the constitutionality of federal intervention.

The Scope of the Federal Proposal

The Federal Proposal, like Meech, addresses the power of the federal government to spend in areas of provincial jurisdiction. The Meech Lake Accord dealt expressly only with "national shared-cost" programs, rather than federal spending generally. The term was not actually defined. The latest Federal Proposals speak of "national shared-cost programs *and* conditional transfers. It may be that the additional words are only intended to make it clear that the provision applies where the federal government is funding provinces according to a formula, as opposed to reimbursing them for actual costs.

A few national "shared-cost" programs still involve the actual sharing of real costs by the federal government; under the Canada Assistance Plan, the federal government absorbs about half of the actual cost of social welfare payments made by agencies under provincial jurisdiction. Under some programs, the federal government underwrites a provincial program according to a fixed formula, which may not correspond to actual costs. The federal government supports post-secondary education and health services in this way.

The Federal Proposal makes it clear that the federal government is not relinquishing any rights it has to spend in areas that are clearly or arguably within provincial jurisdiction. No new limitations would be imposed on payments the federal government makes directly to individuals (e.g., family allowance payments) or organizations (e.g., grants to research institutes). The federal government would retain its current level of freedom in making bilateral agreements with the provinces — e.g., regional economic development deals — as opposed to nation-wide programs.

Conditions attached to federal spending.

The federal government has been very restrained about imposing conditions for the receipt of shared-cost programs. There are essentially no conditions on transfers for post-secondary education, and very few for Canada Assistance Plan payments.

National Medicare is the one high-profile area in which the federal government has insisted on provincial conformity to some important standards. In the *Canada Health Act,* enacted in 1984, the federal government listed five "criteria" which provincial programs must meet in order to qualify for full federal support. They are:

* public administration;
* comprehensiveness: the scheme applies to all insured health services;
* universality: it covers all residents of the province;
* portability: it covers people visiting other provinces;
* accessibility: it provides for insured health services on "uniform terms and conditions and on a basis that does not impede or preclude, either directly or indirectly, whether by [user fees] or otherwise, reasonable access to those services."

The *Canada Health Act* authorizes the federal government to reduce its payments to provinces to the extent that they allow doctors to "extra-bill" — that is, bill patients for more than the provincial health-insurance scheme would cover.

The erosion of the social union through federal cut-backs in shared-cost programs.

National shared-cost programs have been a major element in nation-building. Many Canadians think of Medicare in particular as an important element in defining the nature of Canadian society and maintaining unity. Federal funding in other areas, such as post-secondary education and social assistance, have also been important factors in building a "kinder, gentler" society in Canada. Over the past decade, however, austerity measures by federal governments have begun to erode the extent to which shared-cost programs are contributing to the "social union."

In 1977, the *Established Program Funding Act* (EPF) set out a formula for federal funding for health and post-secondary education; it provided that federal contributions would increase at the same rate as the growth in the economy. For almost a decade federal governments have been trying to limit the growth of federal contributions to post-secondary education and health care. The 1991 budget froze federal contributions until the end of the 1994/95 budget year, and limited increases to the growth rate in the economy *less* three per cent.

In its 1991 report, *Funding For Higher Education: Danger Looming,* the National Council on Welfare pointed out that we are approaching a time when the federal government actually makes no cash payments to provinces at all. The EPF system works like this:

* the federal government has used a general formula to determine how much each province is supposed to get;

* payments to a province are partly or totally made in the form of "tax transfers"; that is, the federal government reduces its taxes on provincial residents and allows the province to increase its rates to make up the difference. Cash payments are only made if the "tax transfers" are insufficient to meet a province's entitlement. As those entitlements would continue to be subjected to federal austerity measures, cash payments would become increasingly "unnecessary" and would disappear entirely in about fifteen or twenty years.

How can the federal government "call the tune" if it is not paying the piper a dime? Cash payments have been the lever that the federal government uses to influence provincial policies. The enforcement mechanism for the *Canada Health Act,* for example, is that the federal government can cut back on its EPF cash payments to the extent that a province is not complying with certain conditions, including a ban on extra-billing. What if the federal government has stopped making any cash payments?

The federal government has already thought of an "answer." Suppose a piper not only plays music, but fixes cars. In the course of negotiating what you will pay him for an engine overhaul, you threaten to pay him less unless he plays "Amazing Grace." This is the approach the federal government advanced in 1991 with Bill C-20. Section 4 would authorize the federal government to cut back on cash payments under any other federal-provincial arrangements if a province has not complied with the *Canada Health Act.* The legality and political legitimacy of such a move is questionable; it may be rejected by both the Courts and provincial governments as an attempt to allow additional federal influence without additional spending. The National Council of Welfare states:

> [We] cannot imagine provinces and territories letting this proposal go unchallenged. The delivery of health care services is within provincial jurisdiction under the Constitution. It is only the federal spending power that allowed federal involvement in this area, and it is difficult to imagine how Ottawa could continue to maintain its presence once the money for Medicare dries up.

The practical "off-loading" of costs onto the provinces, through ordinary legislation, is steadily weakening the social union. The "threat" to many provinces is not excessive federal meddling in areas of provincial jurisdiction; it is the eagerness of the federal government to ease its own fiscal burdens by withdrawing its support for social welfare programs. The next constitutional round ought to be concerned with firming up federal responsibility and authority for maintaining the social union, rather than simply providing the federal government another excuse to withdraw from the social policy field.

"Opting Out" of Shared Cost Programs up to Meech Lake

In the 1960s, the federal government began to offer provinces the right to "opt-out" of some national shared-cost programs. The effect was primarily symbolic. Prior to Meech, "opting out" generally meant that a province would receive tax points instead of cash payments but opting-out provinces were expected to comply with essentially the same federal conditions as any other province. As just mentioned, quite apart from "opting out," the federal government has been increasingly funding programs through tax points rather than cash payments. Prior to Meech, the conditions that "opted-out" provinces were expected to meet were essentially the same as those that were formally "within" the program.

The "spending power provisions" of the Meech Lake Accord were among the most controversial. The original Meech Lake communique, of April 30, 1987, would have allowed provinces to "opt-out" of national shared-cost programs, run their own "programs or initiatives" instead and claim "reasonable compensation" — that is, about the same amount of money they would have received if they had participated in the federal program. The only constraint was that the provincial "programs or initiatives" had to be "compatible" with "national objectives." "Compatible" may imply peaceful co-existence rather than compliance. It was not in the least clear what "national objectives" meant either. The term could have referred only to the objectives of the specific federal program or it could have been interpreted as encompassing the objectives contained in federal legislation generally; allowing a province to take money from a federal education program and spend it on improving its local section of the Trans-Canada Highway. "National objectives" could even have meant the broad aims of all Canadian governments: the safety, welfare and prosperity of the people.

At the "Langevin Block" meeting, in June 1987, First Ministers fought long and hard over the final legal draft of the "spending power" clause. Premier Pawley of Manitoba managed to win some improvements. The revised draft made it reasonably clear that the national objectives were those defined by Parliament when it established the program. In other ways, however, the final draft still left the leadership role of Parliament imperiled. The phrase "compatible with" remained; it was not replaced with something like "conforms to" or "complies with." There was concern as well that the phrase "national objectives" would confine Parliament to insisting on broad policy goals, but disable it from insisting on particular means of achieving them. For example, Parliament might be able to call on provinces to maintain accessible medical systems, but unable to insist on the elimination of all user fees as a means to that end. A province might be able to introduce a "means test" — that is, require everyone over a certain income level to pay a user fee — and still claim its full share of federal Medicare money.

Various would-be reformers of Meech suggested different ways of addressing the remaining problems with the spending power clause. The Federal Liberal Party suggested that provinces must operate a "compatible program which meets minimum national standards." My own approach in *Refashioning Meech Lake* was similar. The 1989 Manitoba Task Force on the Constitution was unable to reach a consensus on any particular draft, and recommended removing the "spending power" clause altogether. Premier Wells adopted a compromise position: "a program" must "accord with the national objectives."

At the end of the day, however, the pro-Meech First Ministers, led by the Prime Minister, tried to force the passage of Meech without any changes, or even any significant promises of change. Elijah Harper in Manitoba and Premier Wells of Newfoundland then concluded that they were left with no choice but to "opt-out" — or more precisely, veto the whole thing.

The Latest Federal Proposal: More stringent than Meech?

The Federal Proposal does not actually present a draft amendment. The discussion suggests that it will attempt these variations on Meech Lake:

* the proposed new "spending power" clause may refer to "national shared-cost programs and conditional transfers." As discussed earlier, the change may simply be to ensure that the provision

addresses programs in which the federal government does not pick up a certain share of actual provincial expenses, but instead provides funding according to a pre-determined formula;

* the proposed new "spending power" clause would require any new program to be approved by the Council of the Federation. In other words, Parliament would not be able to even establish the program unless 7/50 provincial governments agreed. Meech retained the right of Parliament to establish programs unilaterally.

Although I am a strong advocate of having a social union and of the federal government's playing a leading role in shaping it, I can see some advantages in requiring new programs to clear the 7/50 hurdle. The programs are, definitionally, those in areas of exclusive provincial jurisdiction. It does make sense to guarantee a strong role for the governments that will actually operate the programs and contribute much of their own money to financing them. Once they are brought "inside the tent," the provincial governments may be attracted to the idea of playing an active and creative role in nation-building. Furthermore, the case for denying provinces the right to "opt-out" is much better if a program has won the support of not only the federal level of government, but 7/50 provinces.

The existing system does not, facilitate the strong assertion of federal leadership. The federal government is so concerned about provincial objections to the intrusion on their jurisdiction that it tends to provide few or no conditions on its proposals and is most likely to fund programs in which it can play a genuine nation-building role; taxing Canadians so provinces can spend the money cannot possibly remain at the top of any federal government's list of priorities. The proposed "Council of the Federation" may offer an avenue whereby the federal government can gain more political legitimacy for its shared-cost programs while maintaining an active role in shaping policy.

The Federal Proposal for a new spending power clause might allow opting out if the province operates a program that "meets the objectives" of the national program. (The French version is "conformes aux objectifs.") The wording is certainly an improvement on the laisser-faire "compatible with" that was used in Meech. Unfortunately, there is no guarantee that the federal government will not revert, at the drafting stage, to the word "compatible." The net result would then be worse than Meech: the federal government could go to all the trouble of winning the support of 7/50 provinces, and still find itself unable to build the nation-wide social union.

If a program has won the support of the federal government, the House of Commons, the reformed Senate, and 7/50 provinces, there is an extremely powerful case in principle against allowing any "opting out" at all, let alone "opting-out" and claiming federal money. The people of any potentially dissatisfied province would have the chance to voice their concerns through the House of Commons, their senators and their provincial premiers. Even if it is practically necessary to make concessions to Quebec on the "opting out" score, the test should be "conformity with the minimum national standards."

Should the federal government have authority to define minimum standards for the "social union" even if it is not spending money?

To date, the federal government has often been obliged to resort to conditional spending to influence policy in the social area. It is interesting to note that the proposed "economic union" power in the Federal Proposal would theoretically allow the federal government to shape policy without infusing money. For example, the Federal Proposal contemplates the "economic union" power being used to establish "national standards" for labour market training but makes no mention of any federal funding. In practice the federal government might find it very difficult to win the support of 7/50 provinces for a measure that requires provinces to spend more money without federal help.

The Federal Proposal does not define the "economic union" power. Apparently it can include some "people's issues" such as labour market training. It is not clear how far the power to manage the "efficient functioning of the economic union" would extend to establishing national standards in such areas as minimum wages or worker safety. It has been suggested already that the "economic union" power should be better defined and that examples of what it includes is a way of doing so. It would be reasonable to include in the revised definition at least some social issues that are intimately related to economic production — such as labour training, occupational safety and anti-pollution measures.

There is a strong case in principle for directly establishing a federal power to "manage the social union" that would parallel the power to manage the "economic union." Such a power, for example, would permit the federal government, with the Council of the Federation, to define national Medicare standards without having to attach conditions to cash payments.

A number of provinces, including Quebec, would object strenuously to a sweeping and undefined new federal power over the social union; perhaps, however, some progress could be made if the "social union" power were defined by setting out the salient cases to which it would apply — such as establishing Medicare or day care standards.

"Grandfathering" Medicare

The latest Federal Proposal, like Meech Lake, would apply only to "new" shared-cost programs. The comfort offered is small. As we have already seen, the existing Medicare system is already in trouble. The federal government is steadily cutting back on its willingness to fund the system, to the point where its ability to impose any conditions on the provinces is compromised, both legally and politically. Furthermore, a constitutional provision protecting "existing" programs may not protect future attempts to revise those programs. If a "grandfather" clause is to provide any significant protection for what is left of the federal role in the social union, it must expressly extend its protection to future revisions of existing programs. In any event, focusing on the protection of existing programs is misguided. We should be at least as concerned about protecting the on-going ability of the federal government to exercise a creative role in defining and financing the social union. Those who are not concerned about innovation in the future have no business writing constitutions.

Bryan Schwartz LL.B., LL.M., J.S.D.   93

Summary of recommendations

My suggestions for improvement of the "spending power" clause:

   * a "Social Charter" should be included in the Constitution as a solemn political commitment but the interpretation and enforcement of the principles should be left primarily to politically accountable branches of government;

   * the "Social Charter" could be attached to a new "spending power" clause, and placed in a part of the Constitution called "The Canadian Social Union." The existing section 36 of the *Constitution Act, 1982*, which includes a commitment to equalization payments, could be placed in the new "Social Union" section as well;

   * the "Social Union" part should include a statement that the federal government is expected to play a leading financial and creative role in developing the social union;

   * the new "spending power" clause could also be included in the "Social Union" part of the Constitution. It could require new national shared-cost programs to be screened through the Council of the Federation, but it should not allow "opting-out." At the very least, it should require any "opting-out" provinces to conform to the minimum national standards established by the federal government;

   * the federal government's proposed new "economic union" power should be better defined, and could usefully include "social concerns" that are intimately connected with economic production — including worker safety, labour market training and pollution controls standards;

   * the "Social Union" clause could include a "social union" power that would permit the federal level of government, in conjunction with the Council of the Federation, to establish national standards in certain social welfare areas — including national Medicare standards.

It may bear emphasizing again that the federal level of government must have the authority and responsibility to play a leadership role with respect to the definition and financing of actual social programs. Otherwise, there can and will be no meaningful "social union." A generally-worded Social Charter, on its own, would do practically nothing to bring Canadians together. Sharing platitudes does not mean sharing wealth, mutual concern or nationhood. The federal government must have a role if there is to be some real commonality in the quality and nature of programs available to the residents of all provinces.

Transfer of powers to the provinces

The Federal Proposal offers to give away federal powers in a variety of ways. Some are obvious and direct: for example, the federal government will recognize exclusive provincial authority over labour market training. Others, however, are subtle and potentially even more devastating to the authority of the federal government and the equality of the provinces. Some general comments on devolution were offered in Chapter ten. This chapter will focus on some of the specific proposals.

Backdoor routes to special status and decentralization

Most Canadians outside of Quebec want:

* a strong national government;
* no special status for any province including Quebec;
* constitutional reform to proceed openly and only with widespread public support.

The Federal Proposal would provide the federal government with mechanisms to frustrate all three aspirations. The Federal Proposal would offer any future federal government the ability to give its powers away through side-deals with whatever provinces it chooses without having to obtain the consent of other provincial governments, let alone the people. Special status and decentralization could be achieved incrementally. A deal here, a give-way there; immigration, culture, tax collection, agriculture... how can anyone get upset about one little thing? After a while, Quebec could end up running its own show, without paying any price in terms of its influence on national government or its claim on federal revenues. The federal government will not have to go through the spectacle of public hari-kari; it can slowly fade into the sunset. The inconvenient fact that most Canadians want a strong central government and provincial equality will not necessarily stand in the way.

The "side-deal" mechanisms are part of a package that skirts safeguards of provincial equality. Consider the following:

* the proposed "Canada clause" would affirm the "special responsibility borne by Quebec to preserve and promote its distinct society" but no mention of the "equality of the provinces";

* the proposed "economic union" principle contains no guarantee that the federal government will treat all provinces in an even-handed manner. Rather, it exempts "regional economic development" programs from the economic union principle entirely and would allow provinces to "opt-out" from economic union legislation;

* the proposed "spending power" clause would make it more difficult than ever for the federal government to establish national shared-cost programs. These programs tend to distribute money

strictly according to a formula; as a result, they tend to minimize opportunities for the federal government to favour some parts of the country over another. The federal government is proposing no constraints on its ability to cut whatever deal it wants on a province-by-province basis;

* Senate reform is supposed to ensure fairer treatment for less populous provinces; yet the Federal Proposal would deny the reformed Senate any legislative role in taxing and spending matters.

There are a few concessions to the "equality of all the provinces" in the federal package. The Council of the Federation would operate according to the "feds + 7/50" rule; all decisions would require the consent of the federal level of government plus seven provinces with at least half the population of Canada. The formula itself gives no special status to any province. With respect to the amending formula, the federal government is renewing its Meech Proposals, which would have moved more amendments into the category requiring the unanimous consent of all the provinces. Unanimity and 7/50 are both consistent with treating all provinces equally; that is, no single province is intrinsically entitled to more weight than any other.

It should not be forgotten, however, that the federal government tried to revive the "Victoria" amending formula — which gives each of Ontario and Quebec a veto, but not other provinces. Furthermore, the Federal Proposal offers provinces extensive rights to "opt-out" of various decisions that are made under the "feds + 7/50 formula." It will be largely up to the federal government to determine whether an "opted out" province has satisfied any conditions for receiving "financial compensation," and how much money it should receive.

Looking at the package as a whole, there is every legitimate reason to be concerned that the federal government is aiming for a new era of "cut-your-own-deal" federalism. A more attractive-sounding name for such a system would be "asymmetric federalism." The Federal Proposal, however, avoids using any catch-phrases that would alert the public to what it is doing.

A system where every province cuts its own deal might sound attractive at first. What is wrong with "flexibility" or "recognizing that all provinces are not identical and creating special arrangements for the needs of each?"

Of course all provinces are not identical. Provinces do not need different legal powers, however, to act on their differences. Legislatures that have the same authority to make laws can exercise that authority to produce very different kinds of legislation. It is unacceptable, for some provinces to enjoy substantially more local authority than others. People who are relatively immune from the authority of the federal government should not be participating in it as equals, and telling others what to do.

Of course federal programs should respond to differences in actual needs; drought relief should only go to provinces that have experienced droughts. It is unacceptable, however, for a federal government to arbitrarily favour one need over another; it should not have the authority to offer drought relief to an area that has elected a lot of members of the governing party and deny it to another area. Nor should the federal government be able to offer drought relief in one area, and arbitrarily deny flood relief in another.

"Cut your own deal" federalism will lead to more and more balkanization in Canada, more special and privileged status for Quebec, less overall equality among the provinces. If the division of powers is going to be decided by bilateral deals, the biggest winners will predictably be the most powerful provinces. The provincial government of Quebec should be able to exploit the situation to the maximum. Its governments are constantly trying to expand their authority at the expense of the national government. Its people control a quarter of the seats in the House of Commons and usually provide the home base for the Prime Minister. Quebec has often enhanced its clout at the federal level by voting as a solid bloc for a party that is seen as favourable to its interests, rather than dividing its representatives along left-right lines. The fact that the people or the politicians of Quebec are often threatening to pull out of Confederation provides their provincial governments with extra bargaining leverage.

Just look at the 1990 immigration deal between Ottawa and Quebec. It promises Quebec up to 30% of the immigrants to Canada, even though Quebec comprises only about a quarter of the population. It is true enough that the population of Quebec is not growing as fast as some provinces; but other provinces have a population that is actually dwindling. No other province has been promised an extra share of immigrants.

The 1990 immigration deal also promises that the federal government will withdraw from providing reception and integration services for immigrants. The federal government is actually going to "compensate" Quebec for supplanting its role; Quebec is promised up to $332 million dollars in funding over the life of the agreement. The Meech Lake Accord contained a similar federal surrender on immigration — and former Prime Minister Trudeau denounced it as being among the most offensive provisions of the whole Accord. He urged that immigrants be regarded as new participants in Canada, not merely the "distinct society" or any provincial community.

The biggest losers in a "cut-your-own" deal regime are going to be the smaller, less prosperous provinces. They may be unable to afford the assumption of new responsibilities and find themselves in a quasi-colonial situation; politicians from Ontario and Quebec, may be running the programs, even though their constituents are not subject to them. If a smaller province does elect to take over responsibility in an area, its weak bargaining position is liable to be reflected in the amount of money that Ottawa provides as compensation.

One mechanism for "cut your own deal" federalism: entrenched bilateral deals with respect to immigration and culture.

The Federal Proposal suggests the following mechanisms, which presumably would be entrenched in the Constitution. With respect to immigration and culture the federal government would commit itself to negotiating bilateral deals that are "appropriate to the circumstances of each" province. The 1990 immigration deal with Quebec would be constitutionally entrenched. (A similar clause was proposed in the Meech Lake Accord.) On the cultural front, the Federal Proposal states that the federal government intends to retain its authority over national cultural institutions, such as the CBC, National Film Board, Canada Council, and national museums. The federal statement about protecting national institutions is not legally binding on anyone, including itself. Quebec will no doubt use its "distinct society" mandate to try to take over the Quebec aspects of national institutions. Concessions made from time to time by federal governments will be constitutionally protected, and so irreversible.

The other mechanism for "cut-your-own-deal federalism": delegation of federal authority.

The Federal Proposal calls for a constitutional amendment that would permit Parliament and the provinces to "inter-delegate." Parliament could authorize a provincial legislature to pass laws in an area of federal authority and vice versa. Once delegation is constitutionally authorized, powers could be shifted back and forth by ordinary legislation. A legislature that has delegated a particular power would retain the authority to withdraw the legislation.

The idea is not new. Over forty years ago, the Nova Scotia legislature proposed legislation to allow inter-delegation in employment matters. It asked the Courts whether it would be constitutional to do so. The Supreme Court of Canada held that it would not be. Chief Justice Rinfret stated:

> The constitution of Canada does not belong either to Parliament, or to the Legislatures; it belongs to the country and it is there that the citizens of the country will find the protection of the rights to which they are entitled. It is part of the protection [that Parliament and legislatures will each legislate in their own areas].

In his concurring judgment, Mr. Justice Rand made the following points:

* those matters assigned to Parliament are to be regulated in the national interest. Parliament is established to do so, provincial legislatures are not;

* inter-delegation would undermine the federal structure. It is no answer that delegations can be withdrawn. Once a power is transferred, it might be practically impossible to regain it. "Possession here as elsewhere would be nine points of law and disruptive controversy might easily result."

I agree with all these points.

The constitutional division of powers should not be left entirely to bilateral wheeling and dealing. While flexibility and a spirit of experimentation have their merits, some basic structural elements should not constantly be "up for grabs." Changes to the division of powers should be negotiated openly and affirmed only through a formal amendment process that requires a broad level of national support. Provincial legislatures are not accountable to national constituencies and transferring authority to them can undermine the national interest.

Casual power swapping can result in situations that are profoundly offensive to democratic principles. It can lead to the restructuring of Canada through an incremental series of low profile deals, rather than open and honest reform that is based on national consensus. It can result in voters selecting a party on the basis of its position in a particular area, only to see that area delegated to a different order of government. It can and will lead to situations in which some provinces, particularly Quebec, gain more autonomy than other provinces without surrendering any authority in the national government.

Once a power is delegated from Parliament, it will likely be foresworn forever. Quebec politicians in particular would not tolerate the pendulum swinging back. The official position of the Liberal Party of Quebec, which is essentially the Allaire Report, defines radical decentralization as the ideal state of affairs. Many provincial politicians from Quebec — and some at the federal level as well — seem to envision constitutional reform as a one-way ratchet in the direction of almost complete political autonomy for Quebec. The "federalist" position often appears to be that while all this decentralization is taking place, Quebec would continue to elect members to Parliament, share the monetary and economic union (although "opting-out," perhaps, from certain inconveniences) and continue receiving transfer payments from the rest of Canada.

After the Nova Scotia "inter-delegation" case, the Supreme Court of Canada has upheld some limited forms of delegation by Parliament. It can authorize provincial officials to enforce federal laws; indeed the Supreme Court has held that the prosecutorial authority of provincial Crown attorneys is derived from federal delegation. The Supreme Court has allowed Parliament and provincial governments to co-ordinate policy by delegating regulatory authority to the same provincial agency. Marketing boards for natural products sometimes work this way: the federal government assigns its authority over the international and inter-provincial aspects of the trade, the province assigns its authority over local transactions. There is no question that some inter-delegation is allowed in our system; the question is where we draw the line. The direct delegation of authority between Parliament and the legislatures would be likely to seriously and permanently disrupt the overall federal structure.

"Interdelegation" was apparently considered, and accepted by all parties in very broad principle, during federal-provincial negotiations in 1979-80. Negotiations stalled over two points. British Columbia insisted that if Parliament offered a power to any province, it could not refuse to offer the same power to the other provinces. The federal government resisted such a limit on its discretion. Quebec was concerned that inter-delegation would compete with the formal amendment process as a way of restructuring Confederation, and wanted clarification of how the two processes would operate together. My view is that inter-delegation was a bad idea when the Supreme Court of Canada rejected it over forty years ago, and it has not improved with age.

The Federal Proposal should be improved by:

    * requiring the approval of the reformed Senate for bilateral deals of any sort, including regional economic development programs;

    * eliminating any mechanism for automatically entrenching bilateral deals on immigration and culture. The agreements should be routed through the usual 7/50 amending formula;

    * eliminating entirely the provision that would allow the federal government to delegate its authority to the provinces by ordinary legislation.

Federal Residual Power

The *Constitution Act, 1867,* s.91 gives the general authority to govern the country — to pass laws for the "Peace, Order and good Government of Canada" — to Parliament. The exception is that Parliament cannot legislate in areas of jurisdiction specifically assigned to the provinces. The provincial powers are mostly listed in s.92 of the *Constitution Act, 1867.* The framers of the Canadian Constitution were aware of the events leading to the American Civil War and wanted to shore up the pre-eminence of the Canadian national government. Under the American Constitution, the federal government has only the authority specifically assigned to it by the Constitution; anything else is reserved for state governments or the people.

Section 91 contains a list of specific federal powers. But the list does not exhaust the federal authority to legislate; rather the list is provided to make it clear that the larger federal authority unquestionably includes certain matters. Anything on the federal list in s.91 is deemed excluded from the provincial list in s.92.

One point often overlooked is this: Parliament has the general power to legislate, unless an item is on the provincial list. In this sense, the federal level has the "residual" power: that is, the powers not specifically assigned by a section of the Constitution. One of the powers assigned to the provinces, however, is a "miscellaneous" clause: under s.92(16), provinces have exclusive authority over: "Generally all Matters of a merely local or private Nature in the Province." So, if an item is not specifically listed in section 91 or section 92, it does not necessarily fall within federal jurisdiction. If the nature of the matter is "local or private," it falls within provincial authority.

Over the years, the Courts have narrowed the scope of Parliament's power to legislate under the general "Peace, Order and good Government" power. The Courts have tended to insist that Parliament justify its legislation by referring to very specific heads of federal power. The judges feel that this approach enables them to maintain the general federal authority within reasonably clear and reasonably limited boundaries, rather than overpowering provincial autonomy.

A specific head of federal power can arise in either of two ways:

* it can be explicitly listed in s.91 or elsewhere in the Constitution;

* it can be a specific head of power that is found by the Courts to be implicit in the general "Peace, Order and good Government" power. Examples have included federal authority over radio and television broadcasting, aeronautics, uranium mining, narcotics control, the national capital area, and very recently, marine pollution.

The Courts have developed certain tests for inferring specific heads of authority. The proposed federal power should be:

* of national importance;

* reasonably limited and well-defined in its scope;

* not too intrusive on core areas of provincial jurisdiction;

* an area in which the co-operative efforts by the provinces cannot be relied upon to protect the national interest.

It appears that a factor that often weighs in favour of finding federal authority is that the subject matter is regulated by an international treaty to which Canada is a party. Parliament has no general authority to implement treaties in areas of provincial jurisdiction and the Courts appear to work around this "jurisdictional deficit," sometimes by discovering that there are new heads of federal authority.

The judicial doctrine on "Peace, Order and good Government" has never been both clear and settled. Some judges, most notably Chief Justice Laskin, have departed from the "pigeonhole" approach, and advocated a more holistic approach to the federal power. Rather than forcing legislation into specific "pigeonholes" of authority, Laskin urged that it be examined in light of federal authority in its entirety. Specific items of "federal authority," according to Laskin, could be "springboards" towards arriving at the overall conclusion that a statute was within federal jurisdiction.

One of the few things that is well established is that the "pigeonhole" approach does not apply in cases of "emergencies." In a crisis, the federal level of government can,under its general "Peace, Order and good Government" power, assume sweeping powers in the national interest.

The Federal Proposal on the "residual power" is very confusing. The proposal is as follows:

> The Government of Canada proposes to reserve to itself the Peace, Order and Good Government clause to maintain its authority to deal with national matters and emergencies. However, the Government of Canada is prepared to transfer to the provinces authority for non-national matters not specifically assigned to the federal government under the Constitution or by virtue of court decisions.

It is difficult to see how the "proposal" would leave us anywhere different from the status quo. To repeat, the provinces already have a certain residual authority; s.92(16) gives them authority over "Generally all Matters of a merely local or private Nature in the Province." Court cases have held that unallocated matters will be attributed to Parliament only if, among other things, they are of national concern.

Perhaps the federal government has a bigger "give-away" in mind, which will be revealed when it releases the actual draft. Perhaps the federal government is trying to create the impression of activity without actually giving up anything. Or perhaps the federal government is simply somewhat confused at the technical level. The issue of Parliament's residual authority is of great importance. Those who care about the preservation of national authority should be on the look-out.

Labour Market Training

One of the most distressing "give-aways" is labour market training. The federal government itself states that Labour Market training is "key to Canada's future prosperity," that training facilitates mobility of labour within the country, and that a highly skilled labour force is essential for Canada to be "competitive" in the world. The federal government itself had been making noises in the period preceding the Federal Proposal about how it wanted to get more involved in education and training, in order to promote Canada's international economic competitiveness. Labour market training is an area in which the federal government could have a very positive influence. It could concretely demonstrate its interest in the economic prospects of individual Canadians. It could ensure that have-not provinces are not skimping on labour-market training, for fear that its alumni are likely to end up working in other provinces. It could help have-not provinces develop the human capital they need to reduce their dependency.

The Federal Proposal suggests that the federal government might use its new "economic union" power to establish labour-market training standards and objectives. There are grounds for doubting that the "economic union" route will be an adequate substitute for current federal involvement. It will be necessary to gain the support of 7/50 provinces before anything can be done. Even then, provinces could "opt-out"; the federal government is already offering a 3-year "opt-out," and asks the Parliamentary Committee studying the Federal Proposal to consider whether the "opt-out" should be renewable. It is worthy of note that the federal government proposes to maintain a hand in labour market training under its "economic union" power, not its new "spending power" mechanism; is the implication that the federal government is going to "off-load" responsibility without committing itself to financial support?

The transfer of labour market authority is a response to demands from Quebec; what kind of money will Quebec expect from Ottawa when it acquires this new authority? Will it be looking forward to bilateral deals, perhaps under the rubric of "regional economic development," that give Quebec the best of both worlds: more power and generous federal financing? Are we looking towards more "profitable separatism?"

A few weeks after I wrote the foregoing paragraph, the federal government announced that it had concluded "negotiations" with Quebec over a job education program. According to the Winnipeg Free Press, November 5, 1991:

> Ottawa had angered Quebec when it announced last month that it was going to spend $472 in the next few years on job education in Quebec. Ottawa said it would give the money directly to the retraining agencies — something Quebec vigorously opposed. The agreement means Ottawa will still spend the money but will allow the cash to flow through the appropriate provincial agencies.

Labour market training is an area in which the federal government, under the authority of its spending power, if nothing else, currently provides programs directly to Canadians. It is a way of expressing concretely the economic leadership of the federal government and its commitment to advancing the individual opportunities of Canadians. It is dismaying to see the federal government giving up a point of contact with Canadians that is visible and constructive.

The rationalization that the federal government offers for its surrender to Quebec over the issue of labour market training is that "skills training for the labour market is intimately related to the education system, which is an area of exclusive provincial jurisdiction." It could be just as cogently argued that labour market training is "intimately related" to unemployment insurance and to inter-provincial and international trade and commerce.

The current Federal Proposal purports to acknowledge that labour market training is an item of high national priority. The specific proposals on labour market training, the "economic union" and the federal spending power all generate cause for concern about whether the federal government is going to be able to do anything about it. Unless and until the federal government spells out how it is going to maintain a real leadership role in labour market training by other means, its proposal to explicitly recognize provincial authority should be rejected.

Federal Jurisdiction over the Environment

Public opinion polls have shown that the environment is one area where Canadians favour a strong federal presence. The people have it right. The federal government is in the best position to protect the environment against local special interests that can overpower provincial legislatures and against misguided projects sponsored by provincial governments themselves. The federal government is the only one that is well equipped to arbitrate between provinces in environmental matters, to represent Canada internationally and to supervise the nation-wide implementation of international standards and agreements. The current constitution offers the federal government substantial authority over the environment, under various specific heads of power, such as fisheries, navigable waters and its implicit authority to deal with inter-provincial and international affairs.

It would have made eminent sense for the federal government to try to firm up, or modestly expand, its role over environmental protection. The current federal government is not eager to challenge the sensitivities of some provinces, including Quebec, over environmental matters. On close examination, the Federal Proposal includes vague rhetoric about how environmental protection is a Good Thing, and some very specific proposals that will actually reduce the federal role in protecting it.

Here is the "Canada clause" rhetoric:

> a commitment to the objective of sustainable development in recognition of the importance of the land, the air and the water and our responsibility to preserve and protect the environment for future generations.

The specific "give-aways" are lengthy in number.

In six areas, the federal government offers to "recognize the exclusive jurisdiction" of the provinces and "withdraw from these fields in a manner appropriate to each sector and respectful of the provinces' leadership." It is not clear whether the federal government is proposing to actually amend the constitution, or is simply offering to conduct itself in a new manner. The six areas are: tourism, forestry, mining, recreation, housing, municipal/urban affairs. The federal government proposes to "preserve Canada's existing research and development capacity and maintaining constitutional obligations for international and native affairs." *There is no specific protection of the environment as a constraint on federal retreats in these areas.* It looks as though environmental concerns may be "deep-sixed."

There should be no agreement on doing anything constitutional in any of these areas unless and until the federal government tables specific proposals, and there has been ample opportunity for public discussion and input. The Federal Proposal is too sweeping and complicated as it is and devising constitutional amendments in these areas is something that should be left to a later round or not bothered with at all.

The federal government also lists ten areas in which it is ready to "streamline" federalism by placing more authority under one roof. While the Federal Proposal does say that "streamlining" might occur by transfers of authority from the provinces to the federal government, the Proposal begins by assuring the provinces that there are "many areas where the federal government is prepared to delegate its program delivery responsibilities in order to provide better services to Canadians and/or reduce costs."

At least four of these candidates for potential federal withdrawal are environmentally sensitive:

* wildlife conservation and protection;
* transportation of dangerous goods;
* soil and water conservation;

Bryan Schwartz LL.B., LL.M., J.S.D.   103

* inspection programs.

As discussed earlier, allowing Parliament the general authority to delegate its law-making powers is unnecessary and dangerous to the preservation of federal authority and the equality of provinces. A good deal of federal-provincial "streamlining" can be accomplished by existing constitutional means; for example, Parliament can authorize provincial officials to enforce federal laws. Specific proposals for "streamlining" should be considered on their merits, with no pre-disposition in favour of provincialization. In some areas, such as environmental protection, any presumption should be in favour of giving the lead role to the federal government.

The amending formula

General Issues.

The people of Canada should have the final word on any constitutional amendments, via referendums. The vote must be on the text of any proposed package, not some vague question packaged by a government to suit its own purposes. The current system of representative democracy in Canada utterly fails, in theory and in practice, to ensure that constitutional reform corresponds to the wishes of the people.

The Federal Proposal renews federal support for the system proposed in the Meech Lake Accord. That system would tilt the amending formula even further in the direction of provincialism and continue to leave out any requirement of binding referendums.

It is possible to hold a "consultative referendum," that is, to test public opinion even though the result is not technically binding. The latest Federal Proposal makes no promises whatever in this regard. The 1991 Parliamentary Committee on the Amending formula (the "Beaudoin-Edwards" committee) made no commitment to referendums either. It suggested only that Parliament pass an ordinary law which would give the government the option to hold a non-binding referendum; apparently, the timing and precise nature of the question would be left up to the federal government. In my view, no legislature should approve any forthcoming proposal until its people have expressed their views in a consultative referendum. There is no chance that the amending formula will be formally changed in time to make such referendums technically binding; but legislators can certainly regard them as morally binding. The referendum issue will be explored in more detail in the next chapter. This one will recap developments on the "amending formula" generally.

After the failure of the Meech Lake Accord, Prime Minister Mulroney put part of the blame on the amending formula. He complained, among other things, that the three-year period allowed for legislatures to consider amendments was excessive. As a prelude to preparing a substantive proposal, he established the Spicer Commission to canvass public opinion, and called for a Parliamentary Committee to study the amending formula.

The "Beaudoin-Edwards" Committee on constitutional reform held a series of public hearings, and reported in June of 1991. Among other things, the majority on the Committee:

* rejected widespread calls, from both witnesses and the general public, for a "constituent assembly";

* rejected any requirement that proposed amendments be ratified or rejected by the people through referendums. The "Beaudoin-Edwards" Committee took a "referendum-if-necessary-but-not-necessarily-a-referendum" approach. It urged that a federal law be enacted that would

give the federal government the authority to hold a non-binding referendum "to confirm the existence of a national consensus or to facilitate the adoption of the required amending resolutions." Whether any referendum would be held, the timing and the question would presumably be left to the federal government;

* recommended that the general amending formula be changed from "7/50" to the Victoria Formula (the amending formula tentatively agreed upon by First Ministers in Victoria in 1971). Quebec and Ontario would acquire a veto. The consent of any two Atlantic provinces, and of two Western provinces with 50% of the western population would also be required;

* recommended that aboriginal people be given a veto over amendments that directly affect them, that they participate in all constitutional conferences, and that a series of biennial conferences be held specifically on aboriginal issues;

* recommended that the maximum period for legislatures to consider amendments be shortened to two years from the current three;

* recommended that the Constitution be amended to allow the delegation of powers between Parliament and provincial legislatures by ordinary legislation.

Victoria Amending Formula: a "non-Starter"

An amendment to the amending formula requires the unanimous consent of all the provinces. The Federal Proposal acknowledges that the "Victoria Formula" had not gathered the unanimous support it would need. The result should have been no surprise. The "Victoria formula" is based on a theory that Canada is composed of equal regions, not equal provinces. As some favoured provinces, Ontario and Quebec, count as regions in and of themselves, the inequality among provinces is great — and to some, grating. If applied to the amending formula, the "four equal regions" theory would mean that an amendment could never pass over the objections of Quebec, but could proceed despite the objections of British Columbia, or even a combination of provinces such as Alberta and Manitoba. It is not surprising that all nineteen members of the British Columbia New Democratic party expressed their objections to the revival of the "Victoria Formula," or that it did not win unanimous support among premiers.

In the context of Senate reform, the Federal Proposal admits that:

...the reality of contemporary Canadian politics is that *provinces and territories, and not regions,* are basic to our sense of community and identity.

Back to Meech

Having acknowledged that the Victoria formula is going nowhere, the Federal Proposal renews its support for the amending formula contained in the Meech Lake Accord. One of Quebec's "five conditions" for "signing the constitution" had been expanding its right of veto over amendments. The Meech Lake Accord accommodated that demand within a framework of provincial equality. Several matters, including Senate reform and the creation of new provinces, were moved from the list of amendments requiring "7/50" to the list that require unanimity (that is, the consent of the federal level of government and all of the provinces).

The Federal Proposal is wary of incorporating elements that require unanimous consent of the provinces to pass. The federal government wants to be able to process a package through the "7/50" rule, and not risk it being held up by a Manitoba or Newfoundland. Accordingly, the offer in the Federal Proposal is this: if a consensus can be developed in favour of the Meech rules by about March, 1992, the federal government will incorporate it into its formal offer. What if there is no consensus? Apparently, the federal government is willing to consider proceeding with a package that does not include any revisions to the amending formula.

Acquiring a veto was one of Quebec's "five demands," and it would be difficult for Quebec to sign a comprehensive deal that does not include it. On the other hand, unanimity was a sore point with many of Meech's critics last time round. Establishing unanimity on Senate reform may be less difficult, as a matter of practical politics, if a satisfactory deal on Senate reform can be established. (It may not be wise to establish a new institution, and then make it extremely difficult to revise it in light of experience.) Perhaps the federal strategy will be this: put the amending formula aside for now; try to gain widespread acceptance of a package dealing with other things; then at the last moment, re-introduce a Meech-like proposal and dare anyone to upset an almost "done deal" over one new element.

Freezing out the North

There is an exception to the federal government's renewed support for the Meech formula. It concerns the creation of new provinces. The story is best understood in chronological order.

In the beginning, the creation of new provinces did not require the consent of existing ones. The only domestic assent required was that of the federal level of government. In 1982, at the behest of some of the provinces, the rule was changed to "7/50."

The Meech Lake Accord of 1987 proposed to raise the barrier even higher, to unanimity. The change was highly unfair to residents of the North. Many of the would-be reformers of Meech urged that the rules for the admission of northern territories should actually be relaxed, rather than tightened. In May 1990, the "Charest Report," which was supported by members of Parliament from all three federal parties, specifically supported a return to the pre-1982 rule — that is, that the consent of the federal level of government be sufficient to create a new province. At the notorious "roll of the dice meeting" in June 1990, First Ministers proposed that Meech be enacted without changes. The "Stockholm Syndrome" Accord includes the paltry undertaking that First Ministers would have a look at the admission of Northern provinces later on and consider returning to the pre-1982 rules as a "possibility."

In June, 1991, the Beaudoin-Edwards Committee came down on the side of returning to the pre-1982 situation. It found that the consent of Parliament and the territory involved should be sufficient to create a new province. In September, 1991, the Federal Proposal followed federal zigging and zagging with a just plain zog. It proposes that the amending formula for new provinces remain as it is.

"Cut-your-own-deal-federalism"

The Constitution should not be amended to allow greater scope for bilateral deals on the division of powers.

During the Meech round, the Globe and Mail editorial board floated the idea of using s.43 of the *Constitution Act, 1982,* to cut bilateral constitutional deals with Quebec. The proposal was based on a gross misreading of what s.43 says. It does not give an open-ended permission to cut bilateral deals. It has a much more modest purpose. It recognizes that there are certain provisions in the existing Constitution that apply to some provinces, and not others, and that these can be recognized by the approval of the federal level and the affected provinces only.

The next two paragraphs will explain the technical implications of s.43; the reader may feel free to skip over them.

The language in s.43 makes it clear enough that its scope is confined to *existing* provisions of the Constitution that apply to one or several provinces, but not all. The examples given in s.43 make the intent even clearer. The explicit references are to boundaries and to language provisions. The framers were obviously thinking of provisions such as s.23 of the *Manitoba Act* (limited official bilingualism in Manitoba) or s.16(2) of the *Charter* (official bilingualism in New Brunswick).

For section 43 to apply, an amendment must be "in relation to any provision" that applies to only certain provinces but not others. To qualify as an amendment to some existing provision, a provision must address the same subject matter. Thus it would not be lawful to try to bilaterally pass a "distinct society" clause, like that in Meech, by dressing it up as an amendment to s.133 of *Constitution Act, 1867* (which establishes official bilingualism at the federal and Quebec levels). First of all, s.133 is a provision that applies to the federal level of government as well as Quebec, and it is debatable whether s.133 can be conceptually divided into a Quebec part and a federal part, with the Quebec part being amendable by s.43 bilateral procedures. Secondly, the "distinct society" clause in Meech and the "official language" guarantee in s.133 are about different subject matters. The "distinct society" clause addressed the use of French and English in society as a whole, and not only at the official level; s.133 is about official bilingualism only. Finally, the "distinct society" clauses in Meech Lake and the Federal Proposal deal with language use across Canada, and not only in one province. The amending formula that must be used for a "distinct society" clause is unanimity; the Constitution provides that unless s.43 is applicable (and it is not) there must be unanimous agreement to any amendment in relation to "the use of the English or the French language." The Federal Proposal neglects to mention the fact that unanimity is required on language issues; it is hoped that no one will be misled into thinking that the language aspects of the Federal Package can be enacted through the "7/50" formula.

As I recall, there were intimations in a federal strategy paper leaked well before the Federal Proposal that some federal officials were considering the following strategy: cut some bilateral deals with Quebec, claim to entrench them on the basis of a specious reading of s.43, and then dare the Supreme Court of Canada to nullify the "progress" that has been made. My own submission to the Beaudoin-Edwards committee stated:

It is hoped that this Parliamentary committee will forthrightly acknowledge that s.43 exists only for very special and limited purposes, and that the federal government not try to abuse it in the hope of 'getting away with it'.

To my pleasant surprise, the Beaudoin-Edwards Committee did indeed acknowledge that the division of powers cannot be changed using s.43.

Regrettably, the Beaudoin-Edwards Committee recommended another means to achieve "cut-your-own" deal federalism: a proposed constitutional amendment that would allow Parliament to delegate authority to provincial legislatures (and vice versa). The current Federal Proposal renews the call for a delegation mechanism to be established with respect to legislative powers generally and urges the creation of a special "cut-your-own-deal" mechanism with respect to immigration and culture: not only could bilateral deals be made on these issues, but they would form part of the Constitution.

The objections to both these mechanisms are stated in an earlier chapter. To recap them briefly: bilateral deal-making is an easy, low-profile, incremental route to creating special and privileged status for Quebec and massive inequality among the provinces. The winners in "cut-your-own-deal" federalism will be large and prosperous provinces; the losers will be the ones with no bargaining power, that is, the smaller and less populous ones.

As mentioned earlier, a fancier name for "cut-your-own-deal" federalism would be "asymmetrical federalism." *The only tolerable form of "asymmetrical federalism" is one in which a province that "opts-out" or "contracts out" of federal authority must sustain a proportionate loss of influence in the national government and a proportionate loss in the subsidies it receives from taxpayers in other provinces.*

The prospect of bilateral deal-making invites a larger consideration of the merits of "asymmetrical federalism." It is unacceptable in principle for Quebec to acquire special authority over certain matters while maintaining an equal voice in the national government. Such an arrangement is nothing more or less than reverse imperialism. For example, if the rest of Canada had no say over broadcasting in Quebec, then Quebec politicians should not be voting in Parliament on broadcasting policy for the rest of Canada.

Quebec should also have to bear its fair share of the costs of "asymmetry." Running your own show can be more expensive than benefiting from the economies of scale achieved through national programs. If Quebec wants to run a parallel immigration system, complete with offices in foreign countries, substantial additional costs will be sustained. Taxpayers in the rest of Canada should not have to subsidize these extra costs. The federal government should not be forking over "federal money" to pay for incremental separatism. To the extent that Quebec governments want enhanced authority, Quebec citizens should receive tax refunds from the federal government, and the Quebec government should be obliged to directly tax its citizens to pay for the programs. To put it succinctly: the only form of "asymmetry" that would be fair to other Canadians is "Quebec pays as it goes." Every step towards Quebec's independence should be accompanied by a fair and proportionate loss of authority in the national government and loss of federal revenues.

The immigration deal that the federal government just made with Quebec illustrates the opposite approach: "profitable separatism." Taxpayers outside of Quebec actually subsidize Quebec governments to "do their own thing." Under the immigration deal just signed, Quebec acquires a right to a share of immigrants that exceeds its share of the population. The government of Quebec acquired enhanced control over the selection and settlement of immigrants, and the federal government agreed to withdraw from providing settlement services for immigrants to Quebec. In return for the privilege of withdrawing from the area, the federal government has offered Quebec generous funding to administer its own programs.

The "Quebec pays as it goes" principle is the only form of "special status" that is fair to the rest of Canada. It is questionable, though, whether pay-as-you go would hold the country together in the long run. If presented with the opportunity to opt-out of Canada one step at a time, absorbing manageable costs at each step, successive Quebec governments might gradually succeed in extinguishing the remaining bonds of nationhood with Canada, and then find that the final step out the door is relatively easy and painless. "Profitable federalism" might do better in keeping Quebec technically within Canada; the combination of *de facto* independence and on-going influence in national governments and subsidies from it might prove attractive. Many observers, however, think that once de facto independence is achieved, the emotional appeal of becoming a full and equal member of the international community might be impossible to resist.

In any event, the "Quebec pays as it goes" principle may be impossible to implement in practice. It requires Quebecois in the national government to refrain from participating in areas over which Quebec has acquired special status. It will not be easy, however, to determine exactly which federal decisions correspond to Quebec's special status. It will be inconvenient and embarrassing for Quebecois public servants and politicians to have to propel themselves in and out of rooms as issues are being discussed. The decisive practical problem may be that some decisions cut across many different policy areas, and it will be unfair for Quebecois to participate in them and unfair to exclude them. Federal taxation policy is one such issue. A cross-cutting "personnel" issue is the selection of the Prime Minister. If Quebecois are largely running their own show, they should not have an equal voice in determining what the national government is or selecting the Prime Minister. At the same time, as long as Parliament retains some authority over the Quebecois, the people of that province would not likely accept having a less than equal say over the formation of the national government.

My conclusion is that "asymmetrical federalism" is wrong in principle if it amounts to "profitable separatism." The only fair version of asymmetry is that Quebec pays for its progress towards sovereignty with fair and proportionate losses of influence in national government and its share of national revenues. The "Quebec pays as it goes" principle is probably unworkable in practice, one of the insurmountable difficulties being that certain policy and personnel decisions cannot be divided into "pan-Canadian" and "everyone-except-Quebec" ones.

A technical observation: is unanimity required to establish the "cut-your-own-deal" mechanisms?

A mechanism that would permit federal and provincial governments to enter into constitutionally binding deals on immigration and culture would, in my view, amount to a new way of amending the Constitution. Amendments to the amending formula require unanimity; it should take unanimous consent of the provinces, therefore, to create this new mechanism.

There has been some controversy already about the level of consent required to establish the proposed new "delegation" mechanism. Some constitutional specialists have suggested that the new delegation mechanism amounts to a new route to amending the Constitution. It amounts in substance, therefore, to an amendment to the amending formula, and so requires unanimity. As I understand it, some senior federal bureaucrats have disagreed.

My legal assessment is that unanimity is indeed required to establish a "delegation" mechanism. We should not be impressed with arguments to the effect that delegating legislation does not formally change the text of the Constitution. We should be looking at substance, not cosmetics. The transfer of lawmaking authority can amount to a radical alteration of the federal structure. If the Constitution says that Parliament has "exclusive authority" over subject matter X, but that authority ends up being exercised in practice only by provincial governments, the Constitution has, in substance, been amended.

It would make little practical difference, in my view, if the delegation legislation automatically expired after a certain number of years. Once power is delegated to a provincial legislature, it will be administratively and politically difficult to withdraw it; the renewal of delegating legislation would become routine.

Recommendations

The general amending formula is already rigged in favour of the provinces, and should not be further revised to enhance provincial rights. The next chapter will argue that the most needed reform with respect to the amending formula is a requirement that the people express their consent to any changes through a binding referendum. There should also be a new "counting rule" to determine whether enough people in enough provinces support the measure; the next chapter will propose a formula whereby a high level of consensus would be required, and no opting-out permitted.

The Federal Proposal seeks to establish two new "back door" routes for restructuring Canada. These attempts should be rejected. We should not allow formal or *de facto* amendments to the Constitution to be effected through low-profile bilateral deals. "Cut-your-own-deal" federalism is liable to favour the provinces with the strongest negotiating power at the expense of the rest. In the case of Quebec, it will lead to "profitable separatism" — the incremental detachment of Quebec from the rest of Canada, while Quebec retains its full voice in operating the national government and the benefit of federal transfer payments. "Cut-your-own-deal" federalism is liable to produce a patchwork of different schemes that interfere with the efficient operation of the Canadian economic and social union. "Cut-your-own-deal" federalism is inimical to the demands of Canadians for more open and consultative decision-making.

Parliament does not need, and should not be given, a general authority to delegate its law-making authority. Any new constitutional provision to promote bilateral deals on immigration and culture should specifically provide that no province shall receive more favourable terms and conditions than any other, and that the arrangement is only constitutionally protected if it receives the consent of 7/50 provinces.

To the extent that any province is allowed to "opt out" of national programs and standards, the operative principle should not be "profitable separatism" but "pay as you go." The "price" of opting out should in principle include a commensurate loss of participation in making policy at the national level, and following an abatement of federal taxes, the necessity for the "opted-out" province to raise its own revenues to pay for the program.

Chapter

15

The case for referendums

Growing support for referendums at the provincial level

At the provincial level there is growing recognition of the merit of direct democracy and the public demand for it. The National Assembly of Quebec has provided for a referendum on sovereignty to be held no later than October, 1992. This signals a measure of respect to allow people to directly vote on their future. The legislature of British Columbia has already approved legislation requiring a consultative referendum before any amendments are ratified by the Legislature. In the October election in Saskatchewan, voters gave a resounding "yes" to a referendum before their Legislature approved any constitutional deals. The Manitoba Task Force on the Constitution has recommended that a referendum be considered before the Manitoba Legislature decides on any forthcoming package.

Experience under the Existing Amending Formula

I have written books on each of the major post-Patriation amending processes: the aboriginal round from 1982-87 and the Meech round. In both cases, my conclusion was that the process involved was seriously defective.

The aboriginal round was marred by totally unnecessary secrecy and stalling during the preparatory stages, and a frenzy of confused activity at First Ministers' Conferences. The argument that negotiations have to be "confidential" is unwarranted by practice, let alone democratic principle. Secrecy certainly contributes to one's self-importance — knowing something reporters and the public don't. It is fun to trade information with fellow insiders and to slip a morsel to press when it suits one's purposes.

Some of the aboriginal groups, like the Inuit Committee on National Issues, had far more respect for democracy than the general run of governments. They tried hard to keep their constituencies informed. In the meantime, the general Canadian press, public and politicians were largely kept in the dark about what was going on.

I see no evidence whatever that the aboriginal negotiations "worked better" because of the secrecy. If the public had been given the chance to discuss what was going on, the participants might have learned many valuable things from the feedback. Ungrounded fears about the state of public opinion might have been dispelled; areas in which more caution or precision was genuinely necessary, explored. If the texts, and to a large extent, the discussions had been available to the public, there might have been less posturing. Fear of public ridicule might have tempered excessive demands and reduced the extent of stalling and obfuscation from governments.

My criticism of the Meech Lake "bargaining process" seems to have attracted some attention and support. Lest anyone think I was criticising the process just because I didn't like the result, I would recall again that I opposed the efforts of the federal government to unilaterally patriate in 1982 because of a lack of democratic legitimacy. In *First Principles, Second Thoughts*, published in 1986, I had this to say about the aboriginal constitutional conferences:

> Almost entirely left out of the whole process has been the public. It is true that participants at preparatory meetings may be a little more relaxed and a little more candid because they know that proceedings are confidential. There is no adequate justification, however, for governments not releasing their position papers and draft proposals as the process moves along. It is entirely unacceptable for a democratic country to change its fundamental law without enabling the general public to inform themselves of the options and make their opinions known to the decision makers. We accept it, but it is unacceptable.

The flaws in the process were not mandated by the Constitution. They were the product of the manner in which the federal government and others chose to manage the negotiations.

The behaviour of governments, particularly the federal government, during the "Meech Round" was reprehensible. I would be inclined not to recall the matter, having documented it several times already; but sometimes people forget, or at least, allow the same objectionable history to repeat itself. Prime Minister Mulroney was able to pull off his "Meech-style" tactics three times: at Meech Lake, a little over a month later at the Langevin Block, and three years later at the "Stockholm Syndrome" meeting.

The Prime Minister may wish to blame the amending formula. He may pretend that he "inherited" the particular process he used. The fact of the matter is that nothing in the Constitution required any of the tactics he resorted to. They were his choices, and he had no apologies for them in his infamous "roll of the dice" interview. He has made it very clear that his only regrets about Meech is that his tactics did not work.

Among the tactics of the Mulroney government were:

* doing everything possible to promote the myth that Patriation was a stab in the back for the people of Quebec, and that Quebec was "outside" of the Constitution;

* insisting that rejecting Meech would amount to rejecting the people of Quebec;

* attempting to scare people into accepting Meech for fear of the economic fall-out from its failure;

* holding public hearings in which the selection of witnesses and reporting of their comments was slanted in favour of pro-Meech presenters;

* holding last-minute hearings (the "Charest Committee") and then completely ignoring its recommendations once they ceased to suit the government's purposes;

* summoning Premiers to Ottawa, one by one, on the pretence that the Prime Minister was merely investigating whether it was worth holding a conference, when he had already decided that there would be a final "show-down";

* closeting First Ministers in a back-room, once again trying to isolate them from their advisers and their people, and giving them no prospect for release unless and until they signed. The tactic produces a known distortion of thinking called "group think" in which participants eventually limit themselves to, and adopt, the narrow perspective of the tiny group. It is also a form of psychological coercion bordering on torture. Imagine being confined in a room, day after day, where you are told that the country will fall apart unless you sign, when you have no definite

prospect of escaping unless you sign, and when you have no pauses in which to recover your bearings, consult your colleagues, and draw strength from the people back home;

* obtaining a letter from "constitutional specialists" that was supposed to allay concerns about the legal meaning of Meech, when the specialists were employees or consultants of the governments involved in the negotiations;

* procuring a political "side-deal" which would have had grave political consequences, all without a mandate from the people. First Ministers worked out a political accord — call it the "Stockholm Syndrome" Accord — that was supposed to make enough promises about future action that Manitoba, New Brunswick and Newfoundland could ratify Meech without changes. Its most spectacular feature was Premier Peterson's autocratic and inane promise to give away a quarter of Ontario's Senate seats to other provinces if no agreement could be reached on real Senate reform later on.

No doubt many of the supporters of Meech believed that the Accord was tolerable on its merits, or that however flawed, it was a necessary step in "keeping the country together." The end could never justify such means. Indeed, the means would have poisoned the end. A deal procured by such bullying, undemocratic and devious tactics would have left far too many Canadians with a sense of having been coerced and manipulated into submission. Such a climate would have accelerated the disintegration of Canada, not the era of harmony promised by some of Meech's proponents.

Recommendations for change to the amending formula

Ratification should require the consent of the people, expressed through a referendum, to the specific text proposed.

When the *Constitution Act, 1982* was shaped, the "gang of eight" provinces managed to impose what is essentially their amending formula. Not surprisingly, the current amending formula is rigged in favour of decentralization and the accretion of powers to First Ministers. It is time to recognize the ultimate supremacy of the people of Canada. When change is as fundamental and irreversible as formal constitutional amendment, it should proceed only if it has widespread support. There is no substitute for allowing the people to vote directly on actual amendments. Anything else permits intermediaries to ignore what the people say, or "interpret" it in a way favourable to the interests of the interpreter.

It is going to be very hard for the people to wrest the final say from the politicians who control the amending formula at present, and do not want to lose the control over events that go with it. The excuses that the politicians have offered, however, are not supported by either democratic principle or practical necessity.

Let's consider the anti-referendum arguments that might be raised.

Anti-referendum argument #1: "Our system is representative democracy. If you don't like what the people do, vote them out next time."

The points I would make by way of reply may be summarized as follows:

* Constitutional changes are practically irreversible. Throwing out a government at the next election cannot undo the damage;

* On the contrary, constitutional damage tends to build on itself. The system is rigged in favour of

provinces and First Ministers. The beneficiaries of the "fix" will try to change the rules to make it even easier for them to keep "winning";

* Representative democracy has a conflict of interest within it. The "representatives" can increase their power at the expense of the people. Ultimate control, therefore, should remain with the people;

* The requirement of a referendum does not necessarily leave "representative democracy" right out of the picture. If the proposals on which the people vote are framed by elected legislatures, then amendments will have to pass through a representational filter, as well as survive the test of direct democracy.

"Our system" is largely derived from the British constitutional system. Under that system, there was no way of entrenching constitutional amendments. Constitutional change was produced by ordinary legislation, and could be repealed by ordinary legislation. It is more easily arguable, then, that the people can speak at the polls if they don't like something. They can undo the damage. Even the British system, however, has started to use referendums when basic and practically irreversible reform is contemplated. A referendum was held on entry into the Common Market. Another was held on proposed devolution of authority to Scotland.

Anti-referendum argument #2: "Referendums do not allow for the bargaining and compromise of representative democracy. People vote either 'yes' or 'no'."

I would reply as follows:

* Under their current system, the legislatures considering ratification of an amendment must vote "yes" or "no." The authority to finally approve or disapprove must exist somewhere; it is best to vest it directly in the people;

* Giving the people the last word does not preclude negotiating the terms of the proposal. The prospect of facing the people will encourage those formulating a proposal to try to win the broadest possible basis of support;

* It is quite clear that when First Ministers dictate draft amendments, and then try to ram them through compliant legislatures, there is not sufficient incentive to ensure that the people of Canada are consulted, or that there is sufficiently broad support for a change. If the proponent of an amendment faces a ratification vote by the people, that proponent has the strongest possible incentive to try to build a broad basis of support, based on consultation and respect for divergent views.

Anti-referendum argument #3: Politicians are smarter than the people.

I would reply that recent constitutional history suggests otherwise:

* Nothing about recent Canadian experience suggests that First Ministers are, as individuals, superior to the general run of the population in their knowledge of the Constitution and how to reform it. Some of the manoeuvres of the First Ministers — such as signing documents without consulting advisers, colleagues or the people — suggest less common sense than most people would have in buying a car. Some of the proposals that were signed (such as Premier Peterson's attempt to give away Ontario Senate seats while he was agreeing to measures which could have drastically increased its authority) exhibited more zeal than understanding and competence;

* Close to the end of the Meech Lake process, I appeared before a Parliamentary committee. As I recall, the Honourable Lorne Nystrom suggested that people were against Meech Lake because they did not understand it. My reply then, and now, is that opposition to Meech Lake increased steadily because people had three years to find out what it is about and tended to oppose it precisely because they did understand it. I had three years to talk to other Manitobans casually, in classrooms, on phone-in shows, and listen to them at public hearings and read their views in the

newspaper columns. In my view, the quality of public debate was impressive. Those participants in the debate exhibited an understanding of the facts and issues that was every bit as good as that displayed by most politicians. Indeed, the people were often better informed and more insightful than the politicians. Having decided (or been told) that it was "thumbs up" to Meech, many of the politicians were merely concerned with repeating whatever pitch lines they could to sell it, rather than basing their arguments on fact and fair-minded analysis.

Anti-referendum argument #4: "Politicians are enlightened, the people are bigots."

Another possible excuse is that if the people decide, they will react in a knee-jerk way against groups such as aboriginal people or the Quebecois. Politicians can rise above their parochial perspectives, even prejudices and create a just order.

I would again reply that recent constitutional history suggests otherwise.

The history of Meech hardly suggests the moral superiority of politicians when it comes to minority groups. It certainly suggested that it depends on the political power of the minority group. Politicians were eager to support Quebec nationalists. They were largely indifferent to the concerns of the anglophone minority in Quebec. The difference in attitude had more than a little to do with the difference in electoral clout.

Most of the politicians exhibited no regard for the elementary democratic rights of northern Canadians with respect to provincehood. They did not trouble themselves with the well-founded concerns of many Canadians about the ability of the federal government to create new social programs and revise the existing ones. Where was the concern for have-not provinces and have-not people?

There is no good reason to believe that the average politician is any more enlightened on minority issues than the average Canadian. I would suggest, moreover, that the people are far more likely to have a positive attitude towards constitutional reforms on which they have the final say and towards the beneficiaries of those reforms. Reforms that are imposed from the "top down" may be viewed as the work of politicians who are favouring one special interest group at the expense of others. On the other hand, I expect that Canadians would respond well to the opportunity to be trusted with fairly considering the interests of others, and would exhibit the appropriate balance of fairness and generosity.

To those advocates of "representative democracy" who are still not convinced, let me point out again that any referendum would likely be held on a proposal that has been framed by an elected legislature. The representatives of the people will have a chance to screen out oppressive or discriminatory proposals; the question is only whether the people will as well.

Anti-referendum argument #5: "Referendums are divisive."

Some oppose referendums on the ground that the "yes-no" campaign will arouse passions and the results will expose divisions within the nation.

I would reply that the current system of executive autocracy creates more resentment than would a resolution that is open and democratic. Divisions in the nation may in fact be lessened by the open venting of disagreement rather than by having governments suppress or ignore honest differences of opinion. The Canadian people are mature, and can accept "losing" in a fair contest. Free Trade aroused strong passions, but those who lost are surely more able to accept the outcome in light of its being tested in a general election, rather than being autocratically imposed. There would have been more acceptance of the result if it had been put to a straight-out referendum; the last election was distorted by massive and unregulated spending by big business in favour of the free trade deal, and by the splitting of the "anti-free" trade vote between two opposition parties.

If a constitutional deal is going to bring enduring harmony, it should be able to win broad support from the people of Canada. Referendums are feared among politicians partly because they want to push through deals that would not survive the test of direct democracy. National unity cannot, however, be served by imposing changes that the people would oppose in a direct vote after a public debate.

Elections are no substitutes for referendums

It might be urged that an election held before a proposal is ratified can give the people a chance to have a say. Not necessarily. Which federal party did you vote for last time if you were against Meech Lake? All three major parties were in favour of it. Furthermore, our first-past-the-post voting system means that a minority view on a vital national issue can prevail; if everyone in the last election based their vote on the "free trade" issue, they were badly served by our electoral system. The two parties opposed to free trade captured almost 60% of the vote; but they also split that vote, allowing the Progressive Conservatives to form a majority government. Finally, people cannot and generally should not vote on the basis of one single issue. Most Canadians, one would expect, base their vote on a variety of considerations, including the relative competence of the candidates and their national leaders, the record of each of the parties since the last election and the prospects of what they will do on a wide variety of issues.

There must be a binding referendum on the actual texts of proposed amendments, and not merely principles.

It is not a bad idea for governments at times to consult their people through non-binding referendums. There is little merit, however, in the idea that the people should only be consulted at the stage of "principles," and the details should be left to First Ministers to negotiate, and legislatures to approve.

There is no sound way of evaluating a proposal without having the "details." For example, are the people of Quebec in favour of "sovereignty?" Perhaps, but what does that mean? The provinces already have supreme authority in many areas of jurisdiction, and the Courts have used the word "sovereignty" to describe that idea. Does "sovereignty" mean the political autonomy proposed by the Allaire Report — which means that Quebec pretty much runs its own show, but continues to participate in the national government and receive transfer payments from other Canadians? Does sovereignty mean outright independence in the eyes of the international community? Voters must have a specific proposal, complete with details, before they can evaluate the concept.

Is Quebec a "distinct society?" Many might agree but fewer would agree that the "distinct society" concept should diminish rights under the *Charter*. There will be broad disagreement over whether the concept applies merely to matters of language and culture, or has the vast scope ascribed to it by many Quebecois.

Is "aboriginal self-government" a good idea? Many might say yes, but some of them would be thinking of something like municipal government while others would be thinking of something closer to quasi-independence. Some might think it applies only on aboriginal land bases, others might think that aboriginal self-government applies in the cities.

Do Canadians favour "free trade" with the United States? In principle, many did. Much of that support dropped off, however, in light of perceived problems with the particular agreement that was signed.

I am against any idea of conducting a constitutional process that sharply separates "principles" from "details." Only if you have the details can you determine what principles are at stake and how they are being balanced against each other.

The people should be consulted as much as possible while proposals are being formulated but none of that consultation along the way means much unless the people have the final say. Meech Lake proved that. Only if the people have the final word will anything else they say be taken seriously.

What should the counting rule for referendums be?

If and when referendums are established as a necessary route to amendments, there would have to be a rule about how to count support; how much of a national majority is required? In how many provinces must there be a majority?

The referendum-based route to amendment should be accompanied by a reduction in the scope for "opting out" and "vetoes." An amendment that has been directly supported by a vast majority of Canadians overall should generally prevail, even over the objections of particular governments and one or two provincial majorities. Amendments that are passed under the existing formulas have less moral legitimacy, because there is no way of knowing for sure how much underlying support they have. A more legitimate and democratic procedure for measuring consent would command more respect, and warrant reducing the avenues for escaping it.

The current 7/50 test of consent is far too low to be a proper and widely accepted all-purpose formula.

The current 7/50 rule does not require a sufficiently high level of consent to serve as a general purpose, no "opting-out," amending formula. With 7/50, amendments could proceed, for example, over the objections of three Western provinces, or against the wishes of the vast majority of Quebecois.

The all-purpose amending formula should be something like this:
* there must be majority support for the amendment in at least eight provinces;
* the amendment must be supported by at least 40% of the people in every province;
* the amendment must be supported by at least 60% of those voting in the referendum.

Provinces surrendering their veto and opting out rights would be assured that no proposal that was clearly unfair to their province could possibly pass. Only if an amendment mustered the support of at least 40% of the people in a province could it pass, and no "slap in the face" could possibly muster such support.

The rules for proposing referendums

The political energy and economic costs of a referendum should not be imposed lightly. Rules will have to be developed concerning who can put a proposal to the people. I would suggest something along the following lines. Any proposal formally endorsed by either the

House of Commons, or by seven provincial legislatures would go to the people for ratification.

There has been widespread support for a constitutional convention to draft constitutional proposals. The idea is that a specially constituted group of people would debate and formulate amendments, rather than leaving matters to the politicians. Such a process would be no improvement on the status quo if the participants were appointed by the political parties; there would have to be direct elections. The process is an untried one, and the best way to be proceed might be with a controlled experiment. Perhaps a major issue or two, rather than the whole constitutional morass, could be referred to an assembly, and we could see how well the process works.

Referendums during this Round

While I have sketched my own suggestions on what the "counting rules" ought to be for referendums, I am under no illusions that my proposal would win consensus where all others have failed. The Beaudoin-Edwards Committee proposed the following rule for this round: a majority overall, and a majority in each of the four regions (Atlantic, Quebec, Ontario, the West). I see no reason why residents of the four provinces of Western Canada should accept, even on an *ad hoc* basis, a rule that minimizes the importance of their provincial communities. Beaudoin-Edwards proposes a level of consent that is below the 7/50 formula, even if we disregard the fact that the 7/50 formula allows dissatisfied provinces to opt-out. Nor does Beaudoin-Edwards take account of the fact that some amendments would ordinarily require the consent of all ten provincial governments. If a level of consent must be specified in advance, something like 60% of Canadians, including majorities in eight provinces, would be more appropriate.

Even if we cannot agree on the *ad hoc* "counting rule" in advance of a referendum, we could productively hold one anyway. A proposal could be put to the people, and each legislature could make its own judgment about how to proceed in the face of public opinion. Parliament could decide whether the actual level of consent obtained on a nation-wide basis is sufficient to justify its proceeding. Provincial legislatures could, if they wished, simply follow the direction of their own residents.

Legislative hearings are no substitute for referendums.

I would insist that there is no substitute for directly testing popular consent through a referendum. The history of "public participation" via legislative hearings has conclusively demonstrated that government representatives cannot be counted on to give public opinion a fair hearing, let along accept a reasonable measure of guidance from the people. The record of public hearings on Meech is dismal. Quebec held public hearings before the Langevin Block meeting. No other jurisdiction did.

I was a "participant observer" in most of the post-Langevin public hearings. I presented at the Senate, New Brunswick, Manitoba and Charest hearings. I submitted material to the Ontario hearings, and expressed interest in appearing before the 1987 federal hearings as well. On behalf of many other presenters, I wish to emphasize that considerable effort can go into presentations, and most of us do so in good faith, in the hope that our views will be given fair and open-minded consideration, and that the substance of our position will be

Bryan Schwartz LL.B., LL.M., J.S.D.   119

fairly reported. Various attempts to "stack hearings," to misrepresent or ignore what is said, have surely contributed to the anger and cynicism that is so widespread in Canada.

The federal government held three sets of hearings on Meech Lake. The 1987 hearings were marred by the disproportionate exclusion of critics of Meech and the more than generous "air time" for its proponents. In the "steamrolling" spirit of the time, the committee gave the public little time to prepare or become aware of how to participate and did not tour the different regions. The views of the critics who did appear were not fairly reported, let alone given a reasonable response. One contemporary critic, writing in the University of Toronto Faculty of Law Review, concluded that:

> Future generations will look back at the joint committee's Report in anger. They will be angered by the Report's inability to support even its most elementary positions without lapsing into inconsistency, angered by its obscurity, by its denial of plain reality, by the way it verges on outright duplicity.

The Senate held hearings, which critics of the Accord were actually given a fair opportunity to attend but the Report that emerged simply adopted the amendments officially favoured by the Liberal caucus. There is reason to doubt that anything said at the hearings altered its conclusions.

In 1990, the Charest Committee hearings were held. I am grateful for having been given the opportunity to attend, but on the whole, the more numerous critics of Meech again found it more difficult to obtain a hearing than the supporters. The report fell far short of responding to the concerns of the "hold-out" provinces and indeed, of a great many Canadians. Even the very modest changes it did recommend were cast aside by the Prime Minister. He chose instead a strategy of coercing the hold-out Premiers into having Meech passed without changes.

At the New Brunswick hearings, presenters were almost unanimously critical of Meech. Many of the criticisms were fundamental in nature. The report that finally emerged, however, did not even have the fair-mindedness to accurately report on the proportion of presenters who were critical of the Accord or to convey the substance of their concerns. It did not even go as far as Premier McKenna's own criticisms in 1987. The report amounted to nothing more than an endorsement of the new, weaker, position that Premier McKenna had arrived at through his own reflection in light of close consultations with the federal government. (In *A Deal Undone*, Andrew Cohen reports that the proposals Premier McKenna released in March, 1990 "had been written in New Brunswick and Ottawa.") The Prince Edward Island hearings amounted to a low-key production of the same sort of travesty. The Ontario hearings were not much better; long before they concluded, Premier Peterson told critics of Meech they would have to be patient, and wait for the next round for improvements.

The only Meech-related report (apart, perhaps, from Quebec's) that made a reasonable effort to reflect and respond to public opinion was Manitoba's. It can be faulted for minimizing or not responding to some of the problems identified in the Accord, the authors' motive being the desire to set the stage for a compromise by focusing on a limited package of reforms. Overall, however, it attempted and succeeded at reporting the views presented — even ones it did not agree with — and left the people of the province with some sense that their politicians respected them. The Manitoba Report went on to make some valuable proposals. Foremost among them was the idea of a "Canada clause," which would have placed special ethnic and regional identities in the context of building the Canadian nation as a whole. It is an idea that should not be forgotten.

By and large, Committees have simply used people; they have been stage shows to create the illusion of consultation while the real business is done in secret among the elites. I do not think Committees are obliged to tally the views of witnesses, and come down on the side of the majority; I do think they are obliged to display some measure of honesty in reporting and open-mindedness and freedom from party discipline in their deliberations.

In the latest round, the Federal Government has been up to its old tricks.

First, there was the Spicer Commission. The Prime Minister appointed all of the Commissioners including one of his most senior legal consultants during the Meech round. The other federal parties were not consulted, nor were the provincial governments. Not surprisingly, the Commissioners rejected or belittled what Canadians told them on some fundamental points.

Not content with reporting public opinion, the Commissioners felt obliged to say "what they thought" about what the people said. Apparently, not too much:

* The people said they want equality of the provinces; the Commissioners responded that the people are misinformed, and that a fundamental principle of federalism is special arrangements for special needs;

* The people said they are furious at the Prime Minister; the Commissioners admit only to a generalized discontent with leaders in general, or with the federal government in particular, and emphasize that the media must bear the blame for "focusing on divisions." Even Mr. Spicer had to acknowledge in his own introduction to the report that his colleagues had let the Prime Minister off too easily. The issue is not a trivial one; the credibility of the Prime Minister on constitutional issues is entirely relevant to the constitutional reform process that we choose;

* Many Canadians supported a constituent assembly followed by a referendum; the Commissioners coyly leave "serious analysis of that method to specialists with more expertise and time."

* Canadians told the Spicer Commissioner that a large majority favoured maintaining the authority of the national government, or enhancing its authority, rather than giving more powers to the provinces. In their "what we thought of what we heard" piece, the Commissioners do not even acknowledge hearing a strong call for maintaining federal authority. Instead, they begin recollecting calls for "eliminating overlap" and "bringing power closer to the people." The former phrase is part of the decentralist philosophy pushed by the Allaire Report and the federal government. The latter phrase is a decentralist slogan that federal government strategists had unveiled much earlier. The Commissioners do end up urging that the pursuit of "efficiency" and "bringing power to the people" be tempered with some respect for "fundamental social values" and "essential national institutions." The net result is this: for the Spicer Commissioners, the desire of Canadians for a strong national government is not an ideal worthy of positive affirmation, but merely a constraining factor in the pursuit of decentralization.

The "Beaudoin-Edwards" Committee on the amending formula was yet another stage show. The witnesses who believed that constitutional reform should involve constituent assemblies, or mandatory referendums, were wasting their time. Even before the Committee reported its "findings," the federal government announced what the process would be: the federal government would work out its own proposal, and invite public comment on it before yet another government-dominated committee.

The irony should not be lost. The government establishes two processes, Spicer and Beaudoin-Edwards, purportedly to consult the public on constitutional reform, including process. Spicer consists entirely of government appointees. Beaudoin-Edwards is dominated by government members of Parliament. Hundreds of thousands of Canadians took part all in good faith in Spicer and hundreds participated in the Beaudoin-Edwards process. The government did not even bother to wait for the committees to report on how constitutional reform should proceed. It announced that once again Canadians will have the opportunity to be ignored by a government-dominated Parliamentary committee.

The process for developing the Federal Proposal was true to form. The federal government spent hundreds of thousands of dollars polling Canadians on what they think about constitutional reform, used the results but never revealed them to the public. The federal government directed committees of bureaucrats to study the issues and has not released any of those reports either, except through the usual controlled leaks. The "negotiations" to formulate the Proposal were carried out by the federal cabinet, in secret, against a tight deadline. It has already been intimated that the "delicate compromises" reached on such matters as the formulation of the "distinct society" clauses are not to be upset by anything the public could possibly have to say.

The Committee that was established has played true to form as well. It is dominated by members of the government. While the Beaudoin-Edwards Committee stated that only a "directly-elected body" could give a sense of "participation, and ... influence" in constitution-making, the government named unelected Senators to the new Committee. The first order of business was to propose that consulting contracts be given to various political friends of the government. The Committee leaders almost immediately adopted the past practice of making a special effort of giving generous "air time" to interest-groups or "experts" who are likely to sympathize with their position. When a critic of the "distinct society" clause, Mr. Godfrey appeared, he was subjected to abusive treatment that included walk-outs by several M.P.s. In other words, the latest Committee, immediately after its inception, was structured and operated in a way that demonstrated an on-going lack of respect for the Canadian people.

Consultation can never be a substitute for consent. No amount of public hearings could ever guarantee respect for the judgment of the Canadian people; only giving the people the final word can do that. The need for consent, however, can guarantee consultation. If the people do have the final word, then politicians will finally show some real interest and sensitivity to what the people have to say along the way.

House of Commons and Senate reform

Institutional Reform

The Spicer Report acknowledges that Canadians feel the political system is unresponsive to their wishes. Many feel that their elected representatives have "little or no influence or freedom to represent constituents' views." Mechanisms should be developed that encourage representatives to consult their own constituents and that give representatives the freedom to vote accordingly, rather than respond to party discipline.

The federal government suggests that it will develop proposals to:

* modify the "conventions" on what constitutes a "non-confidence vote" — that is, votes in which the defeat of a government motion requires the government to resign. The category would be confined in the future to taxation and supply bills and to pieces of legislation which a government explicitly identifies as being central to its program;

* allow more opportunity for private members' bills (that is, legislation initiated by individual members of Parliament rather than the government);

* allow more scope for Parliamentary committees to consider and amend bills;

* ensure that vacancies in the House of Commons are filled expeditiously.

A number of these proposals appear to be borrowed from the policy program of the Reform Party of Canada, the populist movement that is draining away much Progressive Conservative support in western Canada. Whatever the motive behind them, these measures appear positive. None actually require formal amendments to the Constitution, however, and the government would be better advised to implement them through ordinary legislation or by adopting new practices. Room for further experimentation and innovation should be preserved and any package of constitutional amendments should be as spare as possible, in order to permit Canadians to fully understand and evaluate what it contains.

The government's new-found interest in making M.P.s responsive to their constituents is certainly not being applied to the current process of constitutional reform. The government put unelected Senators on both the Beaudoin-Edwards Committee on the amending formula and then added another batch to the Committee it established to hold hearings on its latest proposals; it has not promised the slightest relaxation of party discipline with respect to its Committees or to the House of Commons when it comes time to vote on constitutional proposals; it has ruled out a constituent assembly, and declined to promise a referendum on any constitutional package. Instead, it will introduce legislation to allow the federal government to hold a referendum if it feels like it and it may be expected that the government will retain the discretion to formulate the question as well.

Bryan Schwartz LL.B., LL.M., J.S.D.   123

Meech Lake and the deformed Senate.

The "Senate reform" provisions of Meech Lake were more than reason enough to reject it. The Meech Lake Accord would have:

* given provincial governments primary control over the appointment of Senators. The federal role would have been reduced to choosing names from lists supplied by a province. The role of a nominator far exceeds that of a final selector;

* done nothing to change the distribution of seats in the Senate, which leaves western Canadian provinces with only a quarter of the seats held by Ontario or Quebec;

* left intact the legal powers of the Senate, which are almost equal to that of the House of Commons;

* given every province, including Quebec, a veto over future constitutional reform.

Put it all together, and the results could have been disastrous. The only thing that restrains the current Senate from exercising its full powers is that it lacks political legitimacy. Its members are patronage appointments by the federal government and are neither elected nor representative of provincial interests. If Meech had passed, Senators appointed under provincial guidance might have felt a moral right to assert a role of guardian of provincial interests. After Meech was signed, Alberta arrived at its nominee by holding a *de facto* Senate election. (Technically, it held a non-binding referendum.) Senators nominated in this way would almost certainly have felt it proper to challenge the House of Commons. Meech Lake could have left us with a Senate fully capable of challenging or paralysing the House of Commons, largely or entirely unelected, and still dominated by Ontario and Quebec. Every single province, including the big two, would have had a veto over efforts to try to fix things up.

The (then) Liberal-dominated Senate's attempt to block the Goods and Services Tax shows how dormant legal powers can come to life. Many Canadians applauded the obstructionist tactics of the left-over patronage appointees of the Liberals but the precedent was dangerous; would we also want the patronage-appointees of the Progressive Conservatives to block some government in the future? The federal government overcame the opposition of the Senate Liberals by filling some Senate vacancies with its own patronage appointees and by invoking a never-before-used section of the *Constitution Act, 1867,* to appoint additional Senators.

If Meech had been in force, the federal government would have been obliged to fill the vacancies (although not necessarily the extra seats) with provincial nominees. Provincial governments in which the vacancies occurred might have refused to nominate anyone who was not openly against the GST. The federal government might have quickly discovered the perils of playing reckless games with national institutions.

Premier Peterson and the Santa clause.

The "Stockholm Syndrome" Accord of June, 1990, contained some bizarre provisions that were supposed to induce Manitoba and Newfoundland to ratify the Accord. At a crucial stage in the negotiations, Premier Peterson offered the following political promise: if Meech were ratified immediately, and the Senate not reformed by 1995, Ontario would give away six of its Senate seats and Nova Scotia and New Brunswick two each. The ten seats would be handed over to the four Western provinces and Newfoundland. Apparently, all the criticism about the autocracy of executive federalism meant nothing to Peterson. He evidently considered that Ontario's Senate seats were his to give away, without consulting his staff, Legislature or electorate. Nova Scotia and New Brunswick agreed to the same "seat sale."

As soon as Meech would have been ratified, the government of Quebec would have had primary control over Senate appointments from that province and a veto over further changes. Legally, it could not be forced to make any concessions whatever to anyone. Politically, it was well equipped to deflect any challenges. The parties had already agreed to a "fall-back" position if no further deals were made by 1995; no one could complain too much if they had to accept an arrangement of their own design. The "Stockholm Syndrome" Accord even gave Quebec a good excuse for rejecting any concessions: it said that Senate reform should reflect Canadian duality. Quebec could argue that it needed its Senate seats to protect the Quebec half of Quebec/rest-of-Canada duality or the French-Canadian half of French/English duality. The fall-back situation was a dream come true for Quebec; it would be left with more Senate seats than Ontario, far more Senate seats than any other province. Ontario itself could hardly be expected to give away any more Senate seats. So the "fall-back deal" would have been the final shape of the Senate — unless it was abolished altogether.

The "fall-back" deal Senate would have been a mess. It would still not be elected. Its powers would still not be reformed. It would eventually be composed entirely of provincial nominees, who might start to throw their weight around. The four provinces of Western Canada would still have ended up with fewer seats than central Canada — even though a raft of Senate studies, including two by the federal government, have established that western Canada should at the very least have parity with the centre.

The Federal Proposal on the Senate: elected.

This time around, the federal government has decided its package must include "something for everyone." There have been complaints from the less populous provinces, including western Canada, that the federal government is structured in a way that practically guarantees undue domination by the two central provinces. We have a "representation-by-population" House of Commons in which Ontario and Quebec representatives control over half the seats. The federations that most resemble Canada have "triple-E" Senates to counterbalance the population dominance of the rep-by-pop Chamber. The United States has a "triple-E" Senate — elected, effective, equally representative of all the states. So does Australia. Canada's original Senate was supposed to provide some extra weight for less populous regions, but has become utterly useless for that purpose. Its members are patronage appointments of the federal government, and seat allocation remains dominated by Ontario and Quebec.

The Federal Proposal acknowledges that "In virtually every federation" there is a second federal chamber that is designed to give "particular weight to regional and minority views." The Federal Proposal calls for a second chamber "designed both to improve regional representation and to increase responsiveness to individuals." The Federal Proposal joins the "consensus" of modern Senate reform proposals that would enable Canadians to directly elect their representatives.

The Federal Proposal directs the Parliamentary Committee to consider various options for election, based on the following principles:

* "the method of election should give expression to the social diversity of the Canadian population, keeping in mind the history of the inadequate political representation of women, aboriginal peoples, and ethnic groups";

* Senate constituencies should be large enough to allow proportional representation;

* in larger provinces, constituencies should be large enough to represent regions.

The first point raises the possibility of constitutionally entrenched quotas for women, aboriginal people and other "minorities" in the Senate.

The idea of "sociological representativeness" had been considered by the Beaudoin-Edwards Committee, in connection with the idea of holding a "constituent assembly." The NDP had recommended an assembly based on guaranteed "gender parity," participation of aboriginal peoples and representatives of various "racial and other ethno-cultural minorities" and other groups. The majority report in Beaudoin-Edwards responded:

> Our concern with this approach is that it assumes that political representation must involve sociological representation; that only members of any particular group can speak for that group. Our experience as politicians is that, on the contrary, social and economic groups contain sharp divisions over political values and policies. No white middle-aged man can claim to represent, politically, all white middle-aged men, because white middle-aged men disagree strongly among themselves over almost any conceivable political issue. The same applies to other groups, whether they are based on gender, ethnicity, occupation, income level or any other sociological category... The only person who can represent an individual, politically, is a person who broadly shares the political values and policy commitments of that individual.

The Federal Proposal sends off mixed signals on the "quota" issue. The "Canada clause" would recognize the "equality of women and men," which some lobby groups might take as encouragement to demand gender parity in allocation of Senate seats. On the other hand, the next statement in the Canada clause is "a commitment to fairness, openness and full participation in Canada's citizenship by all people without regard to race, colour, creed, physical or mental disability or cultural background." The phrase "without regard to" might be read as suggesting an "equality of opportunity" approach, rather than entrenching entitlements based on personal background. In its discussion of aboriginal issues, the federal government commits itself to "guaranteed representation" for aboriginal peoples in any reformed Senate.

My view is that the method of Senate election should be based on real equality of opportunity not "sociological representativeness." In public life, Canadians should have equal opportunities as individuals; they should not be consigned to different categories of citizenship on the basis of personal background. Doing so reinforces divisions and promotes an attitude of seeing people in group categories, rather than as individuals.

Quotas would reinforce the idea that the public interest is best served through a balance of special interests. Senators should see themselves, first and foremost, as servants of the whole nation. Ensuring fairness for your constituents is proper; attempting to selfishly exploit other Canadians is not.

As Beaudoin-Edwards states, "sociological representativeness" discounts diversity within groups. The "group entitlement" approach, like any quota system, is biased against "merit." Individuals may be ruled in or out on the basis of background, rather than individual ability to understand and promote the beliefs of their constituents. Quotas are also undemocratic; they deny Canadians the ability to choose the representatives of their choice.

Our current system uses only geographically-based political units (constituencies, provinces) to apportion representation. Just about every such geographically-based unit contains people of widely varying personal backgrounds. Giving some real clout to provincial communities in the Senate would not add an additional element of national division. We have so far chosen not to officially gerrymander our society along ethnic and gender lines and I do not think we should do so in the future.

Enhanced "representation" for minorities would be better secured by taking positive measures to ensure fair conditions of political competition for all.

Among the possibilities for improvement are using the transferable ballot system. Voters would elect not one, but several Senators at each election. On their ballots, voters would list their order of preference among candidates, rather than voting for just one of them. This form of "proportional representation" makes it much more likely for a person representing a strong minority viewpoint to be elected. The system we currently use for federal and provincial elections is called "first-past-the-post"; each voter in a single-member constituency votes for only one candidate and the person with the most votes wins. The system can result in gross under-representation of political viewpoints. For example, it is entirely possible that most Canadians in the last election opposed the U.S.-Canada Free Trade Agreement, but wound up with a majority government in favour of the deal; the split in the popular vote between the two anti-Free Trade parties enabled the one major party in favour to win most of the ridings. There have been extended periods in which minority parties in Western Canada and Quebec had the support of a large part of the electorate, but were practically unable to elect a member from those regions.

Professor Smiley concludes in a study on the Australian system of Senate elections that:

> Current debate about a reformed Canadian Senate is preoccupied with provincial and regional representation. Yet apart from this, the adoption of any one of the variants of PR for choosing such a body might well have an effect on the enhanced representation of women, members of minority ethnic groups and so on as the parties worked to balance their respective tickets.

It should be noted that the "enhanced effect" referred to by Smiley would be the result of creating a fairer system, refraining from state-imposed quotas and leaving the result up to free political choice.

Another way of increasing the fairness of the system would be election financing reform. There should be even-handed public support for campaign activities and more stringent requirements on the direct and indirect ways that private interests can use money to influence election results. During the "Free Trade" election, the big corporations spent massive amounts of money lobbying for passage of the deal. As they were technically supporting an idea, rather than a party, the spending was not regulated by campaign finance laws.

Public regulation in this sphere should be extended to the way political parties run leadership conventions and nomination meetings. These processes may be at least as important to the selection of leaders as elections; indeed, a leadership convention can, in effect, select a Prime Minister. Yet many qualified candidates may be excluded for lack of finances, and candidates with big money behind them may be able to spend their way to power — without any public disclosure of their backers.

The initiation of a proportional representation system and reform in election financing laws would help to produce Senate elections in which more Canadians have a real, and not merely theoretical, opportunity to compete. The problem of "under-representation" for people of various backgrounds should properly be solved by creating a fairer system, not by turning personal characteristics into a source of public entitlement.

The special case of aboriginal people

The Federal Proposal is clear in proposing "guaranteed representation" for aboriginal people in the Senate. In my view, aboriginal peoples living in the cities should not be lumped into a separate political category and given the right to elect their own Senators. People who have every right to participate as equals in the municipal and provincial politics of wider communities should not be singled out for special treatment on the basis of their ethnicity. They should not have privileges that exceed those of other members of their local communities, nor should they be denied representation by the same Senators who are looking after other local interests. The precedent of special political status for off-reserve people would encourage demands for special political status at the municipal and provincial level, and encourage other groups to demand similar entitlements.

Allocating Senate seats to residents of reserves is a somewhat different matter. The reserves will constitute geographically-based political units, and may eventually have governments with many of the powers of provinces. Grouping together reserves to form Senate constituencies would not be a drastic departure from the traditional basis for allocating representation in Canada — units defined by geographical boundaries and political status.

Again, one "price" that reserve residents would in principle have to pay for having their own Senate districts would have to be a loss of any right to vote in provincial Senate elections. No one should have double representation in the Senate. The "price" will not be inconsiderable. Assuming province-wide Senate elections and no separate aboriginal seats, aboriginal people would have to be taken seriously by a great many "ordinary" Senators.

The fact that reserves will have their own Senate representation, separate from other provincial residents, may create some theoretical, psychological and practical complications.

The interaction among provincial, Senate and House of Commons representatives will be different for reserve residents than all other Canadians. The residents of provinces and provincial governments may view separate Senate representation as yet another way in which reserves are detached from the larger provincial community; there may be some corresponding decrease in the willingness of provincial governments to provide funding for reserve activities, or otherwise concern themselves with the well-being of their residents.

Another complication will be that the grouping together of reserves to form Senate constituencies will not be a straight-forward matter. First Nations communities differ from each other in many ways, including their state of economic development, ethnicity of the people, languages spoken and political traditions. It will likely be necessary to form Senate constituencies that incorporate reserves in more than one province.

Figuring out how many seats to allocate to aboriginal people will be a challenge as well. Now that the door has been opened by the Federal Proposal, aboriginal groups may well demand a number of seats that is equal to that of the other provinces. Perhaps the Federal Proposal had in mind only a few guaranteed seats for aboriginal peoples; the "numbers issue" with respect to these seats is hardly discussed. Now that the federal government has already agreed to guaranteed Senate representation, however, it may find aboriginal demands are greater than it had anticipated.

To sum up, separate Senate representation for reserve-based aboriginal communities is a special case. It would not have to set a general precedent for allocating seats on the basis of ethnicity or gender. The Federal Proposal does not, however, state whether the guaranteed seats would be confined to reserve-based people, how many seats would be allowed, how constituencies would be formed and what method of election would be used. Sorting out answers to these questions will greatly complicate the whole process of developing a reformed Senate.

Guaranteeing the Independence of Senators from the House of Commons Parties

The Federal Proposal's stated purposes for Senate reform, ensuring greater regional representation and making Senators responsive to the wishes of their constituents, would be frustrated if Senators were controlled by existing House-of-Commons-based political parties. Instead, a suggestion is made that would reduce the individual freedom of Senators. It proposes that the Senate be dissolved at the same time as the House of Commons. As Gordon Robertson points out in *A House Divided:*

> Indeed, with the inevitable focus of a general election on the selection of a government, it would be extremely difficult for candidates for the Senate to be seen and assessed on any individual basis. They would be swept in or swept out with stronger tides.

The 1990 proposal by the Canada West Foundation arrives at the same conclusion. Giving Senators a fixed term of office, regardless of what the House of Commons is doing, would help to permit voters to evaluate Senators on the basis of their individual commitments or record in office. Half of the Senators should be elected at each Senate election; Senate elections at regular two year intervals would help the people to be heard between general elections.

The extent to which Senators should be allowed to associate with the House-of-Commons-based parties is a difficult one. There is a strong case in principle for requiring Senators to be strictly independent. Once they chose to run for office, they would have to resign from any House-of-Commons-based parties and decline to accept financial support from them. Otherwise, Senators are liable to fall in with the House-of-Commons-based parties, and lose their effectiveness in representing their regions and their individual constituents.

Bryan Schwartz LL.B., LL.M., J.S.D. 129

There are arguments to be made on the other side. Formal party affiliation is a way for politicians to identify their broad political philosophy, for citizens to make more informed choices. The Beaudoin-Edwards Committee has argued that even if parties are formally banned, their militants can informally gather behind the candidate of their choice. Even if some party affiliation is allowed, there should be constitutional guarantees that would maximize the independence of Senators. Among the possibilities are:

* a constitutional statement that the duty of Senators is to act in the best interests of their constituents and their country, and that no Senator is obliged to follow discipline imposed by any political party;

* a constitutional commitment to the principle that Senate elections, including public financing for campaign expenses, should be conducted in a manner that permits independent candidates a reasonable opportunity to get their message across;

* a constitutional provision prohibiting any Senator from accepting any appointments by the federal government or House of Commons parties during a Senator's term of office, or three years thereafter. A government could easily control Senators by dangling various "carrots," such as cabinet appointments or positions on important committees. (The Federal Proposal would allow Senators to sit in the cabinet.)

Distribution of Senate Seats

The Federal Proposal undertakes to provide "much more equitable provincial and territorial representation than at present." It leaves it to the Parliamentary Committee to consider options on exact numbers.

There are advantages to strict numerical equality. It would give substantial clout to smaller provinces in Senate votes. It would avoid the necessity of adjusting the numbers as provincial populations change. The "strict equality" principle might be rendered more credible by making one exception: Prince Edward Island, with its very small population, would be allotted half the usual quota.

On the other hand, there is a "price" to be paid, both in principle and in practice, for insisting on disregarding population distribution. Representing people as well as provinces would help to give the Senate more democratic legitimacy. In practice, the less weight is given to the large provinces, the more they will insist on denying the Senate any real power.

There are precedents for both strict equality and for weighted voted systems. The American and Australian Senates operate on a strict "triple-E" basis. The German Bundesrat, says the Federal Proposal, uses a graduated voting system: small, medium and large units get 3, 4 or 5 seats respectively. When the European Community provides for majority voting in the European Council, it uses a weighted system as well.

One "bottom line" should be clear. There have been a raft of studies of Senate reform over the past decade or so. All of them have called for either strict equality or a distribution whereby all provinces (except Prince Edward Island) are allocated half as many Senate seats as Ontario and half as many as Quebec. Two federal studies (the MacDonald Royal Commission and the Joint Parliament Committee in 1984) agreed on this formula: 6 seats for P.E.I./24 for each of Ontario and Quebec/12 for each of the other provinces. In *A House Divided*, Gordon Robertson concurs.

The "seats" issue cannot be resolved independently of determining Senate voting rules. The Federal Proposal offers Quebec a "double majority" rule for votes on language and cultural issues; legislation would have to be passed by a majority of Senators from both Quebec and the rest of Canada. There could be a supermajority required for other issues as well. For example, if the 6/12/24 Senate is created, extra protection might be given to the less populous provinces on matters of economic equality. Legislation might require support from a majority of Senators in seven or eight provinces, and not only a majority of Senators, on such matters as determining the formula for equalization payments, setting the level of other federal-provincial transfers, authorizing regional economic development schemes or other bilateral deals with individual provinces, or establishing procedures for government procurement.

Similarly, the "seats" issue will have to be determined in conjunction with the rules for House of Commons "override" of the Senate. A strictly equal Senate would be less threatening to the bigger provinces to the extent that the House of Commons would retain its authority to override it.

Powers of the Senate

The Federal Proposal would turn the "E" for effective into "I" for insignificant. It suggests that:

> Since the Senate would not be a confidence chamber, the Government proposes that the Senate have no legislative role in relation to the appropriation bills and measures to raise funds including borrowing authority.

Taken literally, the suggestion is ridiculous. The whole thrust of the Senate reform movement has been to ensure economic fairness for the less populous parts of Canada. The Senate proposed by the Federal Government would apparently have no authority over federal procurement policy (which would include such matters as the CF-18 contract), no authority over revenue-raising matters (such as the National Energy program). The other major concern of the Senate reformers has been to ensure greater responsiveness to the wishes of individual Canadians; the Senate proposed by the federal government would have had no power whatever with respect to the highly unpopular G.S.T. legislation.

The "justification" for the proposed evisceration of the Senate is a non-sequitur. "Since the Senate would not be a confidence chamber..." is the premise from which the Federal Proposal leaps to the wrong conclusion. All right, let us admit that starting point. Let it be written in the Constitution that a government need not resign merely because its measures are defeated in the Senate. If necessary, let it be conceded that the Senate cannot hold up measures necessary to continue the routine operation of the federal government but it makes a travesty of the Senate to deny it the ability to block changes to the tax system, or new spending programs. By way of comparison, notice that the Federal Proposal would give the Council of the Federation a veto over new shared-cost programs; yet the federal government does not seem to be the least bit concerned about the prospect of paralysis in this regard.

The Senate should not only be given the authority to block federal legislation, but also an on-going mandate to review and report on the operation of current programs. The Senate or one of its committees consisting of one member from each province, should issue a report each year that states how current arrangements are redistributing wealth among areas of Canada and recommend changes that would ensure greater fairness.

The "reviewing" authority of the Senate could be put another way. Premier Rae has suggested that the Senate might have the authority to monitor the extent to which a proposed constitutional Social Charter is being honoured throughout Canada. The suggestion being made here is that the Senate be given an analogous role with respect to the economic union. The principle of the economic union would be defined in a way that clearly prohibits economic discrimination against any province or any part of a province. Favouritism for some provinces, or pork-barrelling in government constituencies, would no longer be permitted. The Senate should be charged with regularly reviewing federal spending and reporting on whether it is consistent with the principles of the economic union. The Federal Proposal must be revised to ensure that the Senate has a strong voice in the legislative process, and if that is done, the Senate would not only be able to monitor federal spending, but prevent recurrences of any abuses that are found. There should be a role for the Courts as well in enforcing the "economic union principle; well"; the Courts would not be called upon to make wide-ranging decisions about taxing, spending and priorities, but simply determine whether a government has clearly violated some basic principles such as non-discrimination. Rather than precluding Court enforcement of the economic union principle, reports from the Senate might assist the Courts in determining whether a violation has occurred.

Matters of Particular National Importance

The Federal Proposal would limit the role of the Senate to a six-month suspensive veto in matters of "particular national importance." That is, if the Senate has not approved a House bill six months after its approval, it would still become law if the House of Commons re-passed it. Such a system is already in place for constitutional amendments; *Constitution Act, 1982, s, 47.* The Federal Proposal does not explain what a matter of "particular national importance" would be. The examples provided are "national defence and international issues." Would the latter category encompass Parliamentary resolutions concerning international treaties? Would the next U.S.-Canada Free Trade Agreement be the sort of matter on which the Senate could be overridden?

The power to delay a measure even for six months is not insignificant. The fact of Senate rejection might be embarrassing to the government, and a six-month delay would give opposition more time to mobilize. On the other hand, federal governments might gradually begin to use the override so much that the political embarrassment of doing so would fade and the Senate would begin to be viewed with derision. There have been proposals in the past that a supermajority in the House of Commons should be required to override the Senate. There have been various suggestions on how big the supermajority must be, including:

* two-thirds of the House of Commons;

* a majority of House members from at least seven provinces;

* a margin of victory in the House greater than the margin of defeat in the Senate.

There may be a narrow category of cases in which even a six-month suspensive veto would be disruptive to Parliament. As has been noted, the Federal Proposal would appear to put taxing and spending measures in this category. Some provision could be made to enable the House to maintain routine government operations and respond to emergencies, but taxing and spending exceptions to the powers of the Senate should not go beyond that.

There may be matters on which the House should be allowed to override a Senate defeat and very few on which it should not have to wait six months. These categories should be narrowly and carefully defined and drastically more limited than they are under the current Federal Proposal.

Ratification of Appointments

Having apparently denied the Senate a voice over money matters and over matters of "particular national importance," the Federal Proposal appears to be looking for something for the Senate to do. It suggests that it might undertake "inquiries" to provide "valuable input on public policy." It then suggests that the Senate might ratify appointments to national institutions. The idea is worth considering. The prospect of a ratification vote would give the public a chance to understand the qualifications and perspective of people who are exercising great authority. There is a good chance that our Senators would not turn the ratification process into the circuses they have been in the United States. Still, there are risks to be considered. One is that the Senate could prove to be unduly aggressive and qualified people discouraged from accepting nominations for high appointed office. Another problem is connected with the prospect of applying the "double majority" rule to ratifications: would the prospect of having to prove acceptable to both majorities tend to screen out anyone with both convictions and courage? For example, if a potential Official Languages Commissioner had to be approved by a double majority, would it be possible to secure ratification for an appointee who had been critical of Bill 178 (the Quebec law requiring that outdoor commercial signs be unilingually French)?

A couple other points:

* if Senate ratification is a good idea generally, why is it not a good idea for Supreme Court appointments? Premier Wells suggested that the federal government still make the appointments but ratification of Quebec appointees would be made by Quebec Senators and ratification of rest-of-Canada appointees would be made by rest-of-Canada Senators. The Federal Proposal would give the provinces and in particular, Quebec, far more influence over these appointments than the federal government;

* would the "double majority" rule indeed apply to ratifications, and if so, to which specific agencies?

Supreme Court of Canada Appointments

One of Quebec's "five conditions" for "signing the Constitution" during the Meech era was consultation on Supreme Court of Canada appointments. Meech would have given Quebec far more. Rather than merely guaranteeing Quebec a right to be "consulted," Quebec was guaranteed a third of the seats of the Court, and predominant control over appointments to those seats.

The set-up of the Supreme Court of Canada is currently determined by federal statute, rather than the Constitution. The modern tradition is that the Court consists of nine judges including three from Quebec which has only a quarter of the Canadian population. On a representation by population basis, it would be alloted only two out of nine seats, or three out of eleven (The number of judges is usually odd-numbered to avoid ties). The current "numbers" distribution is not, however, unreasonable. We need at least three Quebec judges to have a pool of expertise in appeals from civil law judgments in Quebec and having more than nine judges on the court overall would make it more difficult for the Court to develop a coherent body of doctrine. The fact that Quebec is being allotted more than "rep-by-pop" on the Supreme Court of Canada, however, is a fact that should be pointed out if and when Quebec complains about attaining less than "rep-by-pop" in the reformed Senate.

The Supreme Court of Canada is a highly influential national institution. Its interpretation of a constitutional provision may have a larger impact on future developments than the actual words chosen by the framers of the Constitution. How a judge will interpret a constitutional provision depends in no small measure on the judge's personal experience and judicial philosophy. The decision about whom to appoint is of great consequence.

While Quebec only asked for "consultation" in the Meech Lake Accord, the federal government gave it far more. Meech promised that the federal government would no longer make appointments unilaterally. With respect to vacancies from outside Quebec, it would appoint from lists of names forwarded by the common law provinces. With respect to appointments from Quebec, its only choice would be to select from names advanced by that one provincial government.

The net result is that the federal government would be left with less influence over appointments than the provinces generally, and drastically less than Quebec in particular. With respect to the "other nine" provinces, the federal government at least has up to nine lists to choose from. Common law provinces would be encouraged to include on their lists jurists who have a balanced view on federalism; a province that nominated only decentralists would reduce its chances of having any of them accepted. Nonetheless, very qualified jurists may be entirely excluded from consideration; the provincial governments may overlook people who are associated with the "wrong" political parties, or who favour strong national government. The federal government has in the past achieved a balance on the Court by including a mix of centralists, moderates and provincialists; under the Meech system, it may be difficult to include any of the first-mentioned.

In sharp contrast, the Meech system would provide Quebec provincial governments with almost unlimited opportunity to place jurists on the Court whose philosophies strongly favour advancing the authority of provincial governments, rather than promoting national government or minority and individual rights. It would be easy for Quebec to forward a list of names — even a long list — that consists of intelligent, experienced, and reputable jurists who happen to be strong Quebec nationalists. The federal government would be reduced to choosing among personalities who share the same broad outlook. Under Meech, it is not obliged to appoint a person who is unacceptable, and could request an additional list — but doing so would provoke a political controversy without guaranteeing in the least that the next list would be any more balanced. The power of nomination far exceeds the power of final selection. How would you like an "election" in which a government commission chooses the political party that will represent your riding, and your choice is reduced to choosing one of the candidates?

Several non-Meech systems would have satisfied Quebec's demand for consultation. The Victoria Charter of 1971, which Premier Bourassa initially supported, would have allowed both the federal and Quebec Ministers of Justice to negotiate as equals over who would be appointed. In case no agreement could be reached, the appointment would be made by an impartial committee. Perhaps Quebec would have agreed to the sort of system recommended in the McKelvey Report of the Canadian Bar Association; lists of nominees would be prepared by a committee consisting of representatives of not only the federal and Quebec Ministers of Justice, but of the judiciary, bar and general public.

Unfortunately, the latest Federal Proposal renews the Meech offer. There are minor modifications. The Federal Proposal requires that provinces submit a list of five names; Meech did not specify any minimum number or maximum number of names. The Federal Proposal would allow the federal government to proceed unilaterally if a province does not submit names within ninety days of being requested to do so. The Federal Proposal does not explain what happens if the province submits a list, but it does not contain any names acceptable to the federal government. The bottom line is that the Federal Proposal is just as bad with respect to the nomination process as Meech was.

Technical procedures for selecting judges may seem like an obscure matter but seemingly small differences in the procedures used — such as the difference between the Victoria Formula and the Meech Lake Accord provision — may have profound consequences. It would be sad if this flaw in the Federal Proposal were overlooked in all the excitement and confusion generated by the entire raft of proposals. The Supreme Court provisions are a case in point of why constitutional reform should move at a measured pace and deal with a limited and manageable number of issues at a time.

A technical note: The *Constitution Act, 1982* provides that amendments in relation to the Supreme Court can generally be effected through the 7/50 formula. Amendments with respect to the "composition" of the Court, however, require unanimity. The Federal Proposal holds that giving Quebec three of nine seats would be a "composition" issue and so require unanimity of the federal government and all of the provinces. At the same time, the Federal Proposal asserts that giving provinces more input is not a "composition" issue, and could be included in a strictly 7/50 package of reforms. I am sceptical. The word "composition" could be plausibly read as encompassing the method of appointments, and the Constitution could reasonably regard the matter as one of special concern to provinces, especially Quebec, and therefore worthy of a requirement of unanimity. This means that any province (or the feds) could veto the proposal.

Reform of Provincial Institutions

The Federal Proposal contains a striking irony: it plans to devolve more power on to the provinces, yet devotes all of its attention to the idea of making the federal government more responsive and equitable. We are offered a reformed Senate and a greater number of free votes in the House of Commons. The Proposal needs much improvement with respect to reform of federal institutions, but at least the issue is recognized. What about the provinces?

One of the existing checks against abusive behaviour by provinces is the counterbalancing authority of the national level of government. The Federal Proposal would weaken that authority in a number of ways, identified throughout this study. Another check on provincial autocracy is the the *Charter;* the Federal Proposal would actually tip the balance even further in the direction of the Quebec majority at the expense of individual and

Bryan Schwartz LL.B., LL.M., J.S.D.

minority rights. The Federal Proposal should instead try to strengthen the protection of rights. The Federal Proposal would take only marginal steps towards making the "notwithstanding clause" more difficult to invoke; as discussed in Chapter Six, it should go much further. Rather than improving the prospects for fair and accountable provincial government, the Federal Proposal undermines them. The right way to proceed would be to take a number of positive steps to improve the functioning of provincial as well as federal government.

Another reform urged by this study is to require that constitutional amendments be ratified by popular referendums, rather than allowing Premiers to cut deals, and force them through legislatures. Additional reforms worth considering would include:

* the terms of both federal and provincial governments should be limited to a four-year maximum, down from the current five. We should not have to see repeats of this year's spectacle, in which two highly unpopular governments, in British Columbia and Saskatchewan, hung on to office until the very end of their five-year mandates;

* the "economic union principle" should specifically prohibit economic discrimination by both federal and provincial governments against any province or part of a province. "Pork-barrelling," in which government largesse is directed on the basis of political reward or bribery, rather than merit or genuine needs, would be rendered unconstitutional. Federal and provincial programs aimed at regional development would be permitted, but would have to address genuine needs and be administered in an even-handed manner;

* a "freedom of information" clause should be entrenched in the Constitution. It would apply to both federal and provincial governments;

* a constitutional principle should be entrenched that patronage appointments to government jobs are not permissible unless party affiliation is a *bona fide* occupational qualification (e.g., for being an executive assistant to a Minister);

* a constitutional amendment should be made which sets out some fundamental principles on fair election financing; Parliament and provincial legislatures would have to observe them in developing more specific rules and regulations.

One of the most objectionable aspects of the Meech Lake Accord was its strong boost for "executive federalism." Meech would have given provincial Premiers a ticket to an infinite series of First Ministers Conferences on the Constitution and on the economy, and provincial cabinets (which would usually mean the Premier) would have authority over Senate nominations, Supreme Court nominations, and "opting out" of social programs. The latest Federal Proposal may unduly boost the power of Premiers in other ways. Its threat to institute "cut-your-own-deal" federalism means that much policy would be made through back-room deals between the Prime Minister and the Premiers. This study has already argued for the almost total deletion of "cut-your-own-deal" features from the Proposal; if governments decide to proceed with any such features, then democratic checks and balances should be provided.

There should be essentially no "opting-out" of economic and social union measures that are approved by the Council of the Federation. However, if any "opting-out" is permitted, it should require a 60% vote by all members of the Legislature; the Federal Proposal only expressly requires legislative input in the case of "opting-out" of the economic union. Bilateral deals on immigration and culture should not be constitutionally protected unless they are ratified by both the affected Legislatures and a sufficient number of other provinces to satisfy the 7/50 constitutional amending formula. The Federal Proposal to allow Parliament to delegate its law-making authority to provinces should be eliminated from the package altogether. If it is retained in any form — which would be profoundly regrettable — severe restrictions should be placed on it. Each and every act of delegation should have to be specifically approved by the House of Commons, Senate and the Council of the Federation. The federal level of government should be obliged to offer equally favourable terms and conditions to all other provinces. Every delegation of authority would expire after three years with no possibility of renewal.

The Council of the Federation contemplated by the Federal Proposal would involve major decisions being made by members of provincial executives, rather than by Legislatures. There is a solid democratic argument for requiring members of the Council to obtain legislative sanction with respect to each issue before them; they might obtain either specific direction on how to vote, or specific authorization to exercise their discretion.

There may be some practical advantages, however, to not requiring subsequent formal ratification of every decision of the Council of the Federation. One of the advantages is "optical"; such a procedure would look too much like the procedures used for constitutional amendments. Some provinces, including Quebec, might note the expansive "opt-out" and "veto" rights under the amending formula and insist that the same be applied to Council of the Federation decisions. Providing a different process for Council of the Federation decisions might help in clarifying its substantive mandate. These decisions would be confined to ratifying decisions in which the federal level of government has a special leadership role; "opting-out" would be permitted only on a severely restricted basis, or not at all. The current amending formulae, by contrast, to a large extent put provinces on the same plane as the federal government, and offer considerable opportunities for provincial vetoes and opting out.

Conclusion

This study has attempted to analyze the Federal Proposal, find both strengths and weaknesses, and make suggestions for improvement. My conclusion is that the Federal Proposal would have to be changed in many ways if it is to do justice to Canada's future. To highlight a few points:

Building the National Community:

Symbolism: In the "Canada clause," which purports to define some fundamental characteristics of the nation, there must be a clear commitment to a Canadian community that transcends group diversity. The Federal Proposal speaks of the parts, but contains no affirmation of the whole;

The economic union: The proposals to guarantee free trade within Canada are welcome. They are rife, however, with "opt-outs" and exceptions. The statement of the economic union principle and of the federal authority to manage the economic union, should be clarified and rendered meaningful.

The social union: The economic and social unions should be seen as complementary. The Federal Proposal may weaken the framework of social programs and investment in people necessary to build a humane and prosperous nation. The Federal Proposal could be improved by affirming broad social principles but must also provide practical means whereby the federal government can play a leadership role in defining and financing social-welfare programs and investment in "human capital." A "Charter of Social Rights" without strong national government is meaningless.

Democratic Institutions

The proposals on Senate reform are a limited start in the right direction. The proposals in their current form fall far short of assuring the independence of Senators from the control of House of Commons parties.

The proposals should be expanded to clearly guarantee other aspects of improved government at both the federal and provincial levels. These might include: freedom of information, the elimination of patronage, principles of elementary fairness with respect to election financing, and limiting the terms of governments to four years.

The economic union principle should be defined so as to clearly prohibit any government from discriminating economically against the government or people of any other part of Canada. Such a principle would not only ensure a more efficient country but a far less corrupt one. Government pork-barrelling is one of the most corrosive aspects of public life in Canada.

Individual Rights

The Federal Proposal undermines respect for the supremacy of the individual. The "distinct society" clause poses risks to individual rights within Quebec and the "Canada clause" wrongly puts individual and "collective" rights on the same plane. The package could be improved by adding a clear affirmation of the supremacy of the individual and by establishing tighter controls over the use of the "notwithstanding clause" (the provision allowing governments to override the *Charter*).

The Federal Proposal appears to raise the possibility of allocating Senate seats according to ethnic and gender-based quotas. This would be objectionable. Democratic reforms should contribute to real equality of opportunity for all, not gerrymandering on the basis of group affiliation.

Groups

The recognition of Quebec's "distinct society" should be framed in a way that is fair to individual and minority rights. The current Federal Proposal does not achieve this.

Aboriginal peoples should achieve enhanced self-government but we should show some consistency in addressing aboriginal and Quebec demands. Self-government for both aboriginal people and the Quebecois should be realized within the context of a strong national community and a solid measure of political equality among all Canadians. The Federal Proposal indicates some sensitivity to this issue but further clarification is needed.

The Equality of Provinces

One of the most profoundly objectionable aspects of the Federal Proposal is its attempt to pave the way for "cut-your-own-deal" federalism. The idea seems to be to allow the federal government to cut side-deals with various provinces on how much power each will acquire and how much money each will receive in addition. The approach is contrary to the desire of Canadians for equality among the provinces and for openness and consensus-based processes for reshaping the country. Powerful provinces will do well in bilateral negotiations; less populous and wealthy provinces stand to lose out. The prospects are for Quebec to achieve more and more "profitable separation" and for Canada to be rendered incoherent. The provisions in the Federal Proposal for provincial "opting-out" and for cutting bilateral deals should be eliminated or severely restricted.

The "Canada clause" should affirm the principle of the equality of the provinces. The "economic union" principle should be revised to expressly prohibit discrimination against any province or part of any province. The Senate should have real authority over money matters, including a mandate to ensure that federal taxing and spending measures respond in an even-handed manner to real needs.

The Supreme Court of Canada

The latest Federal Proposal would give the provinces more control over appointments to the Court than the federal government and Quebec more far more control than any of the other provinces. It is reasonable to give the provincial government of Quebec, or perhaps its

Senators, major influence over appointments for vacancies from that province; but the federal government should have at least an equal voice.

The Amending Formula

The Federal Proposal revives the "Meech" approach, which would rig the constitutional amending formula even further in favour of provincial interests and deny the people of Canada any direct voice in the outcome. The existing system should be replaced with an amending formula that requires a high level of consensus, no "opting-out" and ratification of amendments by the people, through referendums.

Looking Ahead: Entrench in Haste, Repent at Leisure

This study is intended to reflect a profound commitment to matters of substance. An attempt has been made to evaluate in all seriousness the proposals that are made, and indicate ways in which they could be improved. I hope that commitment to substance gives me a special credibility when I address the issue of process.

The "process" we are currently engaged in is unacceptable. Constitutional reform must be open, deliberate and democratic.

Democracy? So far, we have no commitment from the federal government to hold even an election, let alone a referendum, before the proposals are translated into a constitutional resolution by the House of Commons. The federal government may even try to press ahead for formal ratification of the proposals using the current 7/50 amending formula by the end of 1991.

Without giving people the final word — and the only way to do this is through a referendum — there is little reason for confidence in any "consultative" process. Again and again we have legislative committees which go through the motions of listening to people, only to follow agendas set by the party leaders.

Openness? Quebec will not attend First Ministers' conferences, so all the negotiations with its provincial government are taking place through the usual back-room channels. We can expect to see the same skill of the federal government employed to choreograph public pronouncements by its provincial allies. The federal government prepared its proposals using publicly-funded opinion polls and reports by committees of deputy ministers, both of which have not been publicly released. There is a place for confidential discussion, but only in the interstices of a process in which information and positions are available for public examination.

Deliberation? The federal government is insisting that the pace of reform be the forced march demanded by Quebec. Its Legislature has called for a deadline no later than October of 1992 and the three federal parties are all anxiously participating in a helter-skelter promise to somehow "meet" that deadline. Quite apart from the wisdom and dignity of succumbing to threats, it is profoundly objectionable to attempt to wreak massive constitutional changes in great haste.

These are complex matters, the details count for everything and cannot be resolved on the fly. Take a few "minor" Senate matters. The Federal Proposal would allow Senators to accept cabinet posts, and hold Senate elections at the same time as general elections for the House of Commons. Minor matters? Not at all. The effect of these suggestions would be to seriously erode the ability of Senators to campaign on their individual merits and maintain a strong measure of independence from the parties once elected. Similarly, the manner of appointing Supreme Court judges could have a profound impact on a fundamentally important branch of Canadian government; the difference between the Meech system (feds are confined to choosing from provincial lists) and the Victoria system (feds and provinces have an equal voice) may have a drastic impact on the nature of the Court in the long years to come.

We are dealing with changes that are not only important, but for all practical purposes, irrevocable. "Entrench in haste, repent at leisure." You do not have to be obsessed with process, a stickler for minutiae, to think that constitutional reform should take place at a measured pace. You have to hold some belief, however quaint, that proposals benefit from discussion and reflection and care about the long-term future of the country.

What is the race supposed to accomplish? Is the federal government really expecting to present Quebec with the "binding offer" it is demanding by October, 1992? To do so, Ottawa would have to secure the passage of the exact same resolutions (which Quebec is demanding) by at least six other provincial Legislatures in that limited time. That can only be done by short-circuiting the process of deliberation at the provincial as well as federal level. Perhaps the federal plan is to show enough "progress" so that Premier Bourassa can pass legislation postponing the referendum. Are we then supposed to wait with anxiety for Quebec to announce the next deadline, and once again hurry to meet it? A deal passed in haste, without the approval of the Canadian people and in response to threats from Quebec will not secure a lasting peace. It is likely to be ill-considered and resented.

The federal Leader of the Opposition has frequently expressed the sentiment that he is weary of the constitutional battles and we should settle things and move on to other business. Sure, everyone is sick of the whole business. That is a reason, however, to have a moratorium on constitutional processes, not to accelerate them. Fatigued and traumatized people are not likely to view things with balance and intelligence. There are certainly "other things" to deal with but we will not be able to do so if the authority of the national government has been unduly impaired. In his House of Commons response to the Federal Proposal, the Leader of the Opposition mentioned health care, the environment and competitiveness as the sort of issues that must be dealt with but the Federal Proposal may damage the authority of the federal government to revise Medicare, weaken its authority over a number of environmental areas and leave it unable to take on a meaningful role with respect to labour market training. For better or worse, what the Constitution says actually makes a difference to all of these other issues.

A suggested alternative.

Here is a sketch of an alternative:

There is a strong case for a moratorium on constitutional discussions, but if federal leaders insist on "doing something" before October 1992, their aim should be to establish a legitimate process and to provide it with some real direction. The federal government could even hold a referendum to approve its proposed process. A successful result would ensure that the process is finally a legitimate one.

The plan should be to divide the federal package into manageable parts, and deal with them sequentially — say four parts to be dealt with over about eight years. With respect to each part, the federal level of government could indicate the broad principles that should guide discussion. The promise would be made that each part would, after being shaped by intergovernmental negotiations or a constituent assembly, be submitted to the people of Canada in a referendum. A "part" could include proposals for ordinary legislative change, rather than formal changes to the Constitution. In this way, solemnity and legitimacy could be given to important changes without overburdening the formal Constitution with too much detail. All the way along, Canadians would see immediate and practical changes in the operation of government. By combining referendums with federal general elections, it would be possible to greatly reduce the administrative complications and expense involved. Only a couple of referendums would have to be held in between federal elections.

Let me consider a few objections to this proposal.

One concern would be the reaction of the government of Quebec. During the Meech era, it insisted that all of its "minimum demands" had to be met in one package deal. Might not the government of Quebec react the same way to a step-by-step process? Maybe, but the current government of Quebec is eager to avoid a referendum. Furthermore, it would not be necessary for Quebec, or anyone else, to pass resolutions to formally amend the Constitution until the end of the process. In any event, it would be up to the people of Quebec to decide, by way of a referendum, whether they were interested in giving a gradual process a try.

Another objection might be that if the package is divided, it would be more difficult to make "trade-offs." Each part could be made large enough, however, to allow "something for everyone" or almost everyone. Furthermore, as just suggested, it would be open to provinces or the federal government to withhold formal ratification of any amendments until the last part has been put in place. A province would therefore have some means of enforcing deals that involve making a concession in one round, in order to make a gain in a later one.

I would suggest that the first package submitted to the people should address the issue of "democratic reforms." It would encompass some issues addressed in the Federal Proposal, such as House of Commons reforms and others — such as reform of election financing at both the federal and provincial levels, and measures to reduce government pork-barrelling and patronage. Restoring the trust of the Canadian people in their governments would be the best possible start for an on-going process.

The end of mutual blackmail

A nation held together by threats is not worth keeping together. It is time for politicians in the rest of Canada to stop panicking every time Quebec threatens to separate. Conversely, the people of Quebec should not be told that the only alternative is outright independence with no economic association with the rest of Canada and territorial dismemberment of Quebec. If the people of Quebec prove to be uninterested in the gradual renewal of the current system of federalism, than the time will have come to consider more radical alternatives — but still in a rational and constructive spirit. Quebec should not under any circumstances be offered a situation in which it continues to be a full partner in the national government while acquiring special autonomy at home. Some form of "pay as you go" sovereignty-association might be the most satisfactory alternative. Quebec's enhanced autonomy would be balanced by a fair and proportionate loss of influence in the national government and claim on its treasury. If the people of Quebec do not wish to participate as equals in a federal system with a strong national government, then the rest of Canada would be relatively better off if Quebec achieved partial separation.

Looking Ahead

I feel a strong sense of irony as a "federalist." Looking at the way federal governments actually operate, there are strong grounds for joining the rush to dismantle their authority. The routine operations of government are marred by an electoral system that favours big money over people. Resources that are needed to build public institutions and programs are wasted on patronage appointments and projects that respond to partisan politics more than to real needs. The perceived necessity of simultaneously responding to Canadian and Quebec nationalism has had a corrosive effect on the integrity of public institutions. It has been commonplace for leaders to present one face in Quebec, another to the rest of the country, and for public resources to be directed to Quebec for the purposes of forestalling separation.

I feel a further irony in that the federal parties have not spoken up for the nation-building side of balanced federalism. During Meech, provincial governments were put in the awkward role of having to defend national institutions and programs when the federal parties were all pushing hard for the passage of the Accord. It remains to be seen whether we are going to see any conviction or fortitude from the federal opposition parties this time. While Mr. Chrétien won the leadership of the Liberal Party largely because he was critical of Meech, he put heavy behind-the-scenes pressure on the "hold-out" provinces to compromise their strongly-held beliefs. Mr. Chrétien now appears very eager to have done with the constitutional issue before the next election. Will he actually pursue his avowed commitment to strong national government, the protection of individual and minority rights and the principle of holding a national referendum? Or will he settle for some minor amendments — to "show the flag" — declare victory, and ask the rest of us to move on? It also remains to be seen whether the New Democratic Party has a commitment to building the national community; will it display any conviction with respect to such matters as protecting the federal role in the social union and the environment, or will it be satisfied with a "Social Charter" that consists of unenforceable platitudes?

I have sometimes argued that Canada is a place where government has shaped the people as much as the people have shaped the government. We seem to be an extremely diverse people. Potential fissures exist along geographical, economic, linguistic, religious and ethnic lines. The assimilative pull of the United States is always powerful. It would seem that the existence of a sense of shared identity in Canada must stem partly from government programs and institutions, and the on-going viability of the country depends on the existence of a strong national government.

Bryan Schwartz LL.B., LL.M., J.S.D. 143

The remarkable thing is that a sense of shared identity in Canada and the desire for an effective national government have survived actual political experience, to have a coherence and resonance that has withstood continuing disappointment in the operation of national politics. The lesson for the future, however, is not that Canadian unity can withstand the further erosion of national government. A tree that has withstood gloom and tempests needs sunshine, not more of the same. If we continue on our current path, alienation will increase in all parts of the country. Eventually, the things "holding Canada together" will prominently include such uninspiring factors as inertia, fears of the economic costs of transition to anything else and restrictive American immigration laws.

The ultimate touchstone of the value of any system of government is its effect on the lives of the individuals within it. I continue to believe that balanced federalism offers the best prospects for securing the freedom and prosperity of all of Canada's people. It also offers something extra for the spirit; the chance to enjoy the intimacy of local communities, but still participate in a larger enterprise. Rather than further eroding the programs and institutions of national government, let us see if we can reform and improve them. If this round is to be the "Canada round," it cannot and should not amount only to the appeasement of more special interests. It has to be a creative and constructive period of reform for national institutions and programs. The federal government should have the authority and responsibility to build the economic and social union. It must be structured so that it proceeds openly, democratically, deliberately and honestly. Our ability to achieve such a result depends crucially on whether we employ a process that embodies those qualities which we are trying to impart to the national government itself.

I think there was a tee-shirt slogan that read "I'm no longer angry, just amused." I guess that after "amused" might come "indifferent." In my view, though, it is almost always too early to give up. You never know. The Federal Proposal raises the right issues. Some of its features are objectionable or downright intolerable but others are first steps in the right direction. Despite everything that has come before, it is still worth trying to arrive at a process and at a result that is worthy of the Canadian people.

The manuscript of this book was completed in early November, 1991. Virtually all of the issues identified and suggestions made remain live ones. Just as the edited version of this book was going to press, however, a Parliamentary Committee issued its own report on the Federal Proposal.

The "Beaudoin-Dobbie" report is not strictly binding on the Federal government; it is, technically speaking, a report of a committee composed of ordinary MPs — Conservatives, Liberals and New Democrats. The federal government will, apparently, issue its own revised proposals later in Spring 1992. The "Beaudoin-Dobbie" report is, however, a strong indication of the latest thinking of the federal government and the leaders of the two major opposition parties.

The addiction to "Meeching It."

The Parliamentary committee set up to study the federal proposals crashed shortly after take-off. Amid charges of disorganization, patronage appointments of staff and stacking the hearings to favour supporters of the proposals, the Committee suspended its proceedings. One of the co-chairs, Mr. Castonguay, resigned and was replaced by Senator Beaudoin. The committee then renewed its series of public hearings. The government decided to intertwine its proceedings with a new experiment, a series of constitutional conferences. Each would be co-sponsored by a different policy institute. Members of the Beaudoin-Dobbie Committee would attend but so would members of various special-interest groups, officials of federal and provincial governments, academic "specialists" and "ordinary Canadians."

The Beaudoin-Dobbie Committee quickly returned to the old habits of Meech-era committees. As usual, the leaders of the Committee were happy to hear from "academic experts" who were predictable supporters of the package, and in some cases, active consultants in its preparation. Those likely to criticize the package had far less success in securing invitations. The Committee strictly adhered to the deadline of February 28 for its report. In a series of frantic, lengthy and exhausting "Meech-style" meetings at the end of February, the final report of the Committee was assembled in closed meetings under intense time pressure with inadequate opportunity for reflection and consultation and under the shared assumption that there must be a consensus. The Committee not only disregarded much of what Canadians told them during "consultations" but made proposals with respect to areas of jurisdiction such as energy, family policy, bankruptcy and fisheries that were never publicly discussed in the original Federal Proposals or any time in between. The final report was slapped together in such a frenzy that in many places, it is obscure or internally inconsistent; the text sometimes suggests one thing, the draft amendments another.

Bryan Schwartz LL.B., LL.M., J.S.D.   145

It was "Meech time" all over again. Can we soon expect the Prime Minister to be back at it again; summoning together First Ministers, closeting them in a back-room and bludgeoning them with threats of Quebec separation unless they sign?

Did the series of constitutional conferences make any difference? At the one I attended, in Calgary, members of the Committee were active and assertive in trying to shape the advice that emerged. The conferences contained a considerable element of having Committee members advising themselves. In addition to politicians, government officials, technical specialists and representatives of special interest groups, a relatively small number of "ordinary Canadians" were permitted to attend the conference. The latter category included some thoughtful and articulate people but was too small to give much indication of the views of the wide Canadian public. Indeed, it may be that a great many Canadians do not trust the federal political parties to respond to their views, are fed up with the current constitutional obsession and had no interest in attending. In any event, the federal government actually did receive some unwanted advice. The Halifax Conference on the division of powers, for example, affirmed the need for a strong central government. The majority apparently rejected the notion of offering powers to all provinces and of making side-deals with any. The preponderance of opinion favoured offering powers only to Quebec; some of those within that majority (such as former President of the Canadian Broadcasting Corporation, Mr. Al Johnston) very clearly voiced the notion that any such special powers must be accompanied by a commensurate loss of federal subsidies and influence in the national government.

Notwithstanding anything said at any of the conferences, Beaudoin-Dobbie continues the federal government's game plane from the very beginning. The centre-piece of the report of the Beaudoin-Dobbie Committee is "cut-your-own-deal federalism." The federal government will attempt to maintain the illusion of equality among the provinces, while creating easy new routes for individual provinces to grab power and revenue from the federal government. Quebec in particular could be expected to exploit these new means in order to attain more and more special status while maintaining its full share of federal subsidies and influence in national institutions. With respect to the crucial issue of the division of powers, the Beaudoin-Dobbie report would settle nothing; it would create a dynamic and endless process for dismantling the federal government, creating radical inequalities in power among provinces and, in particular, enabling Quebec to pursue profitable separatism within Canada.

I will now try to briefly survey the various features of the Beaudoin-Dobbie report. As will be seen, there are several genuinely encouraging developments amidst profoundly disturbing ones. It is important that the positive features be acknowledged and appreciated; the inclination of the federal government will likely be to abandon them in a desperate attempt to satisfy demands from Quebec.

The Canada Clause and the Distinct Society

The Beaudoin-Dobbie Report proposes placing a new preamble in the Constitution as well as a "Canada clause". The text of *Opting In* condemns the original Federal Proposal for failing to put any Canada in the Canada clause; that is, for emphasizing only diversity, and no sense of shared national purpose. The Beaudoin-Dobbie Report does contain some suggested improvements in this respect. The new preamble would recognize that there is a Canadian people. It would "value our diversity" but also affirm that we are a "free and united country." The revised "Canada clause" would contain many of the usual references to various communities within Canada but it would also speak of "renew[ing] our historic resolve to live together in a federal state"; of "reaffirm[ing] our profound attachment to the principles and values that have drawn us together [and] enlightened our national life."

Opting In has condemned the original Federal Proposal for discounting the ultimate importance of individual rights and playing up collective rights. The "collective rights" of the Quebec majority would have been unequivocally favoured at the expense of the rights of members of the anglophone minority. The Beaudoin-Dobbie recommendations are much improved in their protection of individual and minority rights. The Beaudoin-Dobbie Preamble would speak of the "dignity of each individual." Unlike the original Federal Proposal, the "Canada clause" proposed by Beaudoin-Dobbie does not import the jargon of collective rights into the constitution.

The Beaudoin-Dobbie "Canada clause" would speak of the "vitality and development of official language minorities." So would the Beaudoin-Dobbie version of a "distinct society" clause that would appear in the *Charter*. The new proposals are very welcome. Unlike Meech and unlike the Federal Proposals, Beaudoin-Dobbie would no longer ruthlessly relegate the position of language minorities to second-class constitutional status. Instead, governments would be committed to fostering their "development and vitality." The *Canadian Charter of Rights and Freedoms* is affirmed as "the solemn expression of our national will and hopes."

So the Beaudoin-Dobbie proposal does amount to progress with respect to the supremacy of the individual, the dignity of linguistic minorities and the symbolic (though not practical) affirmation of shared national purpose. The question now is this. Will these improvements stick or, in the face of complaints from Quebec, will the federal parties abjectly revert to the divisive and anti-individualist framework of Meech and the original Federal Proposal?

Particularly worth watching is Mr. Chrétien and the Liberals. Mr. Chrétien's Janus-like activities during the Meech Lake period are notorious. While actively campaigning for the Liberal Leadership on a "reform-Meech" platform, he put heavy behind-the-scenes pressure on "hold-outs," such as Premier Wells, to weaken or abandon their positions on fundamental issues. In his "reform Meech" public statements, Mr. Chrétien emphasized first and foremost the protection of individual and minority rights under the Charter. Will he stand by the improvements in the Beaudoin-Dobbie Report with respect to individual and minority rights, and the symbolic affirmation of Canada or, will he do whatever backing-and-filling is necessary to achieving his apparent goal of getting the constitutional issue off the agenda, and winning the next federal election on the basis that he is, quite simply, not Mulroney?

One key element still deplorably missing in the Beaudoin-Dobbie proposals is any reference whatever to the principle of the equality of provinces. As we shall see, the omission is deliberate. Beaudoin-Dobbie is even more explicit than the original Federal Proposal in contemplating a future of "cut-your-own-deal" federalism.

The Division of Powers — side door routes to decentralization and special status.

The Federal game plan since the failure of Meech has been to permit the federal government to re-arrange the division of powers, including providing special status for Quebec, through side-deals between the federal government and individual provinces. The aim is to maintain the illusion of equality — every province has the theoretical right to ask for more money and power — while providing an easy route to decentralization and special status.

Formal constitutional amendment is the difficult road to decentralization and special status. It attracts public attention, requires the consent of at least "7/50" provinces and most Canadians outside of Quebec do not want significant decentralization or special status. As discussed in *Opting In*, the Federal Proposal proposed two mechanisms for "cut-your-own-deal" federalism: bilateral agreements and delegation. The mechanisms are spelled out in more detail in Beaudoin-Dobbie.

Once we descend into a regime of "cut-your-own-deal" federalism, the long run is gloomily predictable. Quebec will continue to press for more and more decentralization. Given the electoral clout of Quebec, and apparently endless threats of separation, the federal parties will continue to prove themselves incapable of resisting those demands. Quebec will take over authority and civil servants from the federal government, while receiving on-going federal subsidies as "compensation" and undiminished influence in the national government. Other large and powerful provinces may follow suit. Canada will become increasingly a crazy-quilt, with different provinces exercising sharply differing authority. The lines of political accountability will be increasingly confused.

The position of smaller provinces will not be a happy one. Their bargaining power with Ottawa is weak. They cannot achieve the same economies of scale as larger provinces, and may find it prohibitively expensive to assume responsibilities. As the larger provinces pull out, the quality of federal programs is likely to decline. As programs apply to fewer provinces, the federal government will cease to achieve economies of scale. Federal politicians and bureaucrats will pay less attention to programs that do not apply to major provinces. Smaller provinces could end up in a quasi-colonial situation: having poor-quality federal programs being managed by bureaucrats and politicians who come from provinces where the programs do not even apply.

The mechanisms are spelled out further in the Beaudoin-Dobbie Report. Constitutionally binding side-deals would be available in any area the parties choose. For example, the federal government could cease to provide labour market training programs in Quebec and transfer the money and civil servants involved to Quebec. Once the agreement is approved by both Parliament and a provincial legislature, the agreement would have "the force of law" and "could not be amended or revoked" by either side — unless the agreement permits the parties to back out, or unless the parties reach a new agreement.

The side-deals would have priority over "any inconsistent laws" passed by Parliament or the legislature, before or after. They could be of very long, or permanent duration, and binding on Parliaments in perpetuity. So what is the difference between a constitutionally-protected side-deal and an amendment to the Constitution? A side-deal would probably have to be consistent with other parts of the Constitution, such as the Charter. Other than that, it would have all the characteristics of a constitutional amendment: superiority over other laws, immunity from unilateral change. I would think that any politician or court with an ounce of intellectual integrity would have to conclude that side-deals amount to amendments to the constitution. The creation of a side-deal mechanism therefore amounts to a new amending formula, and so can only be changed with the consent of all provinces. It is quite likely, however, that the federal government will try to pretend otherwise and press ahead using only the consent of 7/50 provinces.

There are no safeguards in the "agreement-making" route. Its availability is not limited to a few areas of jurisdiction. There is no limit on how long agreements can last. There is no requirement that other provinces be consulted or approve.

It might be thought that the Senate could block an excessively "sweet deal." Not necessarily. Senators from the major parties might defer to orders from the House of Commons leaders. Even if they do not, the majority view of the Beaudoin-Dobbie Report is that the House of Commons should be able to override Senate opposition. However, they do not take a stand on how much support in the House of Commons is needed to override the Senate. A simple majority might suffice. Suppose, that a 60% vote were needed in the House to override the Senate. The governing party in 1984-88, under Prime Minister Mulroney, could have mustered more than that all on its own. During the Meech era, it proved easy to procure over 90% support in the House of Commons for excessive give-aways to Quebec — despite the opposition of most Canadians.

Quite simply, no single Parliament with one province can be trusted to effect substantial and practically irrevocable changes to the Constitution of Canada. A broad level of national support should be required — preferably through a referendum, but at least through a process that involves legislatures in other provinces. The proposal for constitutionally-protected side-deals should be rejected.

Delegation

The Beaudoin-Dobbie proposal offers another route to balkanizing Canada in general and providing special status for Quebec in particular. Parliament would be authorized to give away any of its powers to any province it wishes. In case anyone was wondering whether this will lead to "profitable separatism," Beaudoin-Dobbie clears up the uncertainty: it certainly will. Beaudoin-Dobbie makes absolutely no provision for a province acquiring power to surrender any subsidies from tax-payers in other provinces, diminish its "share" of federal public servants, or relinquish any claim to tell other Canadians what to do. On the contrary, Beaudoin-Dobbie makes it very clear that a province has the right to pursue "profitable separatism." A draft clause would provide that:

> Parliament or a legislature that delegates authority under this section shall provide reasonable compensation to the government that administers legislation enacted under the delegated authority, taking into account the costs of enacting and administering the legislation.

There you have it: a firm guarantee of profitable separatism. Quebec can take power from Ottawa, but retain its full share of bureaucratic and political authority over the rest of Canada. In assuming a particular power, Quebec will probably be increasing the total costs of administering programs. The federal government will likely lose economies of scale and there will be costs putting in place Quebec's bureaucrats, polices and procedures for a relatively small population. Does Quebec absorb the increased financial costs? Is there some fiscal deterrent to dismantling the national government and creating extra administrative expenses? Not at all. The rest of us are apparently supposed to give Quebec the money its citizens would have received if the feds still had authority — and then extra money to cover the added costs of running a relatively small and inefficient operation.

If a province is going to "opt-out" of the national framework, it should strictly be on a "pay-as-you-go" basis. It should, to the extent it has divorced itself from the rest of Canada, surrender its subsidies from tax-payers in other provinces and diminish its influence over national policy. If Quebec wants to opt-out of a national program, its tax-payers should, at most, be relieved of the taxes they would otherwise send to Ottawa for that program. The tax-payers should not receive the money they would ordinarily have obtained from Ottawa, which could include an element of subsidy from tax-payers in the rest of Canada. Quebec should then be entirely responsible for raising taxes to pay for the program. Quebec should also sustain a proportionate reduction in its representation in the federal public service and in the right of its MPs and cabinet ministers to participate in policy decisions.

Beaudoin-Dobbie offers some ludicrously inadequate safeguards against the abuse of the delegation power. Parliament has to give one year's notice before delegating a power, and to allow public hearings. Some safeguard! Anyone remembering the Meech era will know that Parliament can hold public hearings, hear protests from Canadians and other provincial governments and still proceed to make excessive give-aways to Quebec. Another woefully inadequate safeguard is that the delegation automatically expires after five years, unless renewed. Once a power is given to Quebec, what federal party is going to dare take it back? What government of Quebec will ever acquiesce in restoring a power to Ottawa? We are witnessing a process in which provincial governments of Quebec define constitutional "success" primarily in terms of wresting powers from Ottawa. Given the Allaire report, the ideal, and indeed, the eventual, outcome contemplated by even the "federalist" provincial Liberals is provincial authority over virtually everything.

Culture

Beaudoin-Dobbie makes a proposal in one area for straight-out special status for Quebec. It would be given exclusive jurisdiction over "culture in Quebec." No definition of "culture" is provided. One existing section of the *Constitution Act, 1982*, defines culture as including "education." The term "culture" could very well be interpreted by Quebec governments, and eventually by the courts, as extending well beyond the world of arts and entertainment — including the funding of all academic research in the humanities. The text of Beaudoin-Dobbie suggests that national institutions such as the Canada Council, the CBC and the National Film Board would continue to be able to carry on operations in Quebec. The draft amendment, however, says nothing of the sort. There is a principle of legal interpretation that the specific takes precedence over the general; as worded, the Beaudoin-Dobbie amendment might be used by Quebec as a political and legal tool to virtually oust any federal cultural presence in Quebec — apart from sending cheques to Quebec governmental agencies. At the same time, the Beaudoin-Dobbie proposal would permit officials from Quebec — from bureaucrats to MPs to cabinet ministers — to remain fully entitled to participate in shaping cultural policy in the rest of Canada.

Beaudoin-Dobbie suggests that Quebec and Ottawa could enter into a bilateral agreement to define their respective roles over culture in Quebec. The bilateral agreement would be modelled on the "existing Canada/Quebec agreement on immigration — an area where shared responsibility is explicit in the Constitution." So much for consistency and logic. Immigration is an area in which all provinces have some jurisdiction, and the federal government has paramount authority. With respect to culture, the actual draft amendment proposed by Beaudoin-Dobbie would grant power to one province, but not others, and would make no provision whatever for retaining a federal presence.

The dissenting proposal by the Liberal Party is much better. It would make "cultural matters" an area in which both orders of government have authority. Provinces would have paramount authority, subject to the "federal power over national cultural institutions and the federal power to make payments directly to individuals and organizations." The Liberal amendment should be further improved by providing a reasonably limited definition of "cultural matters."

Other Specific Proposals on the Division of Powers

With respect to a number of matters — housing, tourism, forestry, mining, recreation, municipal affairs — Beaudoin-Dobbie would commit the federal government to entering into side-deals with provinces to affirm their jurisdiction and determine what the remaining federal role is. Beaudoin-Dobbie also offers each province the choice of whether "labour market training" should be expressly added to the constitutional list of its powers. A province that chooses to acquire the label is free to negotiate bilateral deals with Ottawa which would spell out how much federal money the province gets and what standards, if any, should apply.

At least the issues just mentioned were discussed in the original federal proposal. Beaudoin-Dobbie suddenly and inexplicably adds several more areas on which federal and provincial governments should make side-deals. They are "family policy" and "energy." We are never told what these labels mean, where they came from or why they are particularly appropriate for bilateral deal-making.

In another last-minute out of the blue development, Beaudoin-Dobbie also calls for the provinces to acquire new authority over inland fisheries and personal bankruptcy. Parliament would retain its existing jurisdiction and have paramount authority in case of conflicts.

Beaudoin-Dobbie elects not to tamper with the federal "residual" power, which is good news. Unfortunately, the majority on the Committee affirm the Federal Proposal to abolish the federal declaratory power.

The majority of the committee recognizes that health, education and social services are under provincial jurisdiction but suggests that the federal government continue to deliver its existing Canada-wide programs in these matters.

Bryan Schwartz LL.B., LL.M., J.S.D.

151

The Social Union

Beaudoin-Dobbie responds to demands from Premier Rae for a Social Charter by suggesting that broad principles be inserted in the "equalization" part of the Constitution Act, 1982. Governments would commit themselves to "fostering":

* comprehensive, universal, portable, publicly administered and accessible health care;
* adequate social services and social benefits;
* high quality education;
* the right of workers to organize and bargain collectively;
* the integrity of the environment.

The principles would be implemented by legislatures, rather than the courts. There would, however, be some sort of specialized commission that would report periodically on how well governments are performing.

The position I have taken is to welcome attention to the "social union"; to agree that it should be developed politically, rather than through the courts; but to emphasize that there can only be a Canadian "social union" if the federal government retains significant authority to spend money and shape policy.

The many provisions for "cut-your-own-deal" federalism seriously undermine my confidence that the federal government will continue to operate in the social policy area, or any other, with integrity and vitality.

As far as specific provisions for national shared-cost programs are concerned, Beaudoin-Dobbie leaves things in much the same state as the original Federal Proposal. The federal government's offer remains essentially this: a province can opt-out of a national shared-cost program, and claim the money it would have received, as long as it runs a program or initiative that "meets the objectives" of the national program. The current federal position is an improvement on Meech Lake; it holds provinces to a higher requirement of co-operation with the national program. The province must now "meet" the objectives of the national program; Meech required only a "compatible" provincial activity. It would be better, however, if the new provision spoke of "minimum national standards," rather than merely "objectives." In any event, it remains to be seen whether the federal government will stand by even this limited improvement in comparison to the Meech Lake Accord.

The Economic Union

The Federal Proposal would have created a new authority for the federal government to "manage the economic union." In the face of strong protests from various provinces, including Quebec, the federal government has abandoned its effort to acquire any new legislative power. Beaudoin-Dobbie propose an economic counterpart to the Social Charter; that is, a statement of broad economic commitments that would be pursued by all governments. The "economic covenant" would include the following goals:

* working co-operatively to strengthen the economic union;
* ensuring the mobility of persons, goods, services and capital;

* pursuing the goal of full employment; and

* ensuring all Canadians have a reasonable standard of living. to be implemented by governments (not the Courts) and a "specialized agency" to report on the state of progress.

The "economic covenant" would not be enforceable in the Courts; it would be monitored by some sort of "specialized agency," according to Beaudoin-Dobbie. Why? What is the necessity of creating expensive new agencies, which will inevitably be filled with patronage appointments, to monitor either the economic or social union? Why could oversight not be turned over to a committee of the reformed Senate, perhaps one consisting of an equal number of Senators from each province?

The original Federal Proposal also proposed entrenching in the Constitution the basic principle that Canada is an economic union; that is, that there should not be internal barriers to the movement of goods, services, capital and people. *Opting In* agrees with the general idea, and suggests ways in which this economic union principle could be clarified and enlarged. Beaudoin-Dobbie moves in the opposite direction. It offers a definition of the principle that is even weaker and narrower than in the original Federal Proposal. Then it greatly expands the list of exceptions. The establishment and functioning of government-owned monopolies are entirely exempt. So are marketing boards and provincial laws aimed at reducing disparities within the province. There continues to be a huge loophole for federal "regional economic development" programs. Beaudoin-Dobbie does not provide any procedure whereby a government can be granted permission to operate a specific program that deviates from the economic union principle. Then again, who would ever need one?

The Beaudoin-Dobbie Report calls for "federal provincial agreements" to arrive at national standards or otherwise enhance the mobility of persons. We should not leave things entirely to such negotiations. As *Opting In* recommends, the economic union principle should specifically include a guarantee that governments (and agencies such as universities, schools and professional bodies) will give reasonable recognition to the professional credentials, product standards and judicial decisions rendered by other provinces. Such a guarantee would be enforceable even if provinces fail to arrive at specific agreements on these matters.

Institutional Reform: House of Commons, Senate, Supreme Court of Canada.

Beaudoin-Dobbie makes it clear that reforms to the House of Commons will take place without formal constitutional amendments and does not discuss them further. I continue to advocate limiting the term of Parliaments and Legislatures to no more than four years and entrenching a constitutional commitment to fair election financing.

The Supreme Court of Canada provisions of Beaudoin-Dobbie are a severe disappointment. At the Calgary conference, a number of working groups stated clearly that provincial consultation is acceptable but that it is unacceptable to give the provinces a far greater voice than the federal government. One of the co-chairs of the Calgary conference, Peter Lougheed, clearly noted the opposition to the "Meech system" at the plenary session. It would be easy to give Quebec a substantial voice in Supreme Court appointments without going overboard. Beaudoin-Dobbie keeps the "Meech system"; the federal government ends up with far less say over Supreme Court appointments than do the provinces in general and Quebec in particular. The wholly inadequate "improvement" is that Quebec has only 90 days to come up with an acceptable name, or else Ottawa can appoint a judge on its own. In reality, it will be easy for Quebec governments to submit list after list of impressive professional nominees who happen to be hard-line Quebec nationalists. The federal government will have to choose one of them, or else provoke a political crisis. Beaudoin-Dobbie throws a very short rope to a federal government which has placed itself in a very deep hole.

The Senate proposals of Beaudoin-Dobbie are unclear in some respects, clearly inadequate in others. On the "elected" issue, Beaudoin-Dobbie does arrive at some of the same conclusions as I have in *Opting In*: Senators should have fixed terms of office, some form of proportional representation should be used and no quotas established on the basis of gender or ethnicity. Unfortunately, the report does not mention the issue of election financing and provides no assurances whatever that Senators will not be co-opted by the House of Common parties — e.g., by holding out the possibility of cabinet appointments. With respect to the distribution of seats, the report predictably favours "equitable," rather than "equal." The Conservative majority on the committee favours the following distribution, assuming a 109 seat Senate:

Quebec and Ontario: 20 each; B.C. and Alberta: 18 each; Manitoba, Saskatchewan, New Brunswick and Nova Scotia: 8 each; Newfoundland 6, Prince Edward Island 4, Northwest Territories 2, Yukon 1.

The proposed distribution does observe the principle that the provinces of western Canada should collectively have as many seats as Ontario plus Quebec. Compared to most proposals on Senate reform over the years, Beaudoin-Dobbie short-changes Atlantic Canada, and especially Newfoundland. (Prime Minister Mulroney's revenge on Premier Wells?).

The Liberal members of the Beaudoin-Dobbie Committee recommend a distribution that gave more clout to the smallest provinces. It would distribute 100 seats as follows: Ontario and Quebec, 20 each; British Columbia and Alberta, 9 each; five other provinces, 8 each; P.E.I. 4; Yukon and Northwest Territories, 1 each.

(Beaudoin-Dobbie bases its seat distribution on the current populations of Canadian provinces. These figures may change through time. That fact, along with the experimental nature of the reformed Senate, suggest caution about giving any or all provinces a veto over future Senate reform.)

On the "effective" issue, Beaudoin-Dobbie is unable to make a firm recommendation. The Progressive Conservative majority on the committee believe there should be some way for the House of Commons to override the Senate. It is not sure how; a simple majority? A 60% majority? Some other formula? I would suggest that if there is any voting procedure whereby the House of Commons can override the Senate, it should count provinces, and not just people. Otherwise, it would be much too easy for House of Commons members from a big province (Ontario or Quebec) to override opposition from the more regionally balanced Senate. A House of Commons override might require something like a 65% of House of Commons members, including a majority of members from each of eight different provinces.

The original Federal Proposal appears to suggest that the Senate should have no legislative role in matters involving taxing and spending. Beaudoin-Dobbie retreats to a much more satisfactory position; the Senate would not have much authority to block routine supply bills but would have its usual authority over legislation involving significant policy changes.

Aboriginal Self-Government

Beaudoin-Dobbie proposes that the Constitution immediately entrench the "inherent" right of aboriginal peoples to self-government. Unlike the original Federal Proposal, there would be no ten-year delay before the right becomes enforceable in the Courts. According to Beaudoin-Dobbie, recognition of the right to self-government would be accompanied by a constitutional statement that the right "shall be elaborated" in self-government agreements negotiated between federal and provincial governments and aboriginal communities. The possibility remains, however, that the Courts will be asked to help define it and that the Courts will agree to do so.

My view remains that some broad principles concerning self-government should be spelled out in the Constitution. Everything should not be left to further negotiation. Both sides should have a general understanding of how aboriginal self-government fits into the framework of the Charter, the division of powers, and the economic and social union. I continue to believe that we must show some consistency in our responses to the demands of Quebec nationalists and aboriginal peoples. In both cases, we should be seeking a reasonable balance between local self-government and participation in the wider national community. We should expect people to share the responsibilities of Canadian citizenship as well as its benefits; we should ensure that individual and minority rights be respected by all orders of government; and devise reasonably well defined constitutional arrangements. It would have been wrong to entrench an undefined concept of "distinct society" in the Canadian Constitution; should we now entrench "self-government" without substantial definitions of its features?

The Amending Formula

Beaudoin-Dobbie considers a variety of options for giving Quebec wider rights of veto. The "Amending Formula" discussion does not contain a single word about giving the people of Canada a direct voice through binding referendums.

The On-going Process

Beaudoin-Dobbie suggests the possibility of splitting the federal package into two parts. The unanimity elements would be put in one package, elements that can be passed by the 7/50 in another. Why deal with Premier Wells or Filmon if you can go around them?

If the federal government proceeds with the split, there is good reason to fear that it will try to include in the "7/50" package various elements that properly belong in the "unanimity" bag. A new mechanism to allow constitutionally protected side-agreements is, on any honest reading of the constitution, an amendment to the amending formula, and so requires unanimity.

Similarly, any new provision for delegation also amounts to a new amending formula. It should make no real difference that delegations are theoretically revocable after five years. A temporary alteration of the Constitution is still an alteration. Furthermore, delegations can be renewed again and again. As a practical matter, they will be. The delegation mechanism would permit the massive and on-going reworking of the constitutional division of powers. Can it be argued in good faith that such a mechanism is not a new means of amending the Constitution? It would be consistent with past practice of the current federal government, however, for the federal government to try to push through a deal, claim the country has been saved, and take an "I dare you" attitude to any notion that the Supreme Court of Canada would invalidate the deal on technical grounds.

At the end of last year, the federal government seemed prepared to introduce legislation allowing for a consultative referendum. It would not have actually required that the people be directly consulted; it would only have given the government the option of doing so. Even such a tentative step was too much for Quebec nationalists; in the face of their protests, the federal government immediately retreated. Apparently, the national agenda can be set by a Quebec referendum but it is not permissible for the rest of Canada to be consulted. Beaudoin-Dobbie is not prepared to push the matter further:

> We recommend that a federal law be enacted, *if deemed appropriate by the Government of Canada*, to enable the federal government, *at its discretion*, to hold a consultative referendum on a constitutional proposal, either to confirm the existence of a national consensus or to facilitate the adopting of the required amending resolutions.

The other federal parties do not have the courage to firmly recommend that the federal government give itself the option of consulting the people of Canada. Mr. Chretien, who earlier expressed strong support for a referendum, apparently is no longer particularly interested. Beaudoin-Dobbie concludes by assuring Canadians that "we believe that our portrait of Canada is realistic, our diagnosis accurate, and our remedies reasonable." If so, why is the Committee so afraid of consulting the people of Canada?

The initial reaction in Quebec to Beaudoin-Dobbie, from academics and the press, and then Mr. Bourassa and the National Assembly, has been that it falls far short of satisfying Quebec's demands. Some of the gains of Meech have been attenuated, goes the complaint, and Quebec wants substantial new powers right away, not through any future process of negotiation. Is the federal government now going to engage in a panicked effort to sweeten the deal for Quebec? Are the all-party efforts in Beaudoin-Dobbie to satisfy the aspirations of other Canadians going to go the way of the all-party Charest Report of 1990 — that is, will they be declared inoperative by the federal government as soon as Quebec nationalists protest?

In 1990, Lucien Bouchard, a Quebec-first cabinet colleague of the Prime Minister, publicly broke ranks with any efforts to reform Meech and quit the Cabinet. Partly as a result, the Prime Minister tried to push the Accord through without the slightest concession to the dignity or opinion of those who wanted improvements. Will history repeat itself? As far as I know, none of the Prime Minister's Quebec cabinet colleagues has come to the defence of the Beaudoin-Dobbie report. One of them, Marcel Masse, has already condemned it. Are we again going to see the Prime Minister bowing to demands from Quebec nationalists and doing everything possible to bully and manipulate others on their behalf — again?

What a spectacle. Quebec threatens to hold a referendum, and the constitutional agenda and deadline is set for the entire nation. The rest of Canada is not supposed to be consulted because doing so would offend Quebec nationalists. Meech Lake failed because people in the rest of Canada found it gave away too much to the provinces; instead of seeking middle ground, Quebec now increases its demands. The Premier of Quebec remains unwilling to openly participate in negotiations with other provinces. We are not told exactly what "enough" is; apparently, we have to keep offering more, until Quebec finally says "enough for now." Even then the game is not over; even the "federalist" Allaire report defines the ideal as turning the federal government into a cheque-processing centre, and little else.

The federal government may be trying do to the entire country what it likes to do with Premiers: lock 'em in a room and tell 'em nobody leaves unless they give up. The current strategy may be designed to wear down the population as a whole. The federal government has staged a long series of "consultative" processes. It has generally been able to retain control of how the events are staged and interpreted; it has not, and will not, promise that the people will be given a direct voice through a referendum.

Perhaps the expectation of federal strategists is that we will end up feeling so bored, cynical or ineffectual that we will simply yearn for an end to things; that we will say to the elites "just get it done, and leave us alone."

Sometimes, it may seem more important to settle a matter than to settle it correctly. I do not think the Constitution is such a matter or that now is such a time. Suppose, however, that we were to value temporary peace and stability over our highest aspirations for the country. We would be mistaken to think that a deal like Beaudoin-Dobbie offers either peace or stability. The entire catalogue of federal authority would remain up for grabs. Flexibility within federalism can be a virtue but there have to be some elementary ground rules that are reasonable, stable and fair. A package like Beaudoin-Dobbie would offer Quebec (and other large provinces as well) some new and easy avenues for pursuing "profitable separatism" within Canada.

I still believe that you cannot hold a country together by taking it apart. Nor can you unite people by denying them a direct voice in their own destiny.

Selected Bibliography

The books directly quoted in this study include: Bercuson and Cooper, *Deconfederation: Canada Without Quebec* (Toronto: Key Porter Books, 1991); Cohen, *A Deal Undone: The Making and Breaking of the Meech Lake Accord* (Vancouver: Douglas & McIntyre, 1990); Elton and McCormick, Peter. *Western Perspectives...A Blueprint for Senate Reform* (Calgary: Canada West Foundation, December, 1990); L. Grafstein, "Look Back in Anger: The 1987 Constitutional Accord, Report of the Special Joint Committee of the Senate and the House of Commons," 45 University of Toronto Faculty of Law Review, 226; Johnston, ed. *Pierre Trudeau Speaks Out on Meech Lake* (Toronto: General Paperbacks, 1990); Mathews, *Quiet Resolution: Quebec's Challenge to Canada* (Toronto: Summerhill Press, 1990); Robertson, *A House Divided: Meech Lake, Senate Reform and the Canadian Union* (Halifax: The Institute for Research on Public Policy, 1989).

For much of the history of the 1981-82 process, I have relied on Romanow, Whyte, and Leeson, *Canada...Notwithstanding: The Making of the Constitution 1976 — 1982* (Toronto: Carswell/Methuen, 1984).

Readers interested in pursuing the case law on the federal residual power should start with *The Queen v. Crown Zellerbach Canada Ltd*, [1988] 1 Supreme Court Reports 401, and the cases referred to therein. On "Interdelegation," the leading cases include *A.G. Nova Scotia v A.G. Canada*, [1951] S.C.R. 31 and P.E.I. *Potato Marketing Board v H.B. Willis Inc.*, [1952] 2 S.C.R. 392; on "Trade and Commerce," a good starting point is *G.M. v City National Leasing*. Justice Stewart's comment on property rights, quoted in Chapter Six, is from *Lynch v. Household Finance Corp.*, 405 U.S. 538.

My own writings on matters related to contemporary constitutional issues include:

Patriation era:

"General National Agreement: The Legal Sanction for Constitutional Reform in Canada" (1981) 6 *Queen's L.J.* 513; The Patriation Case and the Idea of Canada" 8 *Queen's L.J.* 158 (1982-83), co-author with John Whyte; revised and reprinted in *Canada Notwithstanding*.

Aboriginal issues:

First Principles: Constitutional Reform with respect to the Aboriginal Peoples of Canada, 1982-1984. (Kingston: Queen's Institute of Intergovernmental Relations 1985); *First Principles, Second Thoughts: Aboriginal Peoples, Constitutional Reform and Canadian Statecraft* (Montreal: Institute for Research on Public Policy, 1986); "A Separate Aboriginal Justice System?" (1990), 19 Manitoba Law Journal 77; "The General Sense of Things: A Comment on the Delgamuukw Case" (forthcoming, Institute for Research on Public Policy, in their *Delgamuukw* conference proceedings).

Meech Lake

Fathoming Meech Lake (Winnipeg: Legal Research Institute of the University of Manitoba, 1987); "Refashioning Meech Lake," (1989) 18 Manitoba Law Journal 19; Four essays in Ingle, Lorne ed. *Meech Lake Reconsidered* (Hull: Voyageur Publishing, 1989); Comment on the Meech Lake Accord in Shneiderman, ed., *Language and the State* (Cowansville: Les Editions Yvon Blais Inc., 1991).

The "Canada Round"

During this round, I have so far submitted extensive written material to, and appeared before, the following committees: Manitoba Task Force on the Constitution, February, 1991 (and supplementary submission, June 1991); Parliamentary Committee on the Amending Formula, March 1991; Ontario Task Force on the Constitution, August 21, 1991.

An encapsulation of many of my views is contained in "Canada Cannot be Held Together by Taking it Apart," which is contained in Granatstein and McNaught, editors (Toronto: Doubleday, 1991).

The Supremacy of the Individual

First Principles, Second Thoughts (especially chapter one, "Individuals, Groups and Canadian Statecraft" and chapter twenty-five, "The Application of the Canadian Charter of Rights and Freedoms to Aboriginal Governments"); Comment on "Can a Community Have Rights?" in *Language and the State;* "Individuals, Groups and Community" 8 *Journal of Law and Religion,* 47 (1989), 41 pp; "The Inalienable Right to be Alienated," 1990, University of Toronto Law Journal: and my essay in Devlin, ed., *Canadian Perspectives on Legal Theory,* (Toronto: Emond Montgomery Publishers, 1990).

Civil Liberties

"Woodward's Estate as Nonconstitutional Law," (1978), 4 Queen's Law Journal 124; "George Grant on English Speaking Justice," (1987) 16 *Man. L.J.* 73; "The Charter and Due Process," 1983 *Pitblado Lectures* 31; "The Charter and the Domestic Enforcement of International Law" (1986), 16 *Man. L.J.* 149, with Gordon Mackintosh; "Civil Liberties and Public Inquiries," 1990 Pitblado Lectures (forthcoming).

Existential reflections.

"A Meditation on Bartleby," (1985) 22 Osgoode Hall Law Journal 77.

About the author

Bryan Schwartz is a Professor of Law at the University of Manitoba and the Chair of the Legal Research Institute of the University of Manitoba. He holds a bachelor of law degree from Queen's University and a master's and doctoral degree from Yale Law School. He is the author of four books on constitutional reform, including *First Principles, Second Thoughts* and *Fathoming Meech Lake,* and over thirty articles on a wide variety of subjects. He has received academic awards for achievements in teaching and community service as well as outstanding scholarship and is known to a wider Canadian audience through the many interviews he has provided for newspapers, radio and television.

Dr. Schwartz' commentary has drawn on his extensive practical experience. He is a member of the bars of Ontario and Manitoba, a past chair of the constitutional law section of the Canadian Bar Association, and has participated in constitutional cases argued before the Supreme Court of Canada. He has also been a constitutional consultant or adviser to a number of provincial governments and was actively involved in litigation or negotiations connected with patriation (1980-81), the aboriginal peoples round (1982-87) and the Meech Lake Accord (1987-90).